THE SECRET KNOWLEDGE

THE SECRET KNOWLEDGE

ON THE DISMANTLING OF AMERICAN CULTURE

DAVID MAMET

SENTINEL

SENTINEL
Published by the Penguin Group
Penguin Group (USA) Inc., 375 Hudson Street, New York, New York 10014, U.S.A. · Penguin Group
(Canada), 90 Eglinton Avenue East, Suite 700, Toronto, Ontario, Canada M4P 2Y3 (a division of Pear-
son Penguin Canada Inc.) · Penguin Books Ltd, 80 Strand, London WC2R 0RL, England · Penguin
Ireland, 25 St. Stephen's Green, Dublin 2, Ireland (a division of Penguin Books Ltd) · Penguin Books
Australia Ltd, 250 Camberwell Road, Camberwell, Victoria 3124, Australia (a division of Pearson
Australia Group Pty Ltd) · Penguin Books India Pvt Ltd, 11 Community Centre, Panchsheel Park,
New Delhi – 110 017, India · Penguin Group (NZ), 67 Apollo Drive, Rosedale, Auckland 0632, New
Zealand (a division of Pearson New Zealand Ltd) · Penguin Books (South Africa) (Pty) Ltd, 24 Stur-
dee Avenue, Rosebank, Johannesburg 2196, South Africa

Penguin Books Ltd, Registered Offices: 80 Strand, London WC2R 0RL, England

First published in 2011 by Sentinel, a member of Penguin Group (USA) Inc.

10 9 8 7 6 5 4 3 2 1

LIBRARY OF CONGRESS CATALOGING IN PUBLICATION DATA
Mamet, David.
    The secret knowledge : on the dismantling of American culture / David Mamet.
        p.   cm.
    Includes bibliographical references and index.
    ISBN 978-1-59523-076-8
    1. Right and left (Political science)—United States. 2. Political culture—United States. 3. United
States—Politics and government—21st century. I. Title.
    JK1726.M36 2011
    320.51'30973—dc22   2010049347

Printed in the United States of America

This book is dedicated to the memory of my father.

Most initiations are about the devolution of responsibility. At the same time, initiations often double as a long and confused moment of shared truths. Essentially, what the adults, elders, or senior members of the group share with the initiates is the knowledge they possess, and then they admit to a terrible secret, the secret of the "tribe"—that beyond the knowledge the initiates have just been given there is no special knowledge.

—Anna Simons, *The Company They Keep*

CONTENTS

THE SECRET KNOWLEDGE

1 | THE POLITICAL IMPULSE

All religions stem from the same universal needs. Each contains awe, obedience, grace, study, prayer, and submission. Each religion will order and stress these elements differently, but their root is the same—a desire to understand the Divine and its intentions for humankind.

The political impulse, similarly, must, however manifested, proceed from a universal urge to order social relations.

Emotions may elevate practical partisan differences to the realm of the spiritual or doctrinal, which is to say, the irreconcilable—Democrats, notably, are more likely to credit terrorists taken in battle against our country rather than Republicans, and many liberal Jews to believe the statements of Hamas rather than those of Israel.

In the election of 2008, environmental, social, and financial change were the concerns of both parties. The Right held that a return to first principles would arrest or re-channel this momentum toward bankruptcy and its attendant geopolitical dangers. It suggested fiscal conservatism, greater and more efficient exploitation of natural resources, lower taxes, a stronger military. The Left's view was to suggest that Change was good in itself—that a problem need not be dealt with mechanically (by acts whose historical efficacy was demonstrable) but could be addressed psychologically, by identifying "change itself" as a solution.

The underlying question, common to both sides, was how to deal with this problematic change; the Conservative answer, increased exploitation of the exploitable and conservation of needless expenditure—in effect, sound business practice; that of the Liberals a cessation of the same. Each were and are interested in Security, the Liberals suggesting détente and the Conservatives increased armament; each side was interested in Justice, the Conservatives holding it will best be served by the strict rule of law, the Liberals by an increase in the granting of Rights.

This opposition appealed to me as a dramatist. For a good drama aspires to be and a tragedy *must* be a depiction of a human interaction in which both antagonists are, arguably, in the right.

My early plays, *American Buffalo*, *The Water Engine*, *Glengarry Glen Ross*, concerned Capitalism and business. This subject consumed me as I was trying to support myself, and like many another young man or woman, had come up against the blunt fact of a world which did not care.

I never questioned my tribal assumption that Capitalism was bad, although I, simultaneously, never acted upon these feelings. I supported myself, as do all those not on the government dole, through the operation of the Free Market.

As a youth I enjoyed—indeed, like most of my contemporaries, revered—the agitprop plays of Brecht, and his indictments of Capitalism. It later occurred to me that his plays were copyrighted, and that he, like I, was living through the operations of that same free market. His protestations were not borne out by his actions, neither *could* they be. Why, then, did he profess Communism? Because it sold. The public's endorsement of his plays kept him alive; as Marx was kept alive by the fortune Engels's family had made selling furniture; as universities, established and funded by the Free Enterprise system—which is to say by the accrual of wealth—house, support, and coddle generations of the young in their dissertations on the evils of America.

We cannot live without trade. A society can neither advance nor improve without excess of disposable income. This excess can only be amassed through the production of goods and services necessary or attractive to the mass. A financial system which allows this leads to inequality; one that does not leads to mass starvation.

Brecht, an East German, was allowed by the Communists to keep his wealth and live at his ease in Switzerland—a show dog of Communism. His accomplishments, however, must be seen not as an indictment, but as a ratification of the power of free enterprise. As must the seemingly ineradicable vogue for the notion of Government Control.

The free market in ideas keeps this folly as current as any entertainment reviled by the Left as "mindless." But the fiction of top-down Government Control, of a Command Economy, is, at essence, like a Reality Show, which is to say, a fraud. The Good Causes of the Left may generally be compared to NASCAR; they offer the diversion of watching things go excitingly around in a circle, getting nowhere.

———

Who does not want Justice? Each of us, of course, wants justice for himself, and all but the conscienceless few realize that we deserve well from each other.

The question is one of apportionment, for justice cannot be infinite. There is a finite amount of time, knowledge, wisdom, and money—and to tax the mass endlessly, even in the pursuit of justice, must cause injustice somewhere.

One may be just to the trees of the Northwest, impoverish loggers, and raise the cost of home construction; if all prisoners are allowed unlimited and endless access to all courts, whose time and energy is as finite as every other thing, the court system must stint other applicants. One may extend Justice to the snail darter and cripple the Port of New York; and a legitimate aversion to racial profiling may not only inconvenience but mortally endanger the traveling public.

My revelation came upon reading Friedrich Hayek's *The Road to Serfdom*. It was that there is a cost to *everything*, that nothing is without cost, and that energy spent on A cannot be spent on B, and that this is the meaning of *cost*—it represents the renunciation of other employments of the money. He wrote that there are no solutions; there are only tradeoffs—money spent on more crossing guards cannot be spent on books. Both are necessary, a choice must be made, and that this is the Tragic view of life.

It made sense to me. Now, like the Fibonacci sequence, I began to see it everywhere. Milton Friedman pointed out that the cavil, "It would seem that a country that could put a man on the moon could provide free lunches for its schoolchildren," missed the point: the country could not supply the free lunches *because* it put the man on the moon—there is only so much money. I understood this because I have a checkbook, and my reading inspired me to realize the equation did not differ at the National Level—there was only so much money, and choices must be made.

Money, I further learned, was just an efficient way of keeping track of the production of individuals—of their work and the capacity of that work to benefit their fellows. The more the money moved around, the more the mass benefited. The Government could do little with this product save waste it: it did not produce. It could tax or confiscate, but it could not allocate with greater justice than the Free Market;* it could and should, then, provide only those services of which the Free Market was incapable: the roads, the sewers, the Judiciary, the streetlights, the Legislature, and the Common Defense—the notion that it could do more was an illusion and nowhere demonstrable.† The Government could only profess to do more, its bureaucrats and politicians playing on our human need for

*I do not think I am naïve. I have been supporting myself for quite a while, and, as a young man, took every job I could get. I was very glad to have them, but my happiness was neither gratitude toward my employers, nor insensitivity to the various slights, uncertainties, and thefts to which the unskilled, myself among them, were all subject. I was glad to have the money, and looked (and look) for any opportunity to earn more with less expenditure of effort and in more congenial circumstances. This attitude, I believe, is fairly widely shared, cutting across even the most deeply riven political lines.

†See the educative outpouring of admiration, after September 11, for the police and firefighters, and the military—for those of our fellow Americans actually involved in the *legitimate* operation of Government. See also, *per contra*, Government's affection for privatization—of the Chicago parking system, of various national prisons, of toll roads, of the care and feeding of troops. These among the few, legitimate enterprises of Government have in common a benefit to the citizenry greater through government oversight than would be delivered by the Free Market competition. Privatization is called "outsourcing," but it is merely sale by incumbents of the property which is the people's. Can anyone believe that any franchise has ever been sold by any government anywhere other than with the accrual of some personal benefit to the executives and legislators involved in the sale?

guidance and certainty, and, indeed, our desire for Justice. But these members of Government, Right and Left, were as likely to exploit their position as you or I; and, like Brecht, as likely to mine human credulity as to alleviate human need.

Politics, then, seemed to me, like business, a delightful panoply of deceit and error and strife—a brand-new tide pool for the naturalist.

———

I wrote a political play.

Writers are asked, "How could you know so much about [fill in the profession]?" The answer, if the writing satisfies, is that one makes it up. And the job, my job, as a dramatist, was not to write accurately, but to write *persuasively*. If and when I do my job well, subsequent cowboys, as it were, will talk like *me*.

In order to write well, however, the good dramatist must absolutely identify with his subject. This does not mean to be in "sympathy with," but "to become the same as."

In writing my political play I realized, then, that I was in no way immune from the folly of partisanship, of muddle-headedness, and of rancor in political thought; that I enjoyed the righteous indignation and the licensed spectacle as much as anyone, for the feeling of superiority it gave me. That I was, in short, a fool.

That, for a writer, is an excellent place to begin.

———

A friend came to our house for Thanksgiving. She'd flown from D.C. to Los Angeles, and the first-class cabin of her plane had been occupied by two turkeys "pardoned" by President Bush, and sold or lent to the Disney Corporation, to lead its Thanksgiving parade down the Main Street of Disneyland.

This intersection of these two hucksterisms drew me irresistibly to a fantasy.

All people being venal by nature, and politicians doubly so by profession, was it not clear that a President would not pardon turkeys save for some consideration? My fantasy had a despised incumbent, scant weeks from Election Day with no hope of reelection. His party has stopped advertising his hopeless run. He is asked to pardon a couple of turkeys in return for a small campaign contribution. He becomes inspired and tells the turkey manufacturers he wants two hundred million dollars or he will pardon every turkey in America.

So far so good, and here's the kicker—in order to convince the American People to endorse his ban on turkey, he enlists the genius of his treasured speechwriter. She, a Lesbian, has just returned from China, whither she and her partner had gone to purchase a baby. She says she will write the speech only if the President, in return, will marry her and her partner on National TV. Pretty funny play. And its theme, I believe, is not only that we are "all human," but, better, that we are all Americans.

Here is Clarice Bernstein (the Speechwriter) reading a draft of her speech to Charles Smith, the President:

> The fellow or the woman at the watercooler? We don't know their politics. We judge their character by the simple things: are they respectful, are they punctual, can they listen, "can they get along" . . . we care if they paint their fence. We don't know who they vote for. We don't know what they "do in bed." Who would be disrespectful enough to enquire? If you look at the polls it seems we are a "nation divided." But we aren't "a nation divided." Sir. We're a Democracy. We hold different opinions. But: we laugh at the same jokes, we clap each other on the back when we've made that month's quota; and, sir, I'm not at all sure that we don't love each other. (from November)

There is a final reconciliation of Right and Left, straight and gay, and everything is made right by the *deus ex machina*, Chief Dwight Grackle of the Micmac Nation, who has come to assassinate the President, and the curtain line is "Jesus, I love this country." As do I. And my love increased the more I thought about it. I considered the play a love letter to America.

A local New York paper tried to close the play. Their fellow was outraged, finding it politically incorrect, in which he was, astonishingly, acute.

Now, the plot thickening, the *Village Voice* asked me to write an article on the play's politics. I wrote them an essay titled "Political Civility," which laid out my views as above. I knew, however, that the *Voice* (a) has always been the voice of the Left; and (b) that they, over the years, had generally accepted my work only kicking and screaming. So I schemed to ensnare them. I began my essay on civility and consideration with an anecdote about the *Village Voice*.

Norman Mailer reviewed the first production in America of *Waiting for Godot* in the *Village Voice*. He called it trash. He went home though, and thought about it and returned to see the play again. He recognized it now as a work of genius, and bought a page in the *Voice* renouncing his review, and praising the play. I began my essay with this anecdote.

Aha. The *Voice* took the bait and published the article. They, however, retitled it "Why I Am No Longer a Brain-Dead Liberal." The New York paper, enraged, *rereviewed* my play, giving it a worse notice than the first time around, and I was embraced by the Right.

———

Then I was asked to write a book on politics. And, in the words of Gertrude Stein, so I did, and this is it.

2 | THE AMERICAN REALITY

It was observed, and I cannot remember by whom, that "like all prolific writers, he was very lazy." This is certainly true of me. I am prolific, and look upon my lengthy and various credits as must an inveterate debtor look upon the completed list of his obligations: it fills me with shame. Why? Perhaps because none of it felt like work, but like escape. What sort of sick fool would need to still so many terrifying thoughts by so much production?

In any case, I have been granted the dispensation to spend my days making the unpleasant pleasant.

By whom was I granted this right? By the society in which I live, which found my works sufficiently diverting to pay me to sit alone all day and continue as I had begun.

Leisure for reflection, somewhere near the end of a long career, leads me to thank God for allowing me to live in a society sufficiently free of Governmental control to allow the citizenry expression of its *true* diversity, which is to say, diversity of thought.

For, certainly, my works do not please everyone. But I, discovering that which does not please, am free to chase the market, to persist as before, or to desist entirely. I am, in short, free to fail, which means I am free to succeed, and, if successful, to enjoy any particularities which such success might confer upon me.

This is not only the American Dream—but the American reality, my growing realization of which prompted me to write this book.

———

I spoke with my first conservatives at age sixty. My rabbi, Mordecai Finley, a centrist, and a founding member of his temple, Endre Balogh, took the time to talk to me. I was impressed not by their politics, which, at the time, made to me no sense, but by their politeness and patience. They gave me a book, and the book was *White Guilt*, by Shelby Steele.

It brought to mind an old Providence, Rhode Island, answer to a difficult question, "What do you want, the truth, or a lie . . . ?"

Having spent my life in the theatre, I knew that people could be formed into an audience, that is, a group which surrenders for two hours, part of its rationality, in order to enjoy an illusion.

As I began reading and thinking about politics I saw, to my horror, how easily people could also assemble themselves into a mob, which would either attract or be called into being by those who profited from the surrender of reason and liberty—and that these people are called politicians. My question, then, was, that as we cannot live without Government, how must we deal with those who will be inclined to abuse it—the politicians and their manipulators? The answer to that question, I realized, was attempted in the U.S. Constitution—a document based not upon the philosophic assumption that people are basically good, but on the tragic confession of the opposite view.

I examined my Liberalism and found it like an addiction to roulette. Here, though the odds are plain, and the certainty of loss apparent to anyone with a knowledge of arithmetic, the addict, failing time and again, is convinced he yet is graced with the power to contravene natural laws. The roulette addict, when he inevitably comes to grief, does not examine either the nature of roulette, or of his delusion, but retires to develop a new system, and to scheme for more funds.

The great wickedness of Liberalism, I saw, was that those who devise the ever new State Utopias, whether crooks or fools, set out to bankrupt and restrict not themselves, but others.*

---

*President Obama said, "The individual at some point, must be able to say, 'I have enough money.'" But will Mr. Obama, out of office, say this of himself, and of the vast riches he will enjoy? One must doubt it.

I saw that I had been living in a state of ignorance, accepting an unexamined illusion and calling it "compassion," but that there were those brave enough to work their way through the prevailing slogans of their time, and reason toward a consistent, practicable understanding of human relations. To these, politics was not the manipulation of the ignorant and undecided, but the dedication to the defense and implementation of just, first principles, for example, those of the United States Constitution.

I saw that to proclaim these beliefs in individual freedom, in individual liberty, and in the inevitable evil of surrender of powers to the State, was, in the general population, difficult, and in the Liberal environment, literally impossible, but yet men and women of courage devoted their lives and energies to doing so, undeterred not only by scorn but by despair.*

I will now quote two Chicago writers on the subject, the first, William Shakespeare, who wrote "Truth's a dog must to kennel; he must be whipped out, when Lady the brach may stand by the fire and stink"; the second, Ernest Hemingway, "Call 'em like you see 'em and to hell with it."

---

*The Right and the Left, I saw, differ not about programs, but about goals—the goal of the Left is a Government-run country and that of the Right the freedom of the individual from Government. These goals are difficult to reconcile, as the Left cannot be brought either to actually state its intentions, nor to honestly evaluate the results of its actions.

3 | CULTURE, SCHOOL SHOOTINGS, THE AUDIENCE, AND THE ELEVATOR

Culture predates society, as it evolves before consciousness.

Consider, Friedrich Hayek writes, an unwritten law that is universally accepted and practiced and that both predates and gives rise to verbal codification: in a potentially violent altercation, the party nearest his opponent's home will withdraw.

The Culture, of a country, a family, a religion, a region, is a compendium of these unwritten laws worked out over time through the preconscious adaptations of its members—through trial and error. It is, in its totality, "the way we do things here." It is born of the necessity of humans *getting along*. It does not come into being because of the inspiration, nor because of the guidance, of any individual or group, but it evolves naturally: those things which work are adopted, those which do not, discarded. This evolution has been referred to as "social Darwinism," but, as Hayek teaches, it is not. Darwin observed that the individuals of a species which were better fitted to their environment throve and interbred, thus strengthening their particular adaptation. Those without the effective adaptation died out.

But the evolution of a culture takes place not through the disappearance of those lacking a beneficial adaptation and the interbreeding of its possessors, but through imitation. That culture which has discovered a beneficial adaptation is imitated by those cultures which perceive its worth—the possessors and nonpossessors of an adaptation do not compete on this basis—all may adopt the beneficial behavior and thrive.

———

The greatest endorsement of my Grandparents' immigrant generation was "He is my landsman." Which was to say, "He comes from
my shtetl and my lodge (my culture), and I can, thus, *predict* how he
will act." This is not to say that the landsman was perfect, or that the
prediction was infallible, but that, sharing a culture, one could take a
large amount of energy which otherwise would have been expended
on self-defense, and utilize it more productively. (Cf. the locker room
of a jiujitsu academy, where one may safely leave one's valuables
unlocked and in the open; as the more skilled could easily overcome
the neophytes, and skill has been gained only through attendance
and study—status awarded not only for physical accomplishment,
but, as per the tenets of this particular tribe, for honorable behavior.)

The grave error of multiculturalism is the assumption that reason can modify a process which has taken place *without* reason, and
with inputs astronomically greater than those reason might provide.

Sowell, in *Ethnic America*, points out that the behavior of ethnic groups in America predates their immigration (or transplanta-
tion) to this country; and may be seen as growing out of the ancient
necessities facing these groups in their original lands. For example,
the Jews are an historically stateless people, and so had to invest
their time and wealth in that which could be transported without
confiscation—education; the Irish, living for centuries under foreign
rule and at the whim of invaders, had to form their own hermetic
state-within-a-state, to provide support, protection, and justice,
hence their introduction of and success with what became known
here as ward politics.

These cultural adaptations predate and are the basis for that more
conscious, more sophisticated agglomeration called society, which
might be said to be the appurtenances growing out of culture.* Thus,

---

*Compare Thorstein Veblen, *The Instinct of Workmanship and the State of the Industrial Arts*, 1914: "For the basis of settled habit goes to sustain the institutional fabric of received sophistications, and these sophistications are bound in such a network of give-and-take that a disturbance of the fabric at any point will involve more or less of a derangement throughout. This body of habitual principle and preconceptions is at the same time the medium through which experience receives those elements of information and insight on which workmanship is able to draw in contriving ways and means and turning them to account for the uses of life."

as Sowell writes, the communal culture is a *real possession*, available to all through the efforts of all, not only in the present day, but historically. This possession, as per Veblen (as above) is little different from the individual inheritance of an actual, material tool—though it is not material, it *is* a tool, and an inheritance.

The tool of culture is the capacity to predict the operation of the social environment—a property right little different from a right in land or wealth. This cultural right exists not limitlessly—for any property right is limited, by chance, death, inflation, erosion, theft, laws, confiscation, etc. but, as with a material property right, founded upon an abstract concept: *predictability*, which differs from omniscience, but is of immeasurably greater worth than ignorance. Culture exists and evolves to relegate to habit categories of interactions the constant conscious reference to which would make human interaction impossible.

We have all experienced, for example, the phenomenon of the First Night in a New Home. The myriad bits of information in our possession of which we were unaware: the location and operation of the light switch, the steps-to-the-couch, the meaning of a creak in the floor (is it the house settling, or is it the step of an intruder?), these countless accommodations, worked out over time, and *without the individual's conscious knowledge* either of their content or of their presence, are, in the new home, brought to consciousness, and demand energy, consideration, and response. The cultural cursor has been put back to zero, and the mind and spirit complain, "I can't do all these things at once," and indeed, we cannot. And the first nights in the new home are spent without sleep, and longing for peace.

See *The Fatal Conceit: The Errors of Socialism* (to take another idea and a title from Hayek), prime among which is the misconception that the human mind can (a) conceive, and (b) implement a better way of accomplishing a process worked out over millennia by a mechanism infinitely more suited to the task than the human mind (that process being the interaction of human beings, each of whom want something from the other, and all of whom must live together, which is to say, adapt, which is to say, arrive at a solution).

Our current societal (as opposed to cultural) development is burdened by the presence of "Good Ideas." These ideas are called Good not because their implementation has led to the betterment of life, but in homage to the supposed goodwill or intellectual status of their instigators. Examples will come to mind based upon the individual reader's political or moral complexion, but, for the purposes of illustration in this essay, they may be said to include feminism, birth control, "diversity," free love, and the profusion of "countercultural" innovations spawned in the 1960s.*

This joyous extemporizing of a "new social vision" has brought about an effect not unlike the first night in the new home. It exacts a great cost in bringing to the conscious (unprepared and unskilled) mind those decisions worked out over time. One cost is confusion: angry feminists, lonely aging males, full divorce courts, broken families, grieving children, and a growing disbelief not only in the possibility of domestic accord, but of the efficacy of the free market.

The millennia-long evolution of the human family as a means of dealing with the environment was discarded by my generation of fantasists, in favor of a concept not only artificial, but *inchoate*: "freedom"—the pursuit of which has led to misery. See today's film and television love stories. They, almost universally, feature a man and a woman who despise each other, but come, at the end of the piece, to see that, nonetheless, they, somehow "belong" together, and will "make a go of it."

This is a sad inversion of the traditional story of a man and a woman who love each other, and are kept apart by (and eventually united by their ability to overcome), circumstance. (That is, they are awarded happiness through the exercise of their will.)

The "Good Idea" (the unimplementable concept), fails, for it is the product of a consciousness incapable of recognizing let alone assessing possible variables. When it fails, the conscious mind balks at the necessity of spending further energy on that which was once

---

*See also the grand visions of Urban Planning, which destroyed the Black Neighborhood, Welfare, which destroyed the Black Family, and Affirmative Action, which is destroying the Black Youth.

free; which is to say, unconscious: the culture.* The enlightened, socially aware individual, however, a believer in the primacy of the Individual Mind, now affronted by defeat, regresses to that realm which once supported but has now failed him—his unconscious—and takes revenge. He becomes angry.

One might ask not why mass shootings are happening, but why they are happening in schools. Troubled youngsters from troubled families have, traditionally, had the possibility of solace in those institutions operating in loco parentis. The child and adolescent, denied order and predictability in the home, might find it on offer in the rules of the school; learn your lesson, dress and act appropriately, sit down, shut up. Though the child complains, these are, to him a comfort. For they are predictable, and they are *impersonal*, and, so, he need not (in contradistinction to the enormities of life at home) take them personally. As such they are the perfect inculcator of a respect for law, tradition, and property without which the child can have no success in the wider, less predictable world beyond the school.

If the school and its subjects, rules and regulations, and expectations are *unpredictable,* eventual autonomy becomes, to the young, unimaginable, and the wider world which the adolescent knows himself incapable of dealing with becomes not a phenomenon to be faced after the acquisition of skills, but an immediate and frightening exigency. School, in teaching the mastery of skills (the three Rs) gives the child faith in his ability to master *other* skills—schools devoted to the debatable (social studies, multiculturalism, and other moot topics) weaken the child—for, even as they seem to endorse some inchoate sense of "social justice," they offer the adolescent hungering for certainty a curriculum of pabulum, and reward him for regurgitating the school's positions.†

*Consider the congruent phenomenon of the response to the inevitable failure of Government Programs. These Good Ideas—the Great Society, the War on Poverty, etc.—as above, upon inevitable failure, spawn increased governmental programs to "complete" their "work"—their failure being, inevitable again, ascribed to underfunding.

†The mastery of skills is, more basically, essential, as inculcating the practical *approach* to problems: that is, "What am I trying to accomplish, is it worthwhile, what are its probable

College, once a predictable, practicable course of study designed to fit the individual for self-support, has become, at least in the Liberal Arts, an extension of the bad high school, which is to say, of the terror of adolescence.

The advertisement of "choice"—in curriculum, in behavior (in the glorification of "alternative lifestyles") while a charming idea to the conscious (pleasure-bent) eighteen-year-old mind, is, actually, to him deeply unsettling. For the eighteen-year-old knows that at some point he must abandon even graduate school, and get on in a world which, he knows, the pandering cry of "choice" is not fitting him for. Gender studies, multiculturalism, semiotics, deconstruction, video art, and other such guff, while attractive to the child, as they seem to endorse his "adulthood," are in truth, terrifying as his clock ticks on toward the school's relaxation of its authority, that date on which it will spew the unschooled, confused, skill-less student into a world which, he must know, is uninterested in his capacity for bushwah, and wants to know what he can contribute to the common effort.

Consider college education which, in the Liberal Arts, and in the social sciences, or whatever they may be called today, is effectively a waste of money and time, and useless save as that display of leisure and wealth Veblen called "conspicuous consumption." A Liberal Arts education is essentially a recognition symbol, which, as such *might* theoretically facilitate entrance into a higher class, were entrance awarded on the basis solely of that passport; but see the MAs in English bagging groceries. Higher Education is selling an illusion: that the child of the well-to-do

---

costs, where might I go for guidance, what tools do I require, how may I judge my progress?" These tools are the necessary precondition of any success in the world, whether in changing a tire or in supporting a family. As obvious as it is to state, the test, "How will I know when I am done?" seems to have escaped the voters on the Left. "When," they might be asked, "will there be *enough* 'Social Justice'? When will there be *enough* redistributing of wealth? When will there be enough 'equality'?" This inability, in the electorate, to frame actual, practicable goals is exploited, first by the demagogue, and then by the dictator he may become or who replaces him; for, in the totalitarian state, *nothing* is enough, and, so the "Programs" must always continue.

need not matriculate into the workforce—that mastery of a fungible skill is unnecessary.*

It spews him eventually, even after the most attenuated "graduate study," increasingly embraced by the affluent and confused—into a marketplace the lessons of which he is at a vast disadvantage to face, let alone master, having (a) waited too long, and (b) taught himself that he need not stoop to consider the practical.

The Liberal Arts graduate student has stayed too long at the fair—as the once-nubile career woman finds that her marriage prospects at forty-five are not the same available to her twenty years previously; and as the middle-aged roué discovers that the possibility of domestic love and security have receded with habits formed by decades of dating and "freedom."

Conservative reasoning asks, "What *actually* is the desired result of any proposed course of action; what is the likelihood of its success; and *at what cost*?" (The last, importantly, including the costs of possible failure.) These are, to the social tinkerer, unknowable, their sum being expressed, euphemistically, as "the law of unintended consequences."

———

School shootings and the increased enrollment in postgraduate Liberal Arts studies may be seen as two unconscious attempts at adaptation of a culture evolving away from the exigencies of staffing a trained workforce. For though much has been made of the necessity of a college education, the extended study of the Liberal Arts actually *trains* one for nothing. And the terrified adolescent, abandoned

---

*Liberal Arts colleges have also traditionally sold their wares on the claim that such will allow the students to "discover themselves." It is no accident that decades of such advertising have attracted and produced graduates who are unfitted for society, who can survive only through parental or institutional subvention, as intellectuals, as soi-disant "artists" or as "drifters." Who does not know the thirty-year-old described by his parents as "still searching for himself"? By forty this person is, by his parents, generally not described at all, for to do so would be either to skirt or to employ the term "bum." It is not the purpose of the university to allow or to help students "find themselves," but to fit them to take a place in and contribute to their society. How may endorsing and prolonging the impenetrable solipsism of adolescence do so? It cannot and it has not.

by society, coddled by society, may, if unbalanced, turn to rage and (a) kill; or, if merely clueless, (b) hide in college, as he does not possess the strength to grow up and leave.

———

Which brings me to the elevator.

A group of strangers enter an elevator. They arrange themselves according to not only conscious, but *unconscious* patterns of deference. Contributing to the arrangement are unconscious recognitions of size, gender, age, wealth, social status, and education (as evidenced by dress and attitude), vocation (as suggested by dress and appurtenances), sexual desirability, perceived threat (a function of size, age, race, demeanor)—not only of the individual, but of the individual in that particular group. For an individual will be given preference, deference, or the lack of same based not solely on the above per se, but in consideration of the admixture of persons in the elevator, the time of day, the likelihood of many or few stops; a pattern which changes with each new arrival and departure from the car, at which point the entire company redistributes itself.

This, the preverbal, pre-intellectual process of accommodation, is the basis of all culture. It evolves through the accomplishment of shared but unconscious small objectives, which may be collectivized as the preconscious understanding that "We must get along."

———

Civilization is preceded by culture, which is worked out by innumerable interactions over ages.* Culture may be obliterated by revo-

---

*The intellectual may dismiss their importance (confirmation, baptism, Bar Mitzvah, marriage) but, in so doing, he does not obviate, but merely postpones and camouflages their appearance.

The contemporary youth, pampered in perpetual adolescence through college and graduate school, is spared, or, it may be said, is unaware of the necessity that self-sufficiency is a prerequisite for marriage.

He lives in a serial nonpledged monogamy, in ad-lib cohabitation. This is preceded by no awe-provoking exchange of oaths, or reminder of his (now legal) duties.

When he tires, and eventually marries, the ceremony will be understood as supererogatory—has he not engaged in cohabitation several times before? He knows how to live with a woman, he has done it many times.

The awesomeness of an oath, and the meaning of his signature on a legal document

lution (at which point it is, predictably, superseded by Terror), but it will and can evolve only at its own speed, and in a direction shaped by its own countless interactions—neither in response to individual nor to communal will, but through the mechanism of unconscious interaction and toward an unknowable end.

———

Tolstoy, in the epilogue to *War and Peace*, wrote that the savage, on seeing the railroad train, believes that the train is caused by the puff of smoke, for he sees the smoke first.

But the smoke, he wrote, does not cause the locomotive, and five million Frenchmen could not have marched into Russia because Napoleon suggested they do so. Obviously, then, there must be some deeper force at work, a force we cannot ever understand.

The actual operations of a culture are *deeply* mysterious.*

———

committing him to various responsibilities, will occur to him—though only at the *end* of his marriage. They, in their totality are known as "divorce," which has, in our day, replaced marriage as the culturally determined ritual signifying "leaving home."

The ceremony of beginning one's new home, of separating from one's parents, originally ending in marriage, with desire and joy, has been replaced and is now attended by rancor and shock: the community has finally insisted upon its rights.

*In 1998 Daimler-Benz, and the Chrysler Corporation, of the U.S. were engaged in prolonged negotiations regarding their proposed merger. A sign appeared on the shop floor at Chrysler: "Culture will beat organization every time." (Paul Ingrassia, *Crash Course*)

A guest comes to your house. He mentions that he collects and enjoys rare scotch.

It happens that you have just received a bottle of rare scotch, and it sits, unopened, on your sideboard. "I'm not a big scotch drinker," you say. "I wouldn't know one from another, but I just received this as a gift. It's just going to *sit* there; please, why don't *you* take it?"

The guest may accept or decline the gift. Should he accept he is likely to say: "Thank you, but only on the condition that you share it with me." You open the bottle and the guest pours you both a shot, which you both enjoy with the appropriate comments. When the evening is over, it is not unlikely that the guest will leave without reference to the now-opened bottle. At this point you, the host, are likely to suggest that he take "his" bottle with him. He, again, may accept with thanks, or refuse gracefully. No social norms have been violated.

But consider a similar situation.

The guest arrives, and notes the rare bottle of scotch. You open it, and pour two drinks, and you both remark on its excellence. At the close of dinner you suggest that, as you are not a big scotch drinker, the guest should take the bottle home with him. This is now a gross breach of manners; the guest cannot accept without the taint of greed, he cannot decline without the risk of offense, and, indeed, he *has* been offended, for he has, now, not been offered a gift, but scraps from your table.

_____

Those of us in show business spend our lives trying to understand, subvert, and predict the actions of the audience. It cannot be done.

Not only will the audience endorse what it chooses irrespective of cajolery, but it will communicate its preferences instantly and without apparent intervention of traditional forms of discourse or of cogitation. For the audience reacts preconsciously; it will laugh, cry, fall asleep, gasp, or leave, without reference to reason, as a conjoined entity making its decisions in an unpredictable fashion, according to unstatable goals.

The choices of the audience, of Napoleon's army, of the folks in the elevator, are the working out of a mystery. It may be glimpsed, it cannot be understood, and to tinker with its processes is to court great risk.*

*See the presumption of courts to award custody of small children to mothers; and California's community property law, which, however much it presents itself as gender neutral, is, effectively, an acknowledgment that a woman's period of nubility is limited and irreplaceable. In the above cases the cultural understanding that women and infants must be protected is so deep and ineradicable that even in a climate of supposed "gender neutrality" (see the absurdity of women paying alimony to men), the law assumes the coloration of gender-blindness in order to serve the underlying goal, which is the viability of the culture *irrespective* of those laws enacted for its supposed betterment.

4 | ALCATRAZ

I was in the Fairmont Hotel in San Francisco, looking out of a big picture window at Alcatraz. I asked my ten-year-old, "Do you know what Alcatraz is?" He said, "Yes, it is a tourist attraction, but it used to be a federal prison."

Things change. Isn't it interesting how kids learn? I got my information from Warner Bros. movies; where did he get his information from?

In my racket, show business, one learns through doing and through watching. The second assistant cameraman spends years watching the shot being set up, lit, and prepared. Eventually he learns and advances toward the day he will be director of photography.

There is no way to approximate the experience of failure in front of an audience. It has nothing to do with the censure of teachers who are, after all, paid to be nice to one, or at least, to keep one's custom. Actors and writers stay in school to spare themselves that lesson. And they stay in school because they do not know any better.

Temple Grandin, an animal behaviorist, cattlewoman, and designer of livestock systems, is autistic and writes extensively about the similarities between autism and animal thinking. Both think in pictures. Both learn through observation. A hand-reared animal does not know how to behave in the wild, what is food, what is threat, and how to behave toward its superiors. Stallions, she writes, have a reputation for viciousness but are not vicious because they are stallions, but because they, being valuable creatures, have been raised in isolation. They have never learned the submission and dominance patterns of the group.

College, while it may theoretically teach skills, also serves to delay the matriculation of the adolescent into society. He, thus, does not get a chance either to submit to nor to observe unfettered human interaction. This student, not surprisingly, develops a sense of immunity which, after graduation, often results in either a string of failures and rejections, or in his retreat to the exclusive coterie, and extended college-like atmosphere of protection, this last if he is blessed with the crippling curse of not having to make a living.*

As we live by our brains, and as our brains function best through observation, the absence of actual experience of the world opens the student to formation of some conclusions which have no or only harmful application outside the halls of ivy. If he is rewarded by pleasing the teacher, that is, by repeating an endorsed behavior, he, like any other animal, is going to take his learning out into the world. "George Washington, Father of our country—have a pellet of food . . . Thomas Jefferson, third President, but owned slaves and kept a mistress—have an appointment as a graduate instructor." Light comes on, pull lever, get pellet of food. This is fine for the rat, for the rat lives in the lab. In the wider world, however, the path to food is more demanding and its signals cannot be learned inside the lab. To keep pulling the lever when the technicians are gone is called the Cargo Cult.

The Trobriand islanders profited from the presence among them of the Allied Forces in World War II. The forces left, but the islanders kept building driftwood airplanes in the hopes of luring back the food and support.

"Thomas Jefferson, third President, adulterer, slave owner." In the lab—get a pellet. Out of the lab—no pellet. Obvious answer—never

---

*Why is the MA in English literature, film, gender studies, and so on, bagging groceries? Because he is just too old to begin an apprenticeship. That door has closed, and his college career has ensured his fittedness only for the position it was advertised as obviating: a menial job.

leave the lab. But the Left may supply the pellet for the ex-student. It is now not a grade, but the protection of the herd.

The problem for the ex-student, however, may be different from that of the rat. The rat pulls the lever, but the college student has to supply a *phrase*, and the phrase has semantic content.

Semantics is the study of how words influence thought and action. "Sit down" will have a different response than, "Sit right down," "Sit the hell down," "Oh, sit down," "Please sit down," and so on. The college student is not merely pulling a lever, but repeating ideas. He, of course, comes to prize the ideas whose repetition rewarded him. He thinks these ideas themselves are good. How could he think otherwise? For they have brought him food, and so are good. And so unquestionable.

But like the rat in the wild, looking for something shaped like a lever, the released student/intellectual will and must look for opportunities to exercise his learned behavior, and win a reward. The reward may be status or position. It is, more usually, safety in the group.

Thomas Jefferson, slave owner, adulterer, pull the lever.

Why, then, should the student, raised in captivity, examine either the content or the consequences of this connection?

He is of that group, and rewarded for being of that group which knows that slave-owning is bad. But everyone knows that slave-owning is bad. The owners did as much as the slaves. There is no actual wider benefit or merit in being able to repeat it, so its repetition is useful only as a recognition symbol, allowing its utterer access to those whose thinking process is similarly limited.

Group recognition symbols are essential; that's why we all play, "Oh, do you know . . . ?" That's how our animal minds know whom to trust and whom to kill. But a further cost of these intellectual recognition symbols is a membership in a group trained to repeat rather than to consider.

Thomas Jefferson was an adulterer; so was every President, most likely. That's why men get into politics; it gives them power. Power brings sex, just as it was in the cave days. Politicians are supposed to have a wife. With increased success they can have all the sex they want, so they are invited to commit adultery. And those who do not steal (and many do not, but some do), will bend the laws, some for personal benefit, for contributions, for the benefit of friends, some in the service of their Country, some through folly. Because they have power.

———

What else does power do? How might one abuse power? How does one seek it? Knowing the nature of power, why is one inclined to abdicate any power or reason, blindly praising a person or idea?* Ideas may accrete into a philosophy, which is a coherent ordered view of the world, or they may accrete into an elaborated recognition symbol, a series of degrees like that of the Masons.

Che Guevara was a mass murderer; we have his depiction on the walls of our children's rooms. We do not have there the picture of Charles Manson. Why? Che "sought power for the People." How does one know? One has been told. But wait, as a politician, he was probably no different from Thomas Jefferson, which is to say, he was just a man. Is it different, being a mass murderer and being an adulterer? "Ah, but I have seen Che's photo on the bedroom wall of my son." Would I so mislead my son? Why not? It was done to you. And me.

Kindness is good. No doubt. What, however, is kindness? Kindness to the wicked is cruelty to the righteous. As a child I read of the Tibetan monk who left his home, walked a thousand miles and discovered, hidden in his robe, an ant which only existed in his home village. So he walked the thousand miles back to replace the ant, to avoid doing it violence. But how many ants did he step on on the way?

"Practice random acts of kindness." Is it kindness to give a few dollars to a beggar who is likely to spend it on alcohol? Do I have the interest or ability to determine actually what his problem is,

*Those on the Left, generally, do not understand that they are endorsing a *position*. They understand what, to the Right, would be arguable assumptions, as "beyond question," or, to use a blunter but more accurate term, "taboo."

and if I should, how I should help him? Or is it just easier to give him the money? Of course it is, for it makes me feel good, as I may call it kindness.

Is it kindness to pass a real estate bill, which while rewarding some, harms most and brings our country close to bankruptcy?

The problems of the real world are real problems, and most of us are overprotected beings. You and I may pull the lever of Reward Me for the Right Answer—so far so good. But the effects will be far reaching, as our rewards have a semantic content, and our learned responses which we understand as "basic truths," and, so, beyond question, will affect not only ourselves but others.

"Capitalism is bad"? Not the capitalism that founded and supported Stanford or Harvard or Penn; not that which makes our clothes, and cars and guitars, and brings the food and so on, and not that which employs and supports us, or has supported the parents which supported us; and not those businesses we, in our dreams, would like to create ("Gosh, I've got a billion-dollar idea"). But we have gotten the pellet for repeating that capitalism is bad, Thomas Jefferson was an adulterer, and the loop is closed because we have been rewarded. So let us vote for higher taxes on business, although if we look around, California, with the highest taxes in the country, is broke, having taxed business away. And let us vote for a top-down economy, for certainly Government, which destroys most everything it touches, can run the auto industry better than business-people can. But by what convoluted logic does it make sense that a man who never made a car can make cars better than an industry of carmakers? Do you want your surfboard made by a surfboard maker or an oceanographer? But Thomas Jefferson had slaves.

And this is a racist country. Q. Are you a racist? A. No. Q. When was the last time you heard a racist remark or saw racial discrimination at school or work? Ah yes, but I got the pellet. The pellet was fine, but it came with a price. The price was a limited ability to see the world. Do African Americans think it is a racist country? I'm sure they see subtle and not-so-subtle bias and prejudice every day. A Jew is aware of anti-Semitism of which the non-Jew is not. But under the law, this is *not* a racist country, and what other choice would you have? De facto, and de jure, this is a nonracist country, and the only other test I can see is that any taint of bias, any potential bias, whether it results in discrimination or not, must be eradicated at all costs. So let us enact hate crime laws, as if getting beaten to death were more pleasant if one was not additionally called a greaser. And let us ensure that the Government, to eradicate "hate speech," will become the arbiter on all speech—that same Government whose very return address on the envelope awakens fear. Let's give them more power, because I pulled the lever and I got a pellet. It's a racist country, America is an exploiter. Capitalism is bad. Israel is corrupt.

If we identify every interaction as possessing a victim, (find the victim, get a pellet), we are training ourselves away from the ability to ask what are the issues, how do I know, what are the biases of the reporters, how do the issues affect me, what, if any, is my responsibility?*

———

Perhaps there is another view of the world, in which every transaction need not be reduced to victim and oppressor. What would such a worldview be? What skills might one need to see the world thus, as a flea market rather than a slave market? Identity politics reduce the world to victims and oppressors. But is there another way of looking at the world? Do we want, for example, to judge the rights and wrongs of the Middle East conflict on the basis of the predominant darker tint of one of the party's complexions?

Is not the federal Government which we revile the same Government we want to enlarge? Are not the same taxes we want to increase the same taxes we, every one, scheme to avoid, the same capitalism we are taught to loathe the same capitalism which allows us to thrive?

---

*Is it "a racist country," because some television show was hawking as news a group of deranged skinheads posturing? Let's note the fact that the broadcasters considered it a sufficient novelty to display it as newsworthy. And let us note further that there is *no* position closed to any African American because of his race. Our laws and our culture as a whole have conclusively *rejected* racism. Why does it delight the Left to claim the contrary?

Our task in life is not to guess which lever to pull, but to learn to determine, in the wild, as it were, how to support ourselves. Is this not a return to savagery? Not at all. It is a return to community, for in the free market, success comes only from the ability to supply the needs of others.

We recognize it when the power goes off, or the rains or snow come, and we look to our neighbors for what we need, recognizing we are going to have to reciprocate, and are happy to do so. Will there be abuses? Of course. But our free enterprise system, and the free market in ideas brings more prosperity and happiness to the greatest number of people in history. It is the envy of the world. This envy often takes the form of hatred. But examine our local haters of democracy, and of capitalism, the American Left and their foreign comrades come a-visiting to tell us of our faults. They are here not because we are the Great Satan, but because here they are free to speak. And you will note that when they write they copyright their books, and buy goods with the proceeds.

———

It is said that you don't train the new puppy during the training periods; you're training the new puppy every moment of the day. The puppy is a learning machine, as is the child and the adolescent.

The transition from college marks the end of that period in which the child is effortlessly assimilating knowledge. Past this point, the changing of beliefs will be something of an effort. But there is always new information. Where and how do we learn to think for ourselves? In the world and only in the world. In the free marketplace of ideas, where one can run home neither to Momma nor to the enveloping warmth of the herd which has replaced her.

Who is wise enough to untangle those processes of herd thinking which reward him? This was Freud's question. How does the mind examine itself? How do we learn zero-based thinking? How do we learn to see things as they are and form our own opinions?

In the free market, we learn to follow those courses which support us. We learn not to yell at the boss, to get along with our coworkers, to consider the other guy's side of the story. And we love the victim of colonial oppression and capitalism 'til we're asked to actually work to support or to abide him. And then we may think again, and ask what it will cost; and the vaunted "homeless" of our imagination, on our actual doorstep, may be reidentified as vagrants.

For the Government, that is the men and women, as opposed to the Constitution, is a bunch of slaveholders and adulterers just like you and me.

Society functions in a way much more interesting than that multiple-choice pattern we have been rewarded for succeeding at in school. Success in life comes not from the ability to choose between the four presented answers, but from the rather more difficult and painfully acquired ability to formulate the questions.

5 | LOST HORIZON

The Liberal young are taught to shun work. They, like Marx and his beneficiaries, the French, find it an exercise both odious and superfluous. How could the young think otherwise, as they spend their four to six or seven years in pursuit of a Liberal Arts Education whose content, let alone whose purpose, no one seems quite able to describe (compare Existentialism, Deconstruction, Theory. Those incapable of recognizing bushwa may assume that someone *else* surely knows what these things mean. But, sadly, this is not the case).*

These Liberal Arts victims were, fifty or sixty years ago, likely to be subsumed into actual enterprises and given entry-level jobs. Or, harkening back to their parents' time, taught practicable (or at least merchandisable) skills, allowing them entrance into the various Professions.

Currently, those entry-level or, indeed, make-work jobs once found in business are in minute supply—the economy has shrunk and will continue to shrink. Elective expansion of bureaucracy of

---

*The Liberal child, unexposed to the concept of self-support, is discouraged from, and indeed will not anticipate, the day of its necessity. And see the assumption underlying the Liberal's consignment of his child to a wash in the gentle pool of doctrine: What is it? That "something will turn up"—he, as an adult participant in a sick economy, knows it will not—or that Society will take care of his child. Putting aside the question of "Why should it?" or "Who will pay?" let us ask "With what monies?" The third, unexamined, and, I fear, more prevalent method of dealing with the child's economic future is not to. "Rabbi Judah said, 'He who does not teach his son a craft teaches him brigandage.' " (Gemara Kiddushin 29A, with thanks to Rabbi Mordecai Finley.)

both Government and Management has resulted in a decreased ability to accommodate the skill-less (both the children of the well-to-do anticipating a rise by mere heritage and those at the bottom, hopeful of the reality of the American Dream).

The current economic jollity leaves the protected Liberal kid in a more extensive bind: unlike those of the lower or working classes, he will never dream of setting his hand to actual labor.

He will not, that is, learn to be an electrician, a plumber, a fire-fighter, et cetera, and avail himself of the universal need for these services and their like to supply his living.

———

No, the luckless product of our Liberal Universities, skill-less, will not touch that item his culture named taboo: work. So we see the proliferation, in the Liberal Communities, of counselors, advisors, life coaches, consultants, feng shui "experts," as the undereducated chickens come home to roost. Here we find the "energy therapist," "past-lives counselor," and those occupations just north of candle-maker, but accorded the respect due a skill or profession by community consent.*

This courtesy is unconsciously extended by the Liberal Community to its unemployable young, as its final gift: they cannot be awarded a job, as there are no jobs, and they are inheriting a country bankrupted by their parents' spending.

What is this New Age "worker" selling? He is flattering his clients' vanity through the pocketbook. This is a pretty good example of Mr. Veblen's *Theory of the Leisure Class*. We gain status, he teaches, through the display of wealth. But there is only so much wealth one can display, and the rich, having accrued wealth too copious for their own individual display, must display it through leisure. Sadly,

---

*Note that these endeavors are easily mastered, in a short intensive course of study or of laying-on-of-hands. They are, in this, much like, and indeed are the progeny of, those lei-sure activities once known as Adult Education, and tagged generically, by wits at the time of its emergence just post-war, as "underwater basket weaving." They are not *learned* but *imbibed*, either through the short-course indoctrination or through the individual's magical discovery of his "gift."

though one may have innumerable homes, one can only have a finite amount of leisure—one can do nothing only twenty-four hours a day. But one is limited only by one's purse in employing others to do *more* nothing on one's behalf, their number and uselessness a reflection of their controller's worth and status.

Now we see the Liberal Young not flocking but *stampeding* into film schools. Why the stampede? The movie industry is bust, television has gone to the dogs (reality programming), and no one has yet figured out the transition to Internet distribution. There are, in short, no jobs at the end of this exhaustive four-year course of watching movies.

There is, however, *protection*. The film school student is protected, by his community, in his election *not to work*.

Film, and the Arts in general, have long been exempted from the category of "toil," and so have been the refuge of the Leisure Class. This, however, was understood, if only unconsciously, as a socially acceptable holding area, protecting the males until they got an actual job (in the real, non-showbiz world), the females until they got an actual male.

The jobs are no more, and the females are unlikely to marry a twenty-six-year-old fellow with no skills and no ambition to acquire them.* Only the imprimatur remains.

There is an additional effect of the Liberal, learned aversion to actual work: the young "practitioner" can exist only among his own. His specialized skills can be sold only in the Liberal Communities. He, thus, will quite literally *never*, cradle-to-grave, encounter a Conservative Idea, let alone a Conservative.

These young people have, in the useful if lurid phrase, grown up in a parallel country. They do not know what they do not know, and their insulation, geographically and professionally, ensures their continued ignorance—those they meet, that which they read and see, *nothing* will induce nor force them to confront their inherited cultural assumptions, of which they are unaware, considering them "the nature of the world."

---

*So much for the family.

The world in which they live, in contradistinction to the America which created the wealth to allow their leisure, does not understand the concept of work. It is not that we are becoming, but that we have become two cultures occupying the same space.

There is a good piece of fiction on this phenomenon. It is a novel by James Hilton, *Lost Horizon*. In this beautiful fantasy, a flier, blown off course and crashed in the Himalayas, is rescued and taken to a mysterious, inaccessible lamasery in Tibet.

Here he discovers a perfect land—all its inhabitants are artists and philosophers, there is no disease, a person can, indeed, live as long as he wishes to; there is no want, the people of the Valley have for millennia devoted themselves to the care, physical, material, and sexual, of the folks on the Mountain.

This is a sweet tale by a great storyteller. It is also, less admirably, a Fascist tract. For Mr. Hilton's paradise (he understands, if only subconsciously) can exist only if there are slaves.

Here we see the progression from good ideas to horror, down the path Mr. Hayek pointed out in *The Road to Serfdom*. We will recall that the sibilant in the acronym NAZI stands for Socialist. They, like the Italian Fascists and the pre-Bolshevik Russian Communists, believed, in their beginnings, in Social Justice, and the Fair Distribution of goods. But these sweet ideas are encumbered in execution by the realization that *someone*, finally, has to do the work; their adamant practice will quite soon reveal this: "Oh. We will need slaves."*

These slaves may be called, variously, the Rich, the Jews, the Kulaks, the Gypsies, Armenians, countercultural elements, and so on, but they are chosen not for their odious qualities but for their supine or defenseless nature. And they are enslaved to allow the elite not only exemption from work but exemption from thought.

Originally they are enlisted (fellow travelers, or "useful idiots") or convinced (taxpayers) in order to allow the ideological an exemption

---

*"The wealthy and the powerful no longer have the monopoly of violence they had in the past, and it's driving them up the wall." (Noam Chomsky, *A Hated Political Enemy*.)

from toil and the malleable exemption from thought. As the money dries up, the ideologues are easily supplanted by tyrants and the malleable chained to their oars.

History provides no counter-example. A country which will not work will fall.

Our Hero (Hugh Conway) in *Lost Horizon* discovers, midway through the book, that it was no accident which led him to the lamasery; he, like all the inhabitants, was originally kidnapped—chosen for his "readiness" to unquestioningly accept this new, changeless, and perfect life. Like the young of the Left.

6 | THE MUSIC MAN

Somebody must have power in the state, and it is idle and academic to debate whether those who have power should or should not also have wealth, since they will, in fact, take it. Either you allow people to have power because they are rich, or they become rich through the possession of power. It does not make much difference in practice. Therefore all the common talk about the new equality and the abolition of privilege did not seem to have much meaning. That talk was usually to be heard from the lips of the left-wing writers and politicians who were at the very moment of uttering it busy with establishing new privileges for themselves and their children.

—Christopher Hollis, *Death of a Gentleman*, 1937

A subjective system can never be shown to have failed. If its goals are indeterminate, general, and its progress incapable of measurement, how can its performance be faulted?

Karl Kraus makes this point about Freudianism, describing it as "the disease which presents itself as its own cure." I came across this quote in *Dead Aid*, by Dambisa Moyo, an economist whose work for her native Gambia led her to identify the country's problem not as a structural disposition toward poverty, but as international aid. She makes the case that aid prevents the development of a national economy, the exploitation of national resources, the prosecution of national interests, and leads to the subjugation of recipients to the powers of those agencies, international and domestic, who profit from aid, and, thus, from poverty: bureaucrats, dictators, and thieves.

The distribution of alms, she writes, is based, at bottom, on the notion that it will help—actual evidence to the contrary is stilled by those personally interested in graft, profit, or in a subjective feeling of philanthropy.

Why should Gambia et al. be incapable of self-development? Internationally this supposed lack is attributed to a structural cultural residue of colonialism. But what does this mean, and how might such "structural" inabilities be identified, to what attributed (the United States, Australia, and Canada were all once colonies, Britain a colony of Rome), and how ameliorated?

For if these questions cannot be answered, as Ms. Moyo asks of Gambia and Mr. Kraus of psychoanalysis, and if the underlying assumption cannot be challenged, what possible "cure" other than increased and continued application of that which a reasoned and impartial investigation might identify as the cause of the problem?

If, for example, African Americans are to have a special judicial status because of a legacy of slavery, how might one determine, conclusively, that that legacy has dissipated and it is time to welcome the descendants of its victims back into the general population? (Could such a "legacy" exist for a thousand years? Even the most vehement supporters of the idea would probably say no. Then, for how long? And how might one recognize its absence, and upon what authority announce it?) If Latina women are wiser than white men,* then, in a dispute between the two, to accept the reasoning of the latter rather than the former can always be to risk the accusation of racism.

If a country, a region, a race is in difficulty because of a lack of funds, any new or recurrent failure subsequent to *any* subvention in aid may be attributed to insufficient aid, and provide the rationale for that funding's increase. But it may only do so given the acceptance of the nondemonstrable, indeed disprovable theory that

*In the opinion of Supreme Court Justice Sonia Sotomayor.

government intervention increases wealth. (See also student failure attributable to low teachers' salaries, resulting in increased salaries and benefits for teachers, when there is no demonstrable correlation between student success and teachers' salaries.)

Dambisa Moyo asks, of aid, "What would be enough?"

Kraus asks the question of Freudian analysis: What would be enough? At what point would talking about one's problems for x hours a week, be sufficient to bring one to a state of "normalcy"?

The genius of Freudianism, Kraus writes, is not the creation of a cure, but of a *disease*—the universal, if intermittent, human sentiment that "something is not right," elaborated into a state whose parameters, definitions, and prescriptions are controlled by a self-selecting group of "experts," who can never be proved wrong.*

It was said that the genius of the Listerine campaign was attributable to the creation not of mouthwash, but of halitosis. Kraus indicts Freud for the creation of the nondisease of dissatisfaction. (See also the famous "malaise" of Jimmy Carter, which, like Oscar Wilde's Pea Soup Fogs, didn't exist 'til someone began describing it.) To consider a general dissatisfaction with one's life, or with life in general as a political rather than a personal, moral problem, is to exercise or invite manipulation. The fortune teller, the "life coach," the Spiritual Advisor, these earn their living from applying nonspecific, nonspeci-

---

*The problem, at the end, is that there must be governments, as Moyo says, to pay for things everyone uses but no one wants to fund, like her lamppost. But governments, as they grow, grow corrupt, and aid, as it has corrupted Africa, has corrupted America. We call it taxes.

To make government responsible to the citizens it was originally designed to serve, its size must be reduced, for the invitation to corruption and waste, for personal gain, or from "good intentions" is so great as to be evidently insurmountable. Government must be reduced, not *abolished*, which is the all-purpose canard of the Left. "Do you then vote for anarchy or laissez faire?" But reduced to the point at which the harm it inevitably does can be controlled or reversed. This potentiality is the true worth of the system of free enterprise—the alternative being periodic revolution, where *governments* are overthrown; which is, as Moyo says, the problem with Africa. We elect the worst, on both sides, and then marvel that they steal, subvert, waffle, and do every last thing but obey their oath to defend the Constitution. They are not elected to "do well, " or to "transform" but to serve, protect, and defend the Constitution. And we will only stand a chance of finding those actually dedicated to doing so when we take the money out of it—both theirs to spend and squander, and that accruing to them, on their golden retirement, for all the favors they have done.

fiable "remedies" to nonspecifiable discomforts.* The sufferers of such, in medicine, are called "the worried well," and provide the bulk of income and consume the bulk of time of most physicians. It was the genius of the Obama campaign to exploit them politically. The antecedent of his campaign has been called Roosevelt's New Deal, but it could, more accurately, be identified as *The Music Man*.

---

*"Our thinking and our behavior are always in anticipation of a response. It [*sic*] is therefore fear-based." (Deepak Chopra) Is it too much to suggest that this quote contains the most basic prescription of Liberalism, "Stop thinking"?

7 | CHOICE

There is nothing in the world so difficult as that task of making up
one's mind. Who is there that has not longed that the power and
privilege of selection among alternatives should be taken away from
him in some important crisis of his life, and that his conduct should
be arranged for him, either this way or that, by some divine power if
possible—by some patriarchal power in the absence of divinity—or
by chance, even, if nothing better than chance could be found to do it?
—Anthony Trollope, *Phineas Finn*

Imagine yourself as part of a group placed, magically, somewhere
upon the earth in an environment which is foreign to all—in a wilderness. This group's members have been chosen randomly, they
have no common history, or culture of self-government, or religion.

They have, somehow, never learned to respect or to reward industry; they, somehow, have neither the science nor the technology to
exploit their land, nor to provide defense against real or potential
marauders. They have no wisdom tradition.

So, without science, without wisdom, without tradition, without
any form of traditional government, or the culture to establish one,
they form themselves into a cult.

This cult, while it produces neither sustenance, peace, defense,
nor philosophy, does provide one service, which service unites the
group, and to which all other operations of the group are subservi-
ent: it provides the reassurance that although the actions of the world

may neither be understood nor exploited, fear may be shared out and the stranded group may take comfort in its replacement by denial.

But for denial to replace fear it must be universal, and anyone suggesting notions contrary to those of the group must be shamed, killed, or otherwise silenced—these must be at the very least excoriated as evil. For, indeed, if the group knows neither law nor religion, nor technology, its only good (which is to say its only service) is solidarity. Individual initiative or investigation, thus, is destructive of the group's essence, and so to them *is* evil.

Those things which previous tradition or observation revealed as absolutely good must, by this terrified group, be mocked: individualism and ambition called "greed," development called "exploitation," defense "war-mongering," and use "despoliation."

Inevitable global conflicts are indicted by this group as "nationalism"; strife is brought about by arrogance; and laws sufficiently strict to provide actual guidelines for behavior, "injustice."

This new group will, of course, like any group in history, create taboos and ceremonies of its own. But to ensure solidarity, (for the group, we remember, lives in fear for the fragility of its illusions), these new observances must absolutely repudiate the old; and the cult will indict these previous observances as, for example, paternalism, patriotism, racism, colonialism, xenophobia, and greed.

And it may indict religion as superstition. But man cannot live without religion, which is to say, without a method for dealing with cosmic mystery and those things ever beyond understanding; so the new religion will not be identified as such. It will be called Multiculturalism, Diversity, Social Justice, Environmentalism, Humanitarianism, and so on. These, individually and conjoined, assert their imperviousness to reason, and present themselves as the greatest good; but as they reject submission either to a superior unknowable essence (God), or to those operations of the universe capable of some understanding (science and self-government), their worship foretells a reversion to savagery.

The laws of the seasons, for example, have been studied since human beings first observed that the seasons changed. But the new man, who fears change above all things, has decided that the seasons are now changing in one direction only, toward oblivion, and that this change must be stopped. How may this incomprehensible and awful catastrophe be averted? Only through sacrifice. So the new group, which is the Left, is prepared and is in the process of sacrificing production, exploration, exploitation of natural resources, and an increasing standard of living upon the altar of something called "global warming."

But the earth has, in fact, been noticeably cooling for the last decade, and has, at many times during recorded history, and before any emission of manmade carbon, been markedly warmer than it is now or was prior to this cooling trend. This supposed warming is a story known of old as the history of Chicken Little—it means the End of the World. And to the Left, those denying it are classed as heretics, for who but an evil monster would wish the world to end? And, for the Left, to refer its pressing question to adjudication is to hasten the end of the world. The heretics who would do so are marginalized and dismissed and mocked, even though many are renowned practitioners of science—an ancient social development allowing man to differentiate truth from falsehood by the process of observation and measurement.*

See the Left's inability to discard utterly exploded threats of extinction. In its cosmogony can still be found the theory of Thomas Malthus (1766–1834) that overpopulation will soon and inevitably destroy the world—resulting in mass starvation and the destruction of mankind (birth control); that power must come from "natural," renewable sources (which it, at present, cannot; wind power will

---

*In a conversation with a Liberal Friend, The International Committee on Climate Control had been found to be cooking the books on Global Warming, and its much vaunted "hockey stick" graph showing a marked abrupt increase in the world's temperature incident with the consumption of fossil fuels was revealed as a sham. The Liberal said, yes, perhaps this was true, but would we want to scrap our efforts to control a situation as Serious as Global Warming simply because the phenomenon was proved to be an invention? His argument recalled to me Al Sharpton's championship of Tawana Brawley, whose false accusations and perjury led to the persecution of innocent police officers and the disruption of their lives. When she recanted, and admitted perjury, Reverend Sharpton suggested that though perhaps the testimony was not all it could be *in this case*, nevertheless, he still supported her because of the systematic history, in similar cases, of *supportable* claims of abuse. He was, that is, not interested in the Truth.

not run Philadelphia, and ethanol costs more and pollutes more than gas), and that nuclear power is an unacceptable risk (though it has powered France accident-free for over fifty years); that World Unity and disarmament is the only way to Peace (though the anti-militarism of France and England between the wars led to the conquest of the first, and the near conquest of the second).

All the old canards can be found, as if new-discovered, today on the nearby Volvo: "The Population Explosion: It's Your Baby"; "Wind Power"; "War Is Not the Answer"; "Coexist."

No wonder the Left embraces Socialism, the largest myth of modern times and the most easily debunked; for it is a religion, and the tests of actual membership in any religion are likely to include an endorsement of their Foundation Myths: God in the Burning Bush, Joseph Smith's discovery of the Tablets; the Resurrection of Jesus. This is not to denigrate religions, merely to say that they are all based upon myth and symbol, which is to say that they proclaim at the *outset* their intention to approach toward the unknowable, and toward that over which we have no power. This is, however, necessary in religion, a rather unfortunate basis for a political philosophy.

Observe that to propitiate an unknowable power, the Left, ignorant or dismissive of any society or history but its own, insists upon the primacy of Trees and Soil, Oceans and Animals—theirs is a return to the nature worship of the Savage. To see that this nature worship is not quite the good simple-heartedness they believe it is, but rather a religion, observe its imperviousness to information: polar bears are *not*, in fact, decreasing but *increasing* in population;* the earth is *not*, in fact, warming.†

*"Of the thirteen populations of polar bears in Canada, eleven are stable or increasing in number. They are not going extinct, or even appear to be affected at present. It is noteworthy that the neighbouring population of southern Hudson Bay does not appear to have declined, and another southern population (Davis Strait) may actually be over-abundant." (Dr. Mitchell Taylor, Polar Bear Biologist, Dept. of the Environment, Government of Nanavut, Igloolik, Nunavut, Canada.)

†It is to a dramatist, which is to say, to an unfrocked psychoanalyst, stunning that that which has sustained the Left in my generation, its avatar, its prime issue, has been abortion. For, whether or not it is regarded as a woman's right, an unfortunate necessity, or murder,

The philosophy of the Left is not, in fact, a *love of*, but a *rejection* of wisdom. And it is contrary to common sense.

For where is the wealth to come from? If we are no longer to explore, to drill, to develop or to use the world around us, and those things fashioned from that world; if we are to "cap and trade," that which is, essentially, an imaginary commodity (carbon emissions do not in any way affect the temperature of the planet);* if we are to tax and limit growth in service of a fantasy, who is to chance his time and treasure to produce the wealth, and how?

Carbon dioxide is not harmful to the atmosphere. There have, in the past, been periods, much colder than today, when the CO_2 in the atmosphere was twenty-five times what it is today. Carbon emissions offer no threat whatever to the planet. And, as the Left is opposed to nuclear energy, how are we to provide power?

Where is the power to come from? Where is the wealth to come from? From nowhere. For the Left, this new tribe, self-sufficient in its knowledge, ignorant of history, and unwilling to observe, does not understand economics—that man produces, that man consumes, that man trades—and that the necessary consumption drives trade and its attendant invention and exploration, which produce a civilization's wealth.

The Left (as Thomas Sowell points out in *Intellectuals and Society*) believing in what it calls "social justice," believes that wealth should be "shared," but enters the discussion in its middle. For wealth may or may *not* be shared (in fact, it is shared, as efficiently as possible, through trade), but the a priori question, to the Left, is unasked and unanswered: Where did it *come* from?

---

which is to say, irrespective of differing and legitimate political views, to enshrine it as the *most* important test of the Liberal, is, mythologically, an assertion to the ultimate right of a postreligious Paganism.

*"Aristotle established a general principle of scientific enquiry: 'First we must seek the fact, then seek to explain.' The scientific method is now popularly conceptualised that the science on global warming is settled as a process where authorities balance volumes of opinions. That's it. A phenomenon is now scientifically proven because various authorities and some scientists say so. Evidence now no longer matters." (Ian Plimer, *Heaven and Earth*)

It was not, again, quoting Professor Sowell, descended from heaven, like manna, and spread evenly over the ground. It was created by individual expenditure of effort and individual willingness to undertake risk. The Liberals see wealth as manna from Heaven, falling equally upon all; which, being to them the case, means that for any one to have more of any thing than another, it must have been gotten by cheating—the possessor of "more" must be a thief. To the Left, in spite of one hundred and fifty years of the most extensive and tragic disprovals of Marxism, property = theft.

Rejecting both science and industry, the Left is fearful of man's ability to survive, so it sees scarcity everywhere, and its one answer is to *stop*.

As my generation did not live through the Depression, World War II, and the agony of the immigrants who are our grandparents or great-grandparents; as we were raised in the greatest plenty the world has ever known and in the most just of societies, we have grown lazy and entitled (not unlike Marx, who lived as a parasite upon Engels, and never worked a day in his life). The baby boomer generation, my own, is content, if of the Left, to live out our remaining years upon the work and upon the entitlements created by our parents, and to entail the costs upon our children—to tax industry out of the country, to tax wealth away from its historical role and *use* as the funder of innovation. The religion of the Left is to leave untilled that world whose operations it does not understand and, failing to investigate, fears.

It, therefore, mythologizes uselessness, and praises it.

We have all seen this phenomenon as schoolchildren, in the insecure and self-hating child, raised to think himself weak, who will shrink from effort and from communal activity, attach himself to authorities—the tattletale and the spoilsport, who cannot take the rigors and tests of the schoolyard—the complainer and sanctimonious prig, forever calling out about supposed slights and injustices—his is the all-purpose complaint of the preadolescent "it's not *fair*."

For mine is a generation which never grew up. And we have,

in our short lives, dismantled that necessarily imperfect system of industry and government for which our parents lived and died. We have awarded ourselves for realizing its imperfections—as if any human act or combination were perfect—and have created a culture of guilt and shame—corrosively and compulsively shaming where any human act of individuality may be indicted as wrong (which is to say, destructive of equality or equanimity).

But it is the free individual who alone can provide sustenance for the group. For if there is no effort, no use (called "exploitation"), no reward for initiative (called "greed"), where will the food come from? Malthus, before the invention of the improved plow and before scientific agriculture, "proved" that the world must soon starve.

Socialist Europe is held up as a model of "just behavior"; but the Left forgets that for seventy-five years America defended Europe from the Communist threat, and bore the cost, which would have bankrupted Europe, and which, in the event, bankrupted Communism. The Left looks at the peace of Europe since World War II and forgets that it was not only ensured, but created by American military strength and determination.* And now the Left has elected a President who thinks it good to go to Europe and apologize for our "arrogance," who proclaims the benefits of appeasement both at home and around the world.

This appeasement, called the antiwar movement, the antinuclear movement, One-Worldism, Code Pink, "the end to American Exceptionalism," is, to the Left, another example of the Correct Thinking of the never-involved. They believe that our enemies, like the monsters in *Where the Wild Things Are*, will be so moved by some unnamable but real excellence on our part, that they will forswear their desire for our destruction (recognizing it, now, as an unnecessary expenditure of effort) and beat their swords into plowshares.

But the Left does not stop to consider that if we, the most prosperous country in the history of the world, choose neither to exploit nor to defend our property, someone else will take it, and if we

---

* And funded by the Marshall Plan, which is to say, by a surplus of American industrial wealth.

announce, indeed, *proclaim* our passivity, we will only advance that bad day.

The Left insisted that we abandon, in 1973, a war we had just won in Vietnam, and go on home, as the Left today insists we withdraw from Afghanistan and withdraw from Iraq. Leaving to one side legitimate legislative differences over the strategic worth of any one conflict, what real or potential enemy could possibly misinterpret its possibilities of gain in the light of our absolutely predictable absence of resolve?

Just as the Left, geopolitically, does not recognize enmity (other than on the part of the Right), it judicially does not recognize crime; or that which, historically, was known as crime (that is, behavior transgressive of those statutes enacted for the protection of society), calling it "error," or the effect of "environment," or searching for any artifice to free itself of the mature human necessity of choice and enforcement.* So doing, the Left everywhere relaxes those judicial norms which alone can give some measure of certainty to the populace.

(Note that in Samuel Butler's *Erewhon*, an 1872 Utopian novel, crime was considered sickness, and the criminal coddled and condoled with, while sickness was treated as crime. I will not belabor the similarity to the Left's New Age health movement, which, in its charms, potions, and essences and practices, discards science in favor of "ancient wisdom.")

My generation huddles in ignorance that is felt, on the Left, as a worship of man's "natural state," this supposedly being, all human history to the contrary, one of health and peace, ignoring and in fact rejecting both our imperfections as a species and our differences as individuals.

The random distribution of abilities and ambitions, which has allowed human beings to thrive and communities to grow, and which gives to the group strength and to the individual the pos-

*"The causes are the increased polarization of the society that's been going on for the past twenty-five years . . . larger and larger segments of the population have no form of organization, and no constructive way of reacting, so they pursue the available options, which are often violent." (Noam Chomsky, *Secrets, Lies, and Democracy*, 1994)

sibility of achievement and, so, happiness in the approbation of the group, is derided by the Left as nonsense. To them, each child is born a blank slate, and any difference in subsequent individual accomplishment, status, or wealth, must, thus, be due to some maleficent influence, which is to say, to exploitation.* As if we were created to thrive in a society made exclusively of cobblers, or second basemen, surgeons, or deliverymen. The Left sees trade—the source of wealth—as exploitation; and, each child being born equal, all differences in wealth, again, as theft. (Here forgetting the lessons of the schoolyard—that one child may prefer the orange and the other the candy bar, and, so, both may be made happy by an exchange. Is this simplistic? No, it is simple: left to our own devices, we human beings increase our happiness by unfettered trade, and however much we may vote for Government Supervision [state control] we all delight in barter, and the free give and take of the flea market.)†

To correct this observed inequality, which the Left sees as unnatural, it invented the term "social justice." But a system of Justice already exists, formulated by Legislature, in supposed expression of the will of the people, and administered by the Judiciary. This is called the Judicial System. What, then, is this additional, amorphous "social justice"? It can only mean, as Hayek wrote, "State Justice." Here, though the Left will not follow the reasoning out to its end, the State (operating upon what basis it alone knows, and responsible to no law enacted by the people) confiscates wealth accumulated *under existing laws* and redistributes it to those it deems worthy.

History proves that the worthiest in these Marxist schemes are, or quickly become, those in charge of distribution, which is to say "the State," its constitutional powers usurped by those we know as "dictators."

To the Left it is the State which should distribute place, wealth,

*The poor man is poor because of "structural oppression"; the rich man rich because of "greed."

†"But there must be Laws," the Liberal says. Who would deny it? But the alternative to Statism is not the Left's scareword of *anarchy* but Democracy.

and status. This is called "correcting structural error," or redressing "the legacy of Slavery," or Affirmative Action, or constraining unfair Executive Compensation; but it is and can only be that Spoils System which is decried at the ward level as "cronyism," and lauded at the national level as "social justice." It is nothing other than the distribution of goods and services by the government for ends not specified in the Constitution; and in response to pressure from or in attempts to curry favor with groups seeking preferments or goods not obtainable either under the law, or through those practices of mutual benefit called the Free Market. What obscenities are created in the name of "social justice?" What could possibly be less just than policies destructive of initiative and based upon genetics? (As Thomas Sowell writes, "Are we to say of two babies, born on the same day, that one is born owing something to the other?") Can this Social Eugenicism possibly be corrective of *anything*?

But how, to the Left, to explain the difference in status, in wealth, in happiness, among human beings? (And let us note that the Left, though decrying inequality in the abstract, contains none or few who are willing to redress the differences between their financial state and that of any of their less favored brethren by putting the wealth of the two into one pot and each taking half.)

Proverbs informs us that the poor will always be with us; that, just as one may not, as a judge, favor the rich, neither can one favor the poor, but must do justice according to the law—that is to say, that one must judge whether the *law* has been transgressed, a consideration in which the state of the offender (past his mental competency) must play no part.

The Bible is the wisdom tradition of the West. It is from the precepts of the Bible that the legal systems of the West have been developed—these systems, worked out over millennia, for dealing with inequality, with injustice, with greed, are reducible to that which the Christians call the Golden Rule, and which was, previously, propounded by Rabbi Hillel: "That which is hateful to you, do not do to your neighbor."

These rules and laws form a framework which allows the individual *foreknowledge* of that which is permitted and that which is forbidden. This foreknowledge, a real right-of-property, is that upon which the individual makes decisions. It constitutes a practicable system for dealing with a tragical existence and a deeply flawed human nature: it asserts not the perfection, but the imperfectibility of Man. These assertions (and their attendant investigations and observations, known as philosophy and religion) may be called, in their entirety, the Tragic View.

The Left has abandoned the Tragic View,* and considers life and man as unconstrained in our ability to understand and to supersede all strife and inequality. The Tragic View, however, holds that life is complicated and man flawed, and so, our actions must be guided by laws difficult both of formulation and of observance; that these laws, being the product of Man, will, themselves, be flawed, that they will not cover all instances, that their observation and correct application will often cause anxiety, and, indeed trauma, but that the health of a society (both moral and material) must rest on the attempt to do so.

The tragic view recognizes that it is possible to obviate the necessity of choice only by surrender of responsibility (worship of a dictator, or charismatic figure, guru, politician, or theory)—that between Good and Evil there *is* no choice, and thus moral choice means a choice between two evils.

Having renounced the necessity of dealing with complexity, the Left imagines and endorses a "post-governmental" era, in which the individual need not consider the economic and social results of his actions and his vote. He may choose not to choose, and merely endorse "Change," and reject any request for information about the actual mechanics of this "Change," by referring to "Hope."

In this post-societal world of the new cult, we are told we need not produce, but may merely hope, we need not defend, but may hope, we must not consume, but are allowed, somehow, to hope for sustenance—this sustenance, magically, deriving from some

*As per Friedrich Hayek, *The Road to Serfdom*, 1944.

unspecified actions of a government which, all observe, is at best incompetent and, more usually, self-serving and corrupt, *whoever* is in power.

From the Left's point of view one need not work, and may not only Hope to be provided for, by this government, but may insist upon it. This new post-governmental America, then, may, without guilt, apologize for the arrogance of its prosperity and the beauty of its traditions and culture, and plead with the weak of the world to be allowed to join them.

8 | THE RED SEA

There is another possible interpretation of the parting of the sea by Moses.

Rather than intervening to create a path in a unitary substance, it could be said that he demonstrated that freedom lay in the ability to see distinctions; that is, that life could be seen as divisible into good and evil; moral and immoral; sacred and profane; permitted and forbidden—that the seemingly unitary "sea" of human behavior and ambition could actually be divided.

A slave is not permitted to make these distinctions. All of his behavior is circumscribed by the will of his master. The necessity of making distinctions is the essence of freedom, where one not only can but *must* choose.

This revelation of the long-denied, long-lost necessity was, to the escaping Jews, something of a miracle, inspiring awe, fear, and an attendant shame—shame that they had submitted to enslavement, and shame that they had forgotten the essence of freedom so completely that its possibility seemed to them supernatural. Moses told the Jews to look back at the pursuing army, and said, "Those Egyptians you see today you will never see again"—that is, they would be freed from not only the fact but the shame of slavery as soon as they recognized in themselves the possibility of choice, which is to say, as soon as they entered the sea.

The sea was not the path to freedom, the sea *was* freedom. The essence of freedom was and is choice.

The Jews spent four hundred years as slaves. They were freed with a mighty hand and an outstretched arm, by God; and the world's three Abrahamic religions are founded upon the wisdom text whose center is this story. But when the Jews, within the lifetime of many contemporary readers of story, were again slaves in Europe, suffering and dying, and when we were freed by the West, and formed our own State, much of the West (including, to our shame, many Jews) rejected the lesson of the Bible, and turned our back on the revelation of the possibility of choice, and called this heresy enlightenment, and denounced the State of Israel.

————

Is the State of Israel imperfect? All the works of Man are imperfect.

The Jews were led through the Sea of Reeds and, in the desert, complained, and wished to return to Egypt and slavery. Life in Egypt was by no means perfect; its only attraction was the absence of the necessity of choice. But it made all people equal. No slave need choose between good and evil, morality and immorality, all such anxiety had been usurped by or surrendered to the masters.

The Left embraces Socialism, the herd mentality of slavery, as it offers the, to them, incalculable benefit of freedom from thought. There are, to them, no more disquieting choices, no contradictions, there is only submission to the Group in which the ideas of all (being the same) are equal.

The French Jacobins, similarly, discovered a way to do away with inequalities of stature: they cut off the offenders' heads.

The State of Israel is, in itself, an incurable affront to the Left, for it is a demonstration of the possibility of choice. The slave not only need not persevere in the face of his masters' displeasure or disagreement, he *cannot*—it would cost his life; but the free men and women of Israel persevere in spite of the Left's casuist carping and bellicosity and displeasure, backing their convictions with their lives. An intolerable affront to those preferring equality to liberty.

The urge of the Left to surrender choice and self-government for illusion, to insist upon Statism and Government rule, rather than a Government of Service, is a rejection of the lesson of the Exodus.

For it is obvious to the meanest intellect that the Government cannot make cars, health care, industry in general, better than would individual human beings not only interested in but inexorably tied to the outcome of such operations. The endorsement of the Socialist, Statist system, then, is not a desire for more or better goods and services, but a surrender of this desire in return for an obviation of the necessity of personal choice.* It is a regression not to the *tribe*, but to the herd.

(I am indebted to my son, Noah, for his exegesis on the parting of the Red Sea.)

---

*Most Victorian novels featured the stock character of the profligate son. He was a gambler, and, having run through his inheritance, was constantly appealing to his father to pay his ever renewed gambling debts.

The father inevitably paid, "for the honor of the family." And he paid wringing his hands and cursing his fate. And the son thanked the father, wept, swore to reform, and continued gambling.

Why not, as there was, to him, no cost?

He had been taught, by his father, that there was no penalty for losing.

What worse lesson for a gambler?

For, if losing is cost free, why bother either to (a) learn to gamble or (b) quit?

The serious gambler learns young, and painfully, that he must control his impulses, that he must not pursue fantasy, neither wish for the cards to turn, but learn the odds and husband his resources for those times when the cards or dice *do* favor him.

There is a technical term for the gambler who can neither learn nor quit: he is called a sucker.

Our politicians, left and right, are, to belabor the metaphor, the wastrel son: they are free to spend, to chase fantasies, and to squander resources, *for the resources are not theirs, and there is no penalty for their misuse or loss.*

The wastrel son gambles, at no cost, for the thrill it provides; the wastrel politician does so in pursuit of fantasy (good works), or money. The money may be in direct support for his campaigns, or in free redecorating of his summer home; or it may be issued in the form of plaques recognizing his good works, which plaques, on his retirement from office, may be traded in for money.

9 | CHICAGO

The men of my own stock
They may do ill or well,
But they tell the lies I am wonted to,
They are used to the lies I tell;
And we do not need interpreters
When we go to buy and sell.

—Kipling, *The Stranger*, 1908

Someone once began a question to me commenting that I was from the Midwest, and I interrupted, correcting him, that I was not from the Midwest, I was from Chicago.

It was a rough city, ruled by the Machine Politics, which ruled the state, and currently rules the country. But a turkey at Christmas and a job for your kid on the Force were and are better than the phony-baloney tax rebates, and Alternative Tax "givebacks," and Government "programs" which, in toto, will be less and less important than the Christmas Turkey and the Job.

Folks in my grandfather's generation spoke lovingly about Al Capone and his generosity, but, then, in my experience, most criminals are sentimental. But I would rather deal with a crooked cop than a bureaucrat, and I've had the experience of both. And I loved the rough, matter-of-fact Chicago of my youth, and preferred it to the clean, orderly, self-packaged city of today. When the streets' nicknames go up on the lampposts, the city is dead.

The City then was not the promise of snow removal and an absence of litter, but an amalgam of strivers and hucksters, and I found it, thus, either much like myself, or, more likely, I became schooled by its culture, just like the Mayors Daley and then–State Senator Obama and all the governors and councilmen who went to jail, and Hugh Hefner, building whorehouses which sold everything but sex, and the inspired and depraved of that toddling town. For, of *course*, the athletes and the gunmen and the politicians and the businessmen sat down for a drink together; and the celebrities on the way from New York to L.A. changed trains, and took their doxies to the Ambassador East, and had drinks in the Pump Room with Irv Kupcinet, the talk of the town, and in short it was a growing entity, growing according to the rules of self-interest and self-preservation.

It was so young. When I was born, many were alive whose parents had dealt with the Sauk Indians.*

And there was the Lindbergh Beacon, the most powerful aircraft signal in the world, its light visible for forty-five miles, atop the Palmolive Building, sweeping the sky once-a-minute to make the night safe for air traffic.

Hefner bought the building in 1965 it was renamed the Playboy Building, and they put their logo up, and I used to work there. And the great entertainers worked for him at his Playboy Club around the corner, staffed by the Bunnies in their abbreviated costumes, ears, and cottontails, who were prohibited from dating the customers, but were not prohibited from dating me.

Frank Lloyd Wright designed an open chess pavilion on the beach at North Avenue, and I wrote my first play (*The Duck Variations*, 1972), about two old DPs, sitting there, looking at the lake. A DP was a displaced person, and it was my father's term of opprobrium for an appearance insufficiently put-together. "You look like a DP." Insufficient for what, you might ask, and the answer was "to get on in the world," for why else were we in Chicago?

---

*In the late sixties I was driving a cab, and stopped for a cup of coffee at Mike's Rainbow Café, the cabdriver's all-night joint. I began talking to a fellow driver, a man around eighty, who, he told me, had in his youth driven for Robert Todd Lincoln.

Across the drive from the Chess Pavilion was Lincoln Park, and I used to sit out there and write in my notebook. I dated a wonderful girl who worked for the Mob. She lived in the Belden Stratford Hotel, and in the summer she would sunbathe in the park across from the hotel, by the statue of Shakespeare, and every hour on the hour a bellman would bring her an iced coffee. She drove a Mercedes 280 convertible, and she never locked the car, as, she explained, anyone who wanted to break in would simply slit the roof, so why antagonize them?

The back of her car was ankle deep in parking tickets. She would park on the steps of City Hall. And when the tickets got too deep, she'd collect them in a bag, and give them to somebody who would fix them.

One or two nights a week we would drive to Cicero, and I would watch her doing one of her jobs. She had a ring of keys which let her into the various clubs in which her people were interested. She'd let us in to the deserted clubs, at 4 A.M., and she'd go to the vending machines, open them with the keys on the ring, count and then *replace* the money, lock the machine again, and we would leave.

Her boyfriend followed us, now and then, in his car. She told me he had vowed to kill me, but I'd seen him, and I didn't believe the threat. I don't think this was particularly courageous on my part; he just didn't look the type.

———

We conceive the world not through indoctrination, but through osmosis: a culture is the amalgam and the sum of the unwritten laws: "This is how we do things here." And I believe that, in Chicago, I had a very interesting youth. This is how we did things there: one spiffed the mechanic at the cab garage if one wanted to get a working cab to drive; one paid off the cop who pulled you over, as it was much cheaper than going down to 11th and State and paying the fine; the politicians were corrupt—why else would they be politicians? (the absence of this understanding in the minds of the young baffles me); the Governors, regularly, went to jail, how about that?

And through it all one had to make a living, which meant, and means, learning how to navigate in the wider world—learning to take care of yourself.

For the Government was going to take care of you *at best* to the extent that you took care of *it*: if you wanted X you did Y, if you did not do Y, why in the world would any rational entity give you X?

You wanted to work for the Park District, you kicked back your two weeks' pay; you wanted your kid on the Fire Department, you got out the vote.

The politicians have not changed, but it seems that the electorate cannot locate its ass with a guide dog.

There was, in Chicago, no such thing as Social Justice, there was the Law, and the Law was both made and administered by imperfect human beings, like ourselves; and the operations of the Law *itself* could be and were corrupted. There was such a thing as "the underdog," but anyone *demanding* that status was merely picking up a convenient club to use in the fight. (cf. Saul Alinsky on being a "neighborhood organizer": "The third rule is, 'wherever possible go outside of the experience of the enemy.' Here you want to cause confusion, fear, and retreat." *Rules for Radicals*, 1971.)

The White Neighborhoods got better snow removal? Of *course* they did—it was a segregated city and the councilmen were white. And cries for Justice, the blacks knew, would be less effective than getting a dog in the fight, and getting people on the City Council and into City Hall, and letting the *Whites* gape slack-jawed at the *other* fellow being unfair.*

Was it a terrible thing to be a Black in Chicago in those days? Probably. My people came over from Poland to escape the Pogroms, which is to say, fleeing murderers. Did we, the Jews, feel bad for the Blacks? Yes. What did we do about it? We joined the NAACP. Was this effective, appropriate, insulting, paternalistic? How would *I* know?

Did they do it because they felt "guilty"? The suggestion would have been greeted as psychotic. What did my parents' generation

---

*Which is the essence of "Affirmative Action," however else it may be described.

have to feel guilty about? They came here with nothing, sixty years after slavery's abolition, fleeing their state in Europe as slaves or semislaves, and scant years ahead of Hitler's assassins. They supported the NAACP out of a sense of *tzedakah*, which is to say "righteousness." Was their response insufficient, or misplaced? No doubt. But it was not risible. And the South Shore Country Club, eight blocks from my house, and Restricted, allowing No Jews, was eventually bought by Elijah Muhammad, restricting *all* whites, and life goes on.

But I believe I benefited from the absence of sanctimony.

10 | MILTON FRIEDMAN EXPLAINED

Each party alleges, and its enthusiasts agree, that it has never done anything wrong, and its opponent has never done anything right. Any failures, catastrophes, or absurdities during its tenure are blamed on late-appearing aftereffects of its predecessor's enormities.

Most officeholders and candidates are both politicians and lawyers, and so labor under the *double* anecdotal taint of—I will not say, "mendacity," but "looking on the bright side." The bright side is, of course, that which favors their particular interests and aspirations. If bread, it may be identified by the presence of butter.

Let us assume that in all close elections *each* side will endeavor to steal it (a safe assumption, as it is the case); for what unpatriotic soul would not in the service of National Interest wish to lessen the vagaries of chance?

Let us assume, then, that each party partakes equally of the human capacity for good and bad, for corruption, for misguided compassion, and of overweening cupidity; and that each will suffer failures of projects both good-willed and merely monstrously self-serving.

———

The question, as posed by Milton Friedman, was not "What are the decisions?"—any human or conglomeration is capable of decisions both good and bad—but *"Who makes the decisions?"* Shall it be the Government, that is, the State, or shall it be the Individual?

In some cases it *must* be the Government, which is, in these, the only organ capable of serving and protecting individual liberty and freedom: notably, in defense, the administration of justice, and maintenance of and oversight of Federal Infrastructure, e.g., Roads, Interstate Travel, Waterways, Parks, and so on. But what in the world is the Government doing meddling in Education, Health Care, Automobile Production, and the promotion of dubious, arguable, or absurd programs designed to bring about "equality"? Should these decisions not be left to the Individual, or to a Free Market, in which forces compete, to serve the Individual who will be the arbiter of their success?

But but but, some will interject, "Look at the abuses." Well, some abuses fall afoul of the laws, in which case the provision has been made for their correction which, if not forthcoming, is in the right of the public to demand. Others fall afoul of custom, and will or can be corrected by censure, withdrawal of custom, or attempts at criminalization. Some must be borne, as they would under *any* system of government, business, or administration: someone eventually, inevitably, makes what someone else might characterize as "an error."

But which system, Free Enterprise, or the State, is better able to correct itself?

For this is the essence of the difference between the Free Market (constrained) and the Liberal (unconstrained) view of the world—to use Friedrich Hayek's terms. It is not a difference of preference for plans or programs—in which either side may not only differ but, equally, *be* wrong. It is a difference in appreciation of structure.

The constrained view is that neither human beings, nor any conglomeration into which they may form themselves, are omnipotent, nor omniscient, nor omnibenevolent. We are incapable even of knowing, let alone of implementing, engines to alleviate the true causes of, and indeed of understanding the true nature of, many of the problems besetting us. This is, as Hayek says, the Tragic View. We are not only wrong, but most *often* wrong. The treasured values of one generation (slavery, phrenology, lobotomy, physical discipline of children, women as property, et cetera) are seen now not only as vile but as absurd. As, eventually, will many of the cherished ideas of today. This is tragic, but inevitable.

The question is which of two systems is better able to discard the failed and experiment to find the new; and the answer is the Free Market. It is not perfect; it is *better* than State Control; for the Free Market, to a greater extent, must respond quickly and effectively to dissatisfaction and to demand—if a product or service does not please, to continue in its manufacture in the Free Market is pointless. (Compare Government persistence and expansion of programs proved to have failed decades ago—farm subsidies, aid to Africa, busing, urban renewal, etc.) On the other hand, in a Free Market, every man, woman, and child is scheming to find a better way to make a product or a service which will make a fortune. The garage mechanic, the housewife, the tinkerer, the scientist, the artist, and their kids—*everyone* is always looking for a better way. (Compare the Government employee sitting at his desk. Why is he not looking for a better way to do his job? Why should he? A more efficient way might possibly *eliminate* his job, or that of the superior to whom he owes allegiance.)

Nothing is free. All human interactions are tradeoffs. One may figure out a way to (theoretically) offer cheap health insurance to the twenty million supposedly uninsured members of our society. But at what cost—the dismantling of the health care system of the remaining three-hundred-million-plus? What of the inevitable reduction, shortages, abuses, delay and injustice caused by all State rationing?

There's a cost for everything. And the ultimate payer of every cost imposed by government is not only the individual member of the mass of taxpayers who does not benefit from the scheme; but likely, *also, its intended beneficiaries* (cf., welfare, busing, affirmative action, urban planning).

Well, you will say, it's not Either/Or. And, of course it is not. All civilizations need, and all civilizations *get* Government. Many have inherited, had forced upon them, or in fact *demanded* a real or obviously potential dictatorship (Nazi Germany, Fascist Italy)—these, and their like, began as Welfare States, dedicated, supposedly, to distributing the abundant good things of the Land to all. But they, and all the Communist States, and Socialist States, operated at a cost, for everything has a cost. The cost of these benevolent dictatorships was shortage, famine, murder, and the eventual dissolution of the State. Hayek calls this utopian vision *The Road to Serfdom*. And we see it in operation here, as we are in the process of choosing, as a society, between Liberty—the freedom *from the State* to *pursue* happiness, and a supposed but impossible Equality, which, as it could only be brought about by a State capable and empowered to function in all facets of life, means totalitarianism and eventual dictatorship.

Is the State to decide for the individual, or is the individual to insist upon a reduction of State powers *to that point* at which this power is reserved only for application in those cases, as specified in law, where one individual or group abridges the liberty of another?

The latter is the revolutionary understanding of government spelled out in that Constitution elected officials swear to defend. They are elected as public servants, the public granting them *only* that freedom of action necessary to fulfill that oath. Is it not time for a return to that revolutionary understanding?

11 | WHAT IS "DIVERSITY"?

It is a commodity. Parents purchase it for their children; for as much as they might pay to achieve and brag about their children's membership in a "wonderfully diverse" setting, they all eat in restaurants whose clientele looks just like themselves. As do we all. This is "Pediatric Diversity," or diversity-by-proxy.

Once, in my younger days, I was asked to help out at some fundraising event for some good cause. The event was to raise funds to alleviate hunger. All the attendees bought a ticket, but the tickets were numbered one, two, or three. Those getting number one were entitled to all they could eat; the twos, to a meal consisting of five hundred calories (the supposed caloric intake, for the evening meal, in the area to which the funds were supposed to be sent); the threes got nothing at all. I was passing out tickets at the head of the line. I collected the money from a fellow there with his young son. He leaned in toward me and asked me to give them both a three.

I went home after the event and felt something of a fool. What, I wondered, was this charade in which I was participating? If the fellow wanted his son to know what it felt like to miss a meal, couldn't he have played that charade at home? If everyone had, the event would have had no overhead costs, and everyone would have been able to send all the ticket costs to the hungry. But this fellow was practicing Pediatric Socialism: he, rightly, as a loving father, never wanted his son to be hungry; but, like a loving but overindulgent father, he wanted to purchase for him an approximation of the experience, which, he thought, might make his son a better person.

But how would the two possibly be connected? For the son had not only noticed that a point was made that some people were hungrier than others, and that it was (supposedly) a matter of chance, but that one could appreciate and learn from this unfortunate fact by purchasing a ticket at a game show; and, perhaps (more likely), the son had observed that money and influence could buy *anything*, even a charade of poverty.

How fashionable to wear clothes which are distressed. The young on the Westside of Los Angeles dress themselves in jeans worn, sanded, and razored to resemble something a six-month castaway might crawl ashore in. Why? They are trying to purchase a charade of victimization, as the ethos of the Liberal West holds that these victims are the only ones of worth. But how to go about it? For the jeans can cost over one thousand dollars (one might buy them at Goodwill for two bucks, but, I am informed, they would be "seen through" and, though a closer approximation to true poverty, they are ineffective as a concomitant display of wealth).

It beats me all hollow.

Look at those Old Rich Guys in their Porsche, the young might say; but the Porsche is perhaps not an attempt to display wealth, neither to recapture youth, but to enjoy that which some years of labor have permitted as an indulgence.

———

I think quite a bit about higher education, which, to me, partakes of the ethos both of bottled water and of an "evening of poverty": bottled water because, at least in the Liberal Arts, it is useless; and Ticket Number Three, as the rather universal absence of rigor in courses devoted to "Identity" abandons the children to fantasies of their own omnipotence and oppression (a bad mix). This allows, indeed, encourages them to criticize and dismantle a culture they, in their adolescence, are equipped neither to understand nor to participate in—any more than the young chap receiving Ticket Number Three would have, thus, become an expert on Global Inequality.

I believe the incredible wealth of this country will allow it to survive quite a while on its hundreds of years of production and upon its natural resources and historic culture of productivity. But the Change which Obama's rhetoric referred to preceded and will follow him, accelerated by him and his policies, accepted by a drugged populace and a supine press. It is the unfortunate descent of a productive nation into socialism, which, as I understand it, is robbing Peter to pay Paul. I don't think it's any more complex than that.

12 | THE MONTY HALL PROBLEM AND THE CONTRACTOR

There was, and still may be, a television game show called *Let's Make a Deal*. Its MC, Monty Hall, brought the contestants down to guess behind which of three closed doors the Grand Prize lurked.

The contestant made his guess (e.g., Door One). *Now* Monty opened one of the two remaining doors (e.g. Door Two) to show that it did *not* conceal the prize, and asked the contestant if he wished to stay with his original guess, One, or choose the third door, Three—which had neither been originally guessed, nor subsequently revealed.

The audience would then scream out its intuition: "Change! Don't change! Don't change! Change!"

This seemed a logical choice—between option One and option Two—the odds being ostensibly 50 percent of picking a winner; a decision to change or stand pat, resting, then, but upon sentiment. But the odds were *not* now 50 percent, but two to one, actually, in favor of change.

A mathematician acquaintance of mine explained this to me some years ago, and though convinced, I, when the conversation was over, reverted immediately to my previous, logical perception: There was a choice between two doors. Door Two had been revealed a blank—the prize must therefore be behind Door One or Three. The odds *had* to be 50 percent.

Over the years, I would see the mathematician at parties, and ask him to convince me again, and I would again be convinced during the time of our chat.

The problem, called the Monty Hall Problem, I learned, was quite famous in mathematic circles, and had formed the basis for much new and interesting investigation and speculation regarding probability and perception. For it pertained not only to mathematics, but to *cognition*. It could be proved mathematically, and demonstrated empirically, that the odds were two to one in favor of change, and yet, the lay mind (mine) remained unconvinced. There were two choices; I had picked Door One, Monty revealed Door Two was a blank, and I was offered the choice between my Door One, and Door Three.

But no, I was told, I was offered a choice between Door One, and *all the other doors.*

But "All the other doors," I said, "were *only one* door, Door Three."

One day, I figured it out for myself. For I thought about it not as a mathematical proposition, but as a confidence trick: Having picked *my* door, Monty was going to reveal that one of the two remaining was blank. But of *course* one of the two remaining was blank. One of the two remaining had to be blank, as there was only *one prize.*

Thus, Monty's supposedly generous offer was not generosity at all. As far as any benefit to myself, he could just as easily have made his generous offer *before* revealing the nullity of Door Two. He could have said, "You've chosen Door One, you can stand pat, or trade it for Doors Two AND Three. Which, as the penny dropped, I realized, was exactly what he *was* doing. I had defeated myself by accepting the shiny but destructive misinformation that he, in revealing Door Two, had offered me a gift.

My greed convinced me that I possessed something which I did not in fact possess (more information), and so I seduced myself into a false (and destructive) understanding of the problem. "Oh," I realized, "I am an illogical being." This is sobering but helpful information.

I now compare my escape from Monty's fiendish cunning with my experience with an architect.

My wife and I were renovating a house, and the architect said that there were two ways to figure his payment. We could pay him on a cost-plus basis; *or* we could pay him on an hourly basis.

This seemed to me very sporting, and I was surprised when, near the end of the job, and facing the outrageously mounting costs associated with any building process, I was wrathful and sullen. But no, I reasoned, *correct* yourself—the fellow gave you a choice, the choice was *yours* (I've forgotten which scheme I chose), and now it is your part to live with it.

Which I did. Until some years later it occurred to me that I had (as with the Monty Hall Problem), misconstrued the nature of the choice offered me.

For why, I reasoned, would the architect offer a client a choice which was a fifty-fifty proposition to lose him money? The architect knew or would figure how to best reward himself in *whichever* scheme I picked. I do not suggest duplicity, but merely human nature—if paid on a cost plus basis, he (or you, or I) would indulge a natural passion for the most expensive materials—why not? The house would have his name on it, and expensive materials could only redound to his credit. If paid on an hourly basis, he would express this same passion for perfection by working himself and his staff more hours. It was impossible that it should be otherwise. Neither you nor I would do otherwise.

But why, then, offer me the choice? Perhaps to offer the client two options, each of which would lead to different enthusiasms and the disagreements potentially resultant therefrom.

Perhaps, that is, to dissuade against recriminations. But not, though it might so appear, to offer a bargain.

My greed blinded me to the offer's nature: Had the offer been of a bargain, that is, had it contained any possibility of my gain, the architect would have offered me the choice after the fact: that is, at the *completion* of the job. The architect then might have said, "There are two ways to figure my compensation, you will note that one is higher than the other, which do you choose?" But why would a rational architect offer me a choice which *must* redound to his loss? He would not. There was a choice, but only the illusion of a bargain. Which is the essence of a confidence game.

Someone, and it may have been William Styron, said that a drinking problem is like a little Latin—sooner or later, it will find its way into your writing. That's how I feel about the Monty Hall problem— I worked for it, and darned if I am not going to use it in my writing.

The human body is 55 to 75 percent water, and an equal percentage of our endeavors, after food, clothing, and shelter, are nonsense. I play soccer with my dog, but I cannot fool her, for she cares nothing about my elegant and deceptive movements; she is only looking at the ball.

———

That Iraq was "not another Vietnam" can only be interpreted as a proclamation of identity—else why make the comparison? See also, that the foreseeable bust of 2008 was "not another 1929." There are only so many ways in which things go wrong; there are only so many things one may do with his money, health, and talents. Many make a living suggesting that they hold "the Magic Feather," possessing the hidden knowledge which will spare us toil and grief (Bernie Madoff). And we late-appearing Moderns, and the Trobriand Islanders of 10,000 AD, fall for it every time, e.g., "the New Economy," "Change," "Compassionate Conservatism," "Shark Cartilage."

There was a book called *Sharks Don't Get Cancer*, which recommended that one concerned should buy and ingest shark cartilage in order to avoid the disease, his reasoning contained in the book's title. But neither does a Buick get cancer, and who would suggest the afflicted go lick a bumper? No, we are a crazy bunch of monkeys. We have survived through the adaptive mechanism of a brain which is always trying to find the easy way out, and our devotion to our special skill, having allowed us to flourish, will surely, in God's Good Time, kill us off and allow for another variation.

Quantities may have different meanings. It is hard to divest oneself of their connotations. This may, I think, be accomplished in mathematics, where values are set, but, as the task of philosophy, it is certainly difficult to use reason to determine reason's operations and their worth.

There is, historically, much rancor on the Left against the existence of the State of Israel. And frequent mention is made, and, more destructively, implied, of Israel's "aggression." But what does the State of Israel want? To be left in peace within its borders. What does the Arab world want? To destroy the State of Israel. Whatever allegations or sympathies may otherwise be adduced, these demands, as above, are observable, oft-proclaimed and incontrovertible; Western Sympathy for the Arab cause, then, can only rest upon a sliding scale of Humanity—the Arabs, and, thus, their demands, being of a weight sufficient to nullify those of Israel, though the former wants slaughter and the latter peace. How can we know? Return to the mathematic certainty: Israel has no territorial demands (or was willing in negotiations with Arafat and after to concede any scant and still-disputed land). The Arabs want all of Israel.

There can be a sentiment of sympathy with the Arabs *only* based upon a pre-facto assessment of *them* (rather than their cause) as "better" or more worthy than the Jews.

This illogical sentiment, which can only be called "racism," is found again in the Liberal love of the idea of "apology"—that the Government should apologize for Slavery, Japanese Internment, Coolie Labor, and so on. But the Rabbis teach that no apology is legitimate unless the offender (a) expresses remorse stating specifically what he has done; (b) makes restitution; (c) refrains, in similar circumstances, from again committing the offense.

But upon even the first of these, a governmental apology founders. For who is the "we" and who the "they" of the apology?

Is the American Government of today guilty of slavery? If so, are those African American members of the Government equally guilty? Or, are the American People alive today guilty? If so, which citizens? The Black as well as the White? Is the guilt heritable, or not? If so, then would not those (the great majority of) Americans whose ancestors did not arrive until after slavery be exempt from apology? Are the ancestors of the 300,000 white males who died to defeat slavery excepted from apology? If not, on what basis are the descendants of slaves *entitled* to it?

Is one entitled to apology by genetics? If so, then those making the apology must be tainted by their own blood. Is this an American concept?

How is it that, sixty-some years after the West defeated Nazi Racism, we are enmeshed in a race-based culture, and making governmental decisions on the basis of genetics?

Hermann Goering, head of the Luftwaffe, had, as his second in command, Erhard Milch. It was pointed out that Milch had a Jewish father, and so should not be employed as a Nazi, but rather executed as a Jew. Goering replied, "In Germany *I* decide who is a Jew." Equally, to indulge in any racial preferences is not to award to a *Race*, but to the *State* the power to create differing classes of citizens, and to rule on who shall belong in each class. For all our blood is mixed. Our country, like all in recorded history, engaged for a while in Slavery. It also produced the white, northern males who enlisted and died to eradicate Slavery during the Civil War, and fought it and, again, died during World War II; and the white males who voted in the Fourteenth Amendment and the Civil Rights Act. Is it not evident, after a clinical look, that the desire for Justice cannot be served quite so easily, and that a reduction of human beings to classes deserving differing grades of the same is the beginning of the end of Democracy? It costs politicians and legislators nothing to apologize, but costs us citizens much to award them or ourselves credit for the indulgence.

13 | MAXWELL STREET

Her conclusion was that any human being lies nearer to the unseen than any organization, and from this she never varied.

—E. M. Forster, *Howards End*, 1910

Most legislation aimed at eliminating unhappiness and discontent has resulted in misery. Human beings are flawed, and as unlikely to create contentment with amended or increased legislation as they were to create perfect legislation in the first place. The best we might do would be to create a set of laws which made allowance for the imperfection not only of the legislation but of the judges and the administrators who would pass and implement it, and, indeed, of the Electorate.*

Within the memory of many, groups who believed in their own rationality voted for laws against miscegenation. They did not do so because they were white, but because they were *human*, which is to say, flawed—betrayed by their belief in their own rationality, and compromised by reliance on their own indignant and righteous feelings.

Government is an organic cultural organism. It lives by growing, and it grows by accretion. It will arrogate to itself all the power it can by the apparent mechanism of legislation and the less apparent but more virulent operation of bureaucratic growth, by usage, and precedent.

The Constitution reserves to the Congress the power to declare

*E.g., the U.S. Constitution.

war. But Roosevelt declared war on Japan and asked the Congress to affirm that this state of war existed. The act was reasonable and defensible as a pro-forma inversion of the usual process. But ever since Korea and Vietnam and the War Powers Act and so on, the President has achieved the de facto power to declare war, enshrined not in law but in custom.

The Written Law says Congress has the power, but the Unwritten Law, by which the written law is understood, is that such power has become the Executive's. But, defenders might say, the President may declare, not a "war" but a "police action," or a "widening of the sphere of defense," under such and such conditions and *various new stipulations*. Such an elaboration of detail may stem from a desire for Justice, or from a desire to protect the "spirit" of the Constitution, but it, by demanding an accompanying elaboration of oversight and bureaucracy, merely exacerbates the problem it pretends to address, for it entrenches a new, bigger, more powerful class of bureaucrats, paid by the State to deal magically with the issue of when it is acceptable for a President to declare a war by simply calling it something else (the answer, now, "always"); to enforce *new* rules, which is to say, to meddle and obstruct the possibility of simple rules of human interaction (e.g. "The Congress shall have the power to declare war").

The Liberal state, in the worthy desire to exorcise greed, poverty, and unhappiness, has given birth to a radical view of the world: that it is the responsibility of the State to protect anyone who may claim to be powerless. But what check is upon these champions? And what inducement do they possess to refrain, since to refrain is to diminish their power and, so, their livelihoods? Is it not evident that to be accused before the bureaucrats of OSHA, Equal Opportunity Commission, FDA, Consumer Safety Board, and so on, is to be found guilty, for the organization's first and only responsibility is to grow, and, in contrast to the free market, it is not the populace, but the *government* which characterizes failure and success, and that all government programs must not only expand after success, but expand after failure, in order "to bring about eventual success."

Note that all this hocus-pocus is taking place with the money actually earned by hardworking individuals.

We have abundant natural resources. But if there were a system in which there was no waste, we would all be wearing the same clothes, for our clothes would be chosen for us on the basis of the theory of maximum conservation of resources. As would our cars. But suppose someone wanted a different car. Could he alter it? With what resources, if the State had decided that he had "all that he needed"? But suppose he foresaw a way to make his car even more efficient. Could he experiment on it? Again, using what resources of time or energy? But perhaps as a Hobby. But what if his Hobby required more energy or time than that deemed useful by the State?* Could he stint himself of sleep and food? Why should he, if his eventual invention were to be taken by the State—appropriated for the Good of All? And if his subsequent fatigue robbed the State of his exertion in those activities it deemed more useful?

A fixation on natural resources blinds one to the worth of *human* resources: We live in and are designed to *exploit* (which is another word for "use") the natural world. The Socialist vision constrains human inventiveness and imagination.

Why would the worker on the assembly line come forward with a better idea? Why, if his compensation was always the same, would he even fantasize about it, which is the beginning of all progress?

Socialism is the end of all invention; it is the happy face of slavery. Mankind are greater gainers by suffering each other to live as seems good to themselves than by compelling each to live as seems good to the rest.

—J. S. Mill

*Is this fanciful? Consider the case of Creekstone Farms of Kansas. During the Mad Cow scare of 2003, this beef producer developed and sold to the Japanese its own beef, raised, tested, and guaranteed to be absolutely free of the disease. The United States Government ruled that it was not free to do so. Why? Whom could this ruling possibly benefit, save those meat producers who did *not* choose so to raise their beef; and why in the world would legislators take up their ridiculously transparent and immoral cause if they were not suborned?

14 | R100

The controversy of capitalism versus state enterprise has been argued, tested, and fought out in many ways in many countries, but surely the airship venture in England stands as the most curious determination in this matter.

—Nevil Shute, *Slide Rule: Autobiography of an Engineer*

Nevil Shute was one of the best-selling authors of the twentieth century.

He wrote the novels *On the Beach, A Town like Alice, No Highway in the Sky,* and so on. Many of his books (the above included) were made into very successful films.

By day he was an aircraft designer.

His novels, like those of Dreiser and Trollope, were romantic paeans to those processes the lay populace might presume mundane. Dreiser wrote *The Trilogy of Desire,* some thousands of pages, on the subject of street railway franchises; Trollope wrote the Palliser series about the romance of Parliament dealing with Irish Home Rule, and decimal coinage. Shute, in the main, wrote about aviation.

Aviation was his day job. He was a very successful designer of aircraft. His company, Airspeed Ltd., designed some of the first commercial air transports in the world. He designed the trainer which was used by the RAF until World War II; Airspeed eventually merged with de Havilland. He was the real thing.

In 1925, Vickers Ltd., for which Shute then worked as chief stress engineer, was commissioned, by the British government, to design a rigid airship (that is, a *zeppelin*) practicable for transocean and transglobal passenger travel.

But the British government decided to hedge its bets; it awarded the contract to two groups, Shute's (Vickers), and a governmental group under the auspices of the Air Ministry.

The groups worked independently, but were free to exchange information with each other. Shute's group (makers of the airship R100) learned that the government's group (airship R101) was consistently making choices that were heavier, more complex, and, to the eyes of the free-market Vickers group, unnecessary or, indeed, unsafe.

The certainty of the governmental group drove the Vickers group back to their drawing boards, to retest their results, which they again found technically correct. No, the government ship, R101, was, they determined, too heavy, too complex, and unsafe. The various redundancies and compromises resulting from its design as the work of a government committee had rendered it unairworthy. Shute's group shared its concerns with the government and were told to "go away."

The R100 made the first east-to-west commercial airship crossing of the Atlantic, with Shute on board. The R101 set off to Karachi, India, carrying Lord Thomson, Secretary of State for Air, and Sir Sefton Brancker, Director of Civil Aviation, who were both proponents of the government's plan. It crashed and burned in France, after three hundred miles of travel, and the British airship program was scrapped.

How often must this experiment be tried?

Israel's economy wanes under socialism, and burgeons under the free market; West Germany throve, while East Germany, the slave state, lived in starvation until the fall of Communism; Cubans in Miami grow rich, and the prison they risked their lives to flee continues as an eighteenth-century feudal fiefdom. California taxes its flagship movie industry out of the state, and Toronto, Ireland, and the Czech Republic reap the benefits; the United States taxes the auto industry to Japan, the textile industry to China, and so on, and then wonders at the fall of the dollar.

———

I don't know anything about the auto industry, but I am a member of another big business which has killed itself.

Anyone working in show business for any time—actually working, that is, writing, acting, designing, lighting, crafting—has said to himself, when the middle managers come on the set: "Why are *those* fools elected to do that job?"

The affronted, on continued interaction, comes to see that the problem is not with the supposed abilities or personality of the individual bureaucrat; the problem is the existence of the job itself, which is not only unnecessary to but destructive of actual industry.

In the growth of any successful organization, a now-entrenched bureaucracy may work to change its object from production of a product to protection of its (useless) jobs.

It is inevitable that the bureaucrat, awarded his job as a perquisite of superiors who wish to display their power and provide themselves insulation, will work, not primarily, but *exclusively* to obtain and exercise those same perquisites in his own behalf.

Thus, at the end, Chrysler and GMC were making cars no one wanted for a price that did not repay their manufacture. The car business had been run, both by labor and management, as a sideline of their bureaucracies, each exploiting its own rights (which is to say its position and potential for further exploitation). Who was left designing and producing cars people wanted to buy and drive?

At this point the hag-ridden industry was "rescued" by the only organization in the world *less* equipped to ensure productivity: the Federal Government.

What does this "rescue" mean? That the décor and the staffing of the boardroom will change. That the *tenor* of boardroom life will become more austere is inevitable (see the workers' uniforms adopted by Stalin, Mao, Ho, and so on), but otherwise it will be Business As Usual, which is to say waste (now on an even greater scale), disregard for the consumer, and increased distance from those personally involved with the success of the product offered.

In a rational, which is to say a free-market world, this situation would self-correct: the public would cease to buy a product which no one cared to make attractive, efficient, or affordable, and the business would change or go broke.

The only businesses excepted from this rational progression are those supported by government, and, of course the Government itself, where waste *is* the end product.

———

What are we purchasing with our taxes?

What is Big Government but the Executive's cocaine dream, an activity devoted *solely* to jockeying for position, in which he may find license for malversation, and may take the company treasury and direct it toward those people who will support his continued incumbency—it is within the law. Its street name is "earmarks," but it is theft. Of your money and mine.

The problem is, as with the movie business, not with the identity of placeholders, but with the jobs themselves.

The San Fernando Valley is littered with office campuses housing the executives who supposedly "make" the movies. Many of these buildings occupy space which was, formerly, the lot on which actual movies were once made.

Mismanagement (by labor, capital, and our benevolent government) has driven the actual movie business out of California, and, to the largest extent, out of the country.

What would happen to the movie business if these office campuses and their inhabitants were all to disappear tomorrow?

Nothing.

It is not just that a movie studio could be run by one person with a cell phone, in the back of a limo—that is how they *are* run. The accreted bureaucracy serves the Executive as a Royal Court,* but,

*Compare Keeper of the Royal Bedchamber with the Hollywood studio title Director of Development. For the lay reader: No movie has *ever* been made from "development."

like the Big Government it strives to emulate, it makes nothing but waste. It just exists and grows and grows.

Government is the ultimate bureaucracy, from which has been abstracted not only responsibility for the product, but the product itself.

The price is paid not by the consumer (of what? there is no product) but by Government's *victims*—those taxed—and many taxed literally out of existence—by the bureaucrat's unchecked ability to rape the treasury in buying support for his position, his good ideas, or his reelection.

———

The difference between the Liberal and the Conservative lies, in the main, in the level of abstraction of thought. The Liberal assumes he differs from his opponent on the identity of the person holding the job, and on the content of that person's proposals. The Conservative cannot persuade him to see the problem differently: that it is the *job itself* which must be eliminated. The difference is one not of doctrine, but of philosophy.

The worker on the assembly line, on the movie set, and you and I have the same reaction when the Bureaucrats come slumming by: "If the goddamn Suits would finish their tour, stop nodding wisely, and go away, perhaps I might be able to get the job done."

———

I received, from an auction house, a notice of the auction of a Glenn Curtiss 1915 seaplane. It is, I think, one of the most beautiful objects I have ever seen. Its hull is mahogany in a series of gentle steps, allowing it to plane on the water. It is a pusher biplane—its engine mounted behind the pilot and pushing backward. Its wings and tail structure are aluminum. It seats two. It looks as if it were designed by Brancusi; indeed, it was designed by his equal.

The aircraft business, around this time, a mere decade after Kitty Hawk, was largely the domain of producers and designers not far removed (if removed at all) from the workshop garage.

Planes were made (as Nevil Shute observes in *Slide Rule*) largely from wood, with canvas-covered wings; and it cost little to retool.

A fellow with a saw could design and build his own plane, buying or modifying a cheap gasoline engine to power it.*

This early aircraft business resembled that of the shade-tree mechanics who, in building hot rods, gave rise, then as now, to true advances in automobile design. See also the chopper shops of California, and their influence on the world of motorcycling.

A list of these shade-tree mechanics includes the Wrights, Cyrus McCormick, Henry Ford, Tesla, Tom Edison, Meg Whitman, Bill Gates, Burt Rutan, and Steve Jobs. How would they and American Industry have fared had Government gotten its hands upon them at the outset—if it had taxed away the capital necessary to provide a market for their wares; if it had taxed away the *wealth*, which, existing as gambling money, had taken a chance on these various visionaries? One need not wonder, but merely look around at the various businesses Government has aided. And now it has taken over health care.

*As the Wrights did in their bicycle shop.

15 | THE INTELLIGENT PERSON'S GUIDE TO SOCIALISM AND ANTI-SEMITISM

Socialism and "Social Justice" are a sort of Sunday religion, professed one day a week for many good and bad reasons, but suspended during and due to the pressures of the workweek. One may bemoan the plight of the Palestinians, who have elected a government of terrorists and daily bomb their neighbor to the West, but we realize that any support past the sentimental is elective: we do not want to live there, nor to *go* there, and we blink at the knowledge that monies spent in their support may be diverted to the support of terror, and of organizations pledged not only to kill all the Jews, but to kill Americans and Westerners of *all* faiths.

Where does sympathy stop, and where may it not become sanctimony and hypocrisy?

———

Our American plane has been forced to land at some foreign airport, by the outbreak of World War III. It will not be allowed to depart. Two planes are leaving the airport; we must choose which we want to board. One plane is flying to Israel and one to Syria, and we must choose.

That's where sympathy stops.

No one reading this book would get on the plane to Syria. Why? It is a despotism, opposed to the West, to women, to gays, to Jews, to free speech. It is a heinous Arab version of National Socialism, dedicated to the murder of every person in Israel. And yet one may gain status or a feeling of solidarity by embracing the "Arab cause."*

---

*What, detractors might ask, does this prove? Does it mitigate against the "Crimes" and "Colonialism" of Israel, as popularized by the United Nations? I deny these crimes exist, and

But we embrace it only as an entertainment. In the free market, which is to say, when something is at stake, we will vote otherwise.

My interest in politics began when I noticed that I acted differently than I spoke, that I had seen "the government" commit sixty years of fairly unrelieved and catastrophic errors nationally and internationally, that I not only hated every wasted hard-earned cent I spent in taxes, but the trauma and misery they produced; and yet, I thought "the government" was good. What case could I point to to support my feelings? The Emancipation Proclamation and the Voting Rights Act. Then I would have to stop and think.

It was, of course, easier to worship my own capacity for "good thinking" than actually to think, which is to say to compare my actions with their results. But I tired of it. I tired of hearing Israel condemned by Americans, and hearing Americans condemned by Europeans.

I prefer the company of those who are proud of their country, and proud of their religion—the African Americans have it right, the American Liberal Jews are wrong; there is neither beauty, utility nor safety in identification with one's oppressors.

Liberalism is a religion. Its tenets cannot be proved, its capacity for waste and destruction demonstrated. But it affords a feeling of spiritual rectitude at little or no cost. Central to this religion is the assertion that evil does not exist, all conflict being attributed to a lack of understanding between the opposed.

------

that Israel is an oppressive or colonialist power (to those interested I suggest the following books: *The World Turned Upside Down,* Melanie Phillips; *What Went Wrong?,* Bernard Lewis; and *Myths and Facts:A Guide to the Arab-Israeli Conflict,* Mitchell Geoffrey Bard.)

But, let us assume you feel that Israel is neither a laudable precious democracy, nor an ordinary Western country neither good nor bad, but is guilty of all the horrors alleged of it—I assert that you would still fight with every force and argument at your command to get on the Israeli plane, you and every hard Leftist and every head-shaking misinformed One-Worlder and anti-Semite up to and including Jimmy Carter and Noam Chomsky, would, if the issue were his *life,* suspend his most cherished convictions of Israeli perfidy, and plead for the protection of that state he would then not only acknowledge but *assert* to be his ally, and further assert, as such, that their intercession in his fate was simple human decency toward their own kind—a member of a Western democracy.

There is *nothing* any reader of this book would not say or do to get himself and his family on the Israeli plane. Thus, delight in reviling the Jewish state reveals a certain inconsistency.

Well and good, but this does not accord with the experience of anyone.

People have differing needs. The notion that an honest exchange of views will solve all problems is an *article of faith*; which, like many another, is suspended in our daily lives.

It is fine for the uninvolved to say of everything, "The truth must lie somewhere in between," but who on the Left says so, for example, of Abortion? The Israelis would like to live in peace within their borders; the Arabs would like to kill them all. I do not see where there is a middle ground.

The divorcing husband would like to retain some money and visiting rights to his children, the betrayed wife would like him dead; anyone ever involved in a fight or a lawsuit knows that some conflicts cannot be settled peaceably. The Liberal attitude to our war with Radical Islam is a preference for that action which would end the conflict immediately, and without rancor. That action, unfortunately, is surrender.

American Liberals do not wish to surrender *their* particular country, but many wish Israel to surrender hers; they wish to have someone else (the Israelis) pick up the cost of their own psychological upset:* if the Victim is Always Right, and if the Arabs, being darker and poorer, must be the Victim, then Israel *must* be wrong; further, this being so, the Arab démarches of "land for peace" *must* be a legitimate attempt to solve the problem, for the victim is always right. It matters not that every Israeli swap of land for peace has resulted in increased Arab attacks. To the Liberal there *must* be a peaceable solution, and the good-willed (though not the Israelis) see that that solution must be further negotiation, which is to say further concessions from Israel.

The essence of socialism is for Party A to get Party B to give something to Party C.

---

*What is the Liberal's dilemma? That he is forced to *choose*—to weigh rationally two positions, and base his choice upon an honest assessment of his own probable actions under similar circumstances. He is asked, finally, to be *moral*—the cost, however, of such action, is too high. It is his exclusion from the Group.

The Liberal West would like the citizens of Israel to take the only course which would bring about the end of the disturbing "cycle of violence" which they hear of in the Liberal press. That course is abandoning their homes and country, leaving, with their lives, if possible, but leaving in *any* case.

Is this desire anti-Semitism?

You bet your life it is.

16 | THE VICTIM

Just as the Santa Claus myth is a reiteration in the vulgate of the Christ story, so the Love of the Victim is an attempt at a nondeist recreation of religious feeling. It may be found in its everyday, popular face, in the Woman-in-Jeopardy film.

Here the audience experiences vicarious worry and fear for the lot of the defenseless woman (or child), pursued by implacable Evil.

But with these slice-and-dice gothic and horror films, as with the Plight of the Palestinians, the interchange, in order to please, must be inconclusive. The weak, though they may momentarily triumph at the conclusion of any one film, must be available in their intrinsic state of powerlessness for the next go-round.

The woman's victory over the ax murderer is not a portent of her change from victim to nonvictim, but merely a chance, momentary suspension of that state.

For, in our love of Women-in-Jeopardy films, and in the Left's love of the Palestinians, there is something of the sadomasochistic. (If one truly deplored the fact of an alleged injustice, one might actually do something about it, but the West sees the Middle East conflict as entertainment; and part of our polymorphous enjoyment of the ending is that though the woman prevails, we *know* that she is exploitable again next film.)*

We confuse news with reality, and so do the news organizations.

*The Liberal West "enjoys" the Plight of the Palestinians much as it enjoys the purchase of "fair trade" coffee—it is a stimulant additive—self-righteousness being superadded to the morning's newspaper and caffeine.

They are selling entertainment, and, like any good entertainer, will stress the facts likely to please the audience, and structure the rather confusing and nonconclusive nature of day-to-day existence as a drama.

Six houses were destroyed in the Israeli Army's incursion into the Arab town of Jenin. It was described by the Western news as "The Rape of Jenin," and a photo showing a supposedly wounded Palestinian child cradled in his mother's arms went around the world.

Of less currency was the photo taken from an only slightly wider angle showing the mother and child completely surrounded by photographers, arrayed around the now obviously staged shot.* But that second shot, though a better depiction of the actual state of events, had less entertainment value as part of an enjoyable spectacle of misery; to call attention to this would be as irritating to the consumers of "outrage" as would a film buff in the next seat at a horror movie explaining, shot by shot, how the effects were produced and that the woman screaming on the screen was actually an actress in no danger at all.

To do so would have lessened the viewer's enjoyment of the Rape of Jenin.

For one of two things *must* be true, in the West's abandonment of Israel: either it is known, at some level, that the Palestinian claims are insoluble, exaggerated, unjust, or skewed; or that the audience, in truth, *does not actually care*. For if they cared, they would *do* something, and as they do nothing, one must assume that action would put an end to their enjoyable position as viewer.

Michelle Obama famously declared that America is a "mean, mean country," of which she was never proud until it nominated her husband for President. But this "mean, mean country" sent soldiers from the North to eradicate slavery (an action, I believe, unique in the history of the world), in a war fought at shocking cost, which would confer upon those who willingly risked their lives no ben-

---

*And the video that shows the now smiling child rise and remove his bandage when the still-photographers leave.

efit other than their participation in a cause they knew to be right. More than 360,000 Union soldiers died freeing the slaves. This is an actual abiding and permanent legacy of slavery. They died to extinguish evil.

Many in the West enjoy not the suffering, but the *contemplation* of the suffering of the Palestinians.

For a film one buys a ticket. What is the ticket one buys to enjoy this other spectacle? Its price is the indictment of the State of Israel, in contravention of history, of facts, reason, international law, and affinities, national, cultural, and traditional.

Just as at the movies we would resent the fellow in the next seat explaining the effects, so actual information about the Middle East conflict is considered an intrusion and a distraction from the spectacle. One has made one's choice (bought one's tickets) and would like to be left in peace to enjoy the show.

In films the villain is identifiable because he wears the black hat; in the Middle East spectacle he wears a yarmulke.

In 1895 Theodor Herzl was sent by his paper *Neue Freie Presse* to cover the trial of Dreyfus. Herzl's cultural awakening came in seeing Dreyfus stripped of his badges of rank while the crowd screamed not "death to the traitor," but "death to the Jews."

It was a better story that way in 1895, and it is a better story that way today. But it is just a story.

The question, "Excuse me, what has Israel ever wanted except peace within its borders?" is greeted, largely, in the West, by the response: "Shut up, I'm watching the news."

———

The bifurcation of Humanity (as opposed to *acts*) into two identifiable camps, Evil and Good, is, essentially, a childish act; the notion that one may gain merit from this division, and that this merit makes one the superior of the unenlightened, is the act of an adolescent.

Should such reductionism result in any actual social change, the adolescent intellectual is immediately supplanted by the Man of Action (the Tyrant), as observed by Eric Hoffer in *The True Believer*.

For just as the con man capitalizes upon the reluctance of the mark to ascribe evil motives to a chance acquaintance, the Jacobin, his motives limited to pursuit of power, easily supplants, and, traditionally kills, the fool dreamer who thought he was creating a paradise.

17 | PURITANS

He did not, like a Puritan, torment himself and others with scruples about everything that was pleasant.

—Macaulay, *The History of England,* 1848

Have we turned into a nation of maiden aunts?

Must one, upon risk of exclusion from polite society, decry all life as waste, and all differences of political opinion as heresy? Must the opening salvo of any conversation, interminably, be "Did you see what he/they *did* today?"

For, at least, one could say of Hitler and his assassins, that they *enjoyed* their anti-Semitism. But the Left proceeds, from day to day, in a sort of sad, wistful fury at all the things of life not recognized in its cosmogony.

To them, in an inversion of the *truly,* historically, Liberal philosophy, everything not permitted is forbidden.

But the Talmud cautions that when a man dies, he will be called to account for all the unenjoyed, permitted pleasures of this life, which, after all, were given to him as a gift.

And we have become a nation of noodges.

I have seen visitors at an art exhibition clear their paper plates of the residue of bad cheese, and put the plates in their purse, so as to avoid the waste of paper. Is this fun? Is it productive? Or is it just, rather, the physicalization of that same do-goodishness the apotheosis of which is the bumper sticker?

Do bumper stickers save whales, and free Tibet? By what magical process?

Dennis Prager said that the beautiful one-word haiku, the bumper sticker "Coexist," that cunning exhortation both verbal and pictorial, its letters made of the Islamic crescent, the Cross, the six-point star, et cetera, that this work of art appears in the country on earth and in history uniquely dedicated to and achieving freedom of religion. He remarked, further, that were one to affix this bumper sticker to his car in Iran the car would be keyed and its occupants beheaded.

Macaulay suggests that the Puritans were expelled from England not because of their religion, but because everyone had sickened of their kvetching.

My daughter comes home from her high school music class and reports that the teacher has announced that the mnemonic for the lines in the treble clef will no longer be "Every Good Boy Does Fine," which would be sexist, but "Every Good *Baby* Does Fine."

Bruno Bettelheim, a holocaust survivor, wrote that the genius of the Nazi salute was that it prescribed the constant repetition of an action. It did not ask for belief, it *inculcated* belief, as one, perhaps opposed to the Nazis, but forced to give the salute some hundreds of times a day, eventually tired of the unuttered proviso "but I don't believe it." He tired of feeling like a hypocrite, and came to take out the anger this feeling produced not on his oppressors, but on those who did not salute wholeheartedly—who, that is, preserved a measure of autonomy.

The puritan has become, of late, the totalitarian, where every last thing, thought, and utterance in the Liberal Day must be an assertion of some Liberal Value; One-Worldness, Compassion, Conservation, Equality, the dread of giving offense, and guilt.

What is the actual human mechanism devoted to the dread of giving offense? It is called *culture*. It, in its entirety, consists of rules worked out through human interactions sufficiently successful to have been relegated to unconscious habit.

When all human interactions are brought to conscious consideration, the result is anxiety and fear. Consider any first meeting or ceremony where the forms are unknown: a dinner party, for example, of such formality that one was unsure which fork to use, and how and when to address one's tablemates; a meeting with a head of state, or a celebrity. Human beings, in such circumstances, may be brought to a literal state of immobility through fear of violating a norm and of behaving in a, thus, shameful fashion.

This is the state of the contemporary Liberal world—the fear of giving offense has been self-inculcated in a group which must, now, consider *literally* every word and action, for potential violation of the New Norms. To further compound the dilemma, the norms *themselves* are inchoate: consider a high school teacher coming upon two students kissing in the hallway, in violation of school rules. Suppose the two students are gay. Can you imagine a teacher who would not at the very least hesitate in or mitigate her caution or censure in fear of offending the students? Consider the Black Power agitation and vandalism of the sixties, and the school administrators who allowed it on campus—not out of fear for their person, but out of fear that to defend the actual university culture of civility would be to give offense. It is not the absence of government, but the rejection of culture which leads to anarchy.

18 | THE NOBLE SAVAGE

There is a curious disconnection between the Left's worship of the tribal and its religious belief in the power of Government. It may be that its mythology runs like this: The Noble Savage acts in a manner more in tune with Nature. He is uncorrupted, save by the advent of the Whites, who took his land (Israel, the American West, the British Empire). Prior to their coming, he dwelt in peace, tilling the soil according to immemorial principles, and ruled chiefly by his love of the plants and seasons and their influence upon all things. If he had a religion it was that of God as Nature. And we, Westerners, killed and kill him, through greed for his possessions (natural resources).

But the so-believing, the adorers of Third World music, native crafts, and the disheveled dress of their notional American Native Tribe (the poor, the homeless), these, nonetheless, continue to enshrine Big Government as the only tool capable of returning Man from Hell to Eden.

The same Democracy, then, which, in its nonelected quality (civilization) inexorably populated the world, ever widening the polity, and obliterating the Tribe and its supposed blessings, is held by the Left to be that tool capable of reversing the process and restoring us to the Tribe, its campfire, its wise elders, its superabundance of untouched wilderness and game. We're going to vote on it, and when we have enough votes, we're going to return to the campfire. There will be no more pollution, for we will vote to stop our polluting ways; there will be no more war, as all sovereign States will be subsumed into a large tribe of the mutually understanding (cf.

the United Nations), there will be no more Poverty, because the Earth Holds Enough for All, and lacks only that Wise Leadership which will see to its Just Distribution (a dictator). And all that stands between this utopia and our present state of stupid error are the Conservatives, who believe only in Greed.

How did the Conservatives Get That Way? No one on the Left knows. The generous response was that they must have been dropped on their head as babies, lacking which excuse the Conservative point of view is (to the Left) incomprehensible indwelling Evil.*

For to the Left, Government is the water in which they swim, the underlying belief of their lives: Government is not merely one of the ways in which humanity may be convened to order its various affairs (the others being Religion and the Free Market), but the *only* way. Liberalism is that religion which has, for the Left, replaced Religion, for which the prime purpose of Government is to expand Equality, which may also be stated thus: to expand its own powers.

For if Government is not only good, but the only source of good, why should it not be elaborated and empowered to address any and all issues?

This is the vision of FDR, who elaborated a bad economic downturn into the worst depression in history. In an attempt to Do Good for All, he dismantled the free market, and, so, the economy† and

*The Left's hatred of the Right is based, as is most hatred, upon fear. The Left *truly* does not understand what the Right means—the principles of Conservatism are not merely foreign, and not even, primarily, objectionable, to the Left. They are incomprehensible, and so inspire the fear of the unknown. This fear is expressed as hatred of evil. What is the Conservative position the Left is absolutely incapable of understanding? That we have a *choice*.

†"One aspect of social organization is to be found in economic activity, and this, along with the other manifestations of a group activity is to be found in a P.O.W. camp. . . . [T]hrough his economic activity, the exchange of goods and services, [the prisoner's] standard of material comfort is considerably enhanced . . . he is not merely 'playing at shops.' [This is] a living example of a simple economy [and] its simplicity renders the demonstration of certain economic hypotheses both amusing and instructive. . . . But the essential interest lies in the universality and the spontaneity of this economic life; it came into existence not by conscious imitation but as a response to the immediate needs and circumstances." (R. A. Radford, "The Economic Organization of a P.O.W. Camp," *Economica* vol. 12, 1945.) As does and as must *any* free economic organization.

saddled our country not only with "social programs," but with the deeper, unconscious legacy of *belief* in Social Programs, irrespective of their effectiveness. Roosevelt's great domestic bequest was this syllogism: If anything called a Social Program fails, expand it.

This is the meaning of Social Justice. It means actions by the State in the name of Justice, which is to say under complete protection and immunity from review. Its end is dictatorship. This progression, from Social Justice to Judicial Activism and control of means of production and distribution, can be seen in the history of Nazi Germany, Fascist Italy, the USSR, North Korea, China, Cuba, wherever the Socialists took power and brought terror; and yet the Left, longing for the campfire, votes for collectivism, for bigger and more powerful and more "feeling" Government. Why?

It is not that the Superstate will return one to the campfire, but that the fantasy of the Superstate seems more elegant than the simple arithmetic of the Free Market.

———

The Free Market is not a fantasy. We see its efficiency when the power goes out, when we are stranded in an airport, when we throng to the new exciting business down the block—the desire to exchange goods and services in order to increase individual happiness also increases *group* and *societal* happiness. The curtailment of that freedom leads to shortages, famine, and oppression. But its operation, and the demonstrability of its superiority to top-down control, cannot be embraced without forgoing the fantasy of the Return to Nature and the Campfire.

Friedrich Hayek, in *The Road to Serfdom*, called the view of the Free Market the Tragic View: that man is limited; that government is limited in its power to, *justly*, do more than take care of the infrastructure and adjudicate between conflicting claims according to a mutually agreed upon set of laws; that any may and many do misuse both the goodwill of their fellows and the laws themselves to gain immoral advantage; that elected officials are only human, and must be responsible first for their own election, with all that entails; that once elected they will look first to their reelection, which is to say to their own self-interest; that with residual time and energy and wisdom, they may address the social problems before them, but that even in so doing they are, being human, limited in wisdom and foresight. Laws, therefore, cannot be perfect, and all laws will of necessity discommode, anger, or in fact injure *someone*—that is what a law does. It takes two human behaviors, or wishes—two human approaches to the same problem—and chooses one.

Government is limited, as human foresight, wisdom, energy, time, and knowledge are limited. The Left holds as a path to Eden a large unfettered Government, a World Government, in fact. That any democracy is made of warring factions, each plumping for its *own* vision, does not escape the Left, but that any opposing faction may be a *legitimate* attempt to bring about the greater good, is, to them, a simple untruth. The Left insists on unity and indicts the Republicans, not one of whom in either house voted for the health care bill. How could they have increased this supposed good, "unity"—by ratifying a plan they found monstrous and destructive? The Left longs for the one-party state or dictatorship—this is of course not unity but slavery.

Does Man, then, desire slavery? This is the question Moses asked the Jews—the tragic answer being, time and again, "yes." Can this desire be resisted? It can and it must. That's why this country was founded.

———

Intelligent people may look at the excess of big corporations and be appalled by the lack of connection between the will of the shareholders and the operations of the business. They may be shocked by the out of control executive compensation. Why, they may ask, do the shareholders not take the control which is theirs? But these questioners, on the Left, will not ask the same question of that largest and most bloated of all corporations, the American Government. And well they might.

For our chief executive has just used his prerogatives to empty the treasury, and take on what may prove to be a level of debt lethal to the corporation he was hired to run.

What's the difference?

There is no difference. We all know that though we may be unfit to manufacture a car, or plan a pharmaceutical campaign, we each feel capable of demanding an explanation of those in charge of businesses in which we have invested. But the Left does not feel this of our Government.

Why is the government different, in this regard? It is not magic, it cannot be other than an amalgamation of human beings just like you and me, some good, some bad, some smart, some not, and all liable to corruption or confusion by prerogative and power.

19 | ADVENTURE SLUMMING

For Abbie Hoffman, as for the Mailer and Sartre, Castro's appeal had much to do with the macho image, the condottiere on the white horse—or tank: "Fidel sits on the side of a tank rumbling into Havana on New Year's Day . . . girls throw flowers at the tank and rush to tug playfully at his black beard. He laughs joyously and pinches a few rumps. . . . The tank stops in the city square. Fidel lets the gun drop to the ground, slaps his thigh and stands erect. He is like a mighty penis coming to life, and when he is tall and straight the crowd is immediately transformed."

—Paul Hollander, *Political Pilgrims: Travels of Western Intellectuals to the Soviet Union, China, and Cuba*, 1981

Let us squint for a moment, to see if we may blur the particulars and perceive a familiar outline in an unfamiliar act. A young wealthy woman puts on vaguely military garb and travels to a far-off, less-developed land to participate in adventure. She meets there the more primitive indigenous people, admires their hunting abilities, and, in fact, poses with one of their large guns, famous for having bagged many trophies.

Q. What is she doing? A. Going on Safari.

Essentially, yes. The woman, however, would be appalled had the big gun been used to kill an elephant. But it has not. It has been used to kill American fliers.

Jane Fonda's Adventure Tourism is, then, incorrectly, identified not as a safari but as "Ending the War."

This was a no-cost, exhilarating adventure, all the more attractive because it took place in the purlieus of danger, but contained no danger; and it could be described as "humanitarianism," which is an edifying title, rather than "slumming," which is perhaps less so.

Ms. Fonda did not choose to take her wish for adventure into the veldt, where, after all, the beasts might strike back, but to Hanoi in 1969. At the height of the Vietnam War—to pose with the enemy, secure in the knowledge that her (largely inherited) position would protect her from prosecution for what was, arguably, an act of treason.

In her reliance upon this protection she was, of course, availing herself of that same privilege and culture whose destruction she was endorsing in posing by the gun.

Her pilgrimage, as Mr. Hollander points out, was not unique. Intellectuals through the twentieth century have traveled to see the Potemkin Villages of Stalin's "Workers Miracle," the happy children of China, and the grinning, sun-drenched Campesinos of the Island Paradise. They have believed what they were shown.*

---

*"Perhaps the first thing a visitor to Cuba notices is the enormous energy level. It is still common, as it has been throughout the ten years of Revolution, for people to go without sleep—talking and working several nights a week . . . it seems sometimes as if the whole country is high on some beneficient kind of speed. And has been for ten years."

"Cuban culture lacks any equivalent of the Protestant ethic to draw on; *people must be inculcated* about matters we take for granted." (Emphasis added.)

"Our charge (AMERICAN RADICALS) is seen as not one of forming but of *dismantling* (emphasis in original) a consciousness . . . hence the anti-intellectualism of the brightest kids: their distrust of books, school."

"The sense of community perceived in Cuba was not only nurtured by the political ideology of the system, but had its subterranean reservoirs and supports in the stereotype of the joyful, affirming attitude, attributed to the musically gifted song-and-dance loving natives, their natural and politically engendered vitality" From: Susan Sontag: "Some Thoughts on the Right Way (for Us) to Love the Cuban Revolution," *Ramparts*, April 1969.

There we have from a supposedly intelligent and observant human being, not only a recitation, but an unconscious *confession* of her immersion in a fantasy: The workers, though naturally happy, have not seen the potential increase in their joy brought about by continuous work without sleep; they must be *inculcated* in the new, political reality. American children, likewise, must discard books and schools and intuit their responsibility to dismantle their culture, reverting, thus, to the bliss of the song-loving natives off our coast.

From the Webbs, and Bertrand Russell, to Susan Sontag, Jane Fonda, Vanessa Redgrave, and various movie stars of our day, these happy dupes reward themselves for feeling superior to their own country, from which country they were free to travel, and to which they were free to return, while the smiling folk they visited were locked in slave states.

See also the brave actors who endeavored to boycott, and so close, the 2009 Toronto Film Festival because it offended by showing films from Israel.

This "visiting" and political pilgrimage differs from safari in that one does not here toy with danger. It more closely resembles the Victorian practice of "going among the poor."

It used to be called "passing out tracts."

———

Actors, thriving on publicity, have historically claimed for themselves the right to champion "causes," the term of art being "Their" disease. This hucksterism may, in fact, have done somebody good, and more probably, did harm to nothing save the actor's understanding of his place in the world. But it is the nature and profession of the actor to see himself as the Hero. Without this capacity and inclination, the actor cannot act. His professional indulgence in fantasy is a boon to the community, its elaboration into do-gooderism is, perhaps, inevitable.

We writers, similarly, are professional fantasists. But, rather than imagining ourselves as heroes, we live through delineating the struggle between Good and Bad. We are, essentially, Zoroastrians— for, if we can't adequately differentiate between the good guys and the bad guys, how will we know when to end the story?

Writers have traditionally been the dupes of totalitarian propaganda, as the visions we have been shown and the tales we have been told sound, to us, like the products of our own imagination.

And actors, as above, are easily manipulated, similarly, by the unconscious appeal of a universe resembling their own (in which they are the hero).

No wonder, then, that these two subgroups of my particular

racket, show business, have been trotting the globe for a hundred years, petted by and championing the causes of Tyrants.

No wonder that the Hollywood enclaves of today coalesce around Good Causes, and that these Good Causes seem to be reducible to "saving the world."

But I will note that the brave groups protecting the rights of the Palestinians to destroy the Jews, the rights of Iraqis and Cubans to live under dictatorship, and protesting the American military's mission to protect their lives, that these disaffected are taken, in my business, in the main, from the ranks of actors and writers, and interestingly, contain only a very small number of directors.

Why? A director cannot deal in fantasy. His job is to take the delineation of a fantasy (a script) and transform it into film-in-the-can. He has a certain amount of time and money with which to do so, and no amount of fantasy will stop the sun going down on a day on which he has not completed his assigned filming.

More importantly, a director (I speak as one who has directed ten features, and quite a bit of television), is exposed to something of which the actors and writers may not have taken notice: the genius of America, and the American system of Free Enterprise.

The director sees, on the set, one or two hundred people of all walks of life, races, incomes, political persuasions and religions, and ages, men and women, involved, indeed *dedicated* to doing their jobs as well as possible (indeed the ethos of the film set could, without overstatement, be described as "doing it better that it's ever been done"), in aid of the mutual endeavor (the film). Each brings not only his or her particular expertise and craft, but an understanding of and dedication to the *culture* of filmmaking: work hard, pitch in, never complain, admire and reward accomplishment.

Travel posters of the postwar era proclaimed "See America First." I would recommend this as an anodyne to the Adventure Tourist's Weltschmerz: look around you.

20 | CABINET SPIRITUALISM AND THE CAR CZAR

I am very willing to recognize the good in many men of these two classes, but a politician or a civil servant is still to me an arrogant fool 'til he is proved otherwise.

—Nevil Shute, Slide Rule: *Autobiography of an Engineer*, 1954

A czar is an absolute ruler. The wish to appoint a bureaucrat and name him Czar is an example of magical thinking, for, if government is inefficient, how may it be improved by making it omnipotent?

But perhaps Government is unsatisfactory because it is made of bureaucrats. This "czar," then, will be but another. He will have to deal not only with the bureaucracy he inherits, but with that which he creates—the attempts to amalgamate the two, resulting in an organization inevitably worse than either.

The new group dedicated to the streamlining of Government will be paced by a corresponding group of incumbents ensuring that this takes place within the existing rules (which is to say that its jobs are not threatened), and the net results will be an unavoidable increase in the infighting which is the main occupation of all bureaucrats, and a concomitant increase in the power of the State. The inefficiency of Government cannot be addressed through an elaboration of Government.

The delusion that it can calls to mind the Cabinet Spiritualists of the late nineteenth century. These assured the public that they possessed supernatural powers. Locked in a cabinet and bound, they could, for example, cause musical instruments to play, cause writing to appear upon slates, cause objects to fall from the sky, and so on.

But these feats, they explained, could only be performed under those special circumstances necessary for the intercession of the Spirits. The Spirit World demanded privacy. So, the cabinet in which the acts were performed must be closed. To still the doubts of the unbelievers, however, the Spiritualists would be bound, and the cabinet investigated by an impartial committee of the audience.

Here we have a charming example of codependent thinking on the part of the audience, who, in this figure, represent our Electorate. Their *will to believe* is in direct conflict with their *understanding*. They may enjoy the demonstration only if it is believable, but they know it to be a hoax—what are they to do?

The spiritualist and the politician are essentially magicians, one offering diversion, the other security, in exchange for a suspension of common sense.

For, if the spiritualist could actually cause the instruments to play without his intervention, let him do it in the light—he cannot.

Neither can the politician suspend the natural processes of bureaucracy by *expanding* them. He can at best, and only under special circumstances, perform the *illusion* of doing so—these special circumstances being that period prior to his inauguration, or a time of emergency sufficient to distract the populace or otherwise stay any outside power of verification.*

How, for example, may a new agency, named Homeland Security, offer improvement over that security previously provided by various diverse government agencies, each of which itself originated as an amalgamation of its predecessors in the name of efficiency?

This tendency toward elaboration is, of course, the way of the world. In the mobile society of our Democracy each new stage of elaboration is inaugurated by the selfsame vision: that what is needed is a centralized power, and a revision of laws to allow this efficiency. This is called a return to common sense.

---

*"Never let a good crisis go to waste."—Rahm Emanuel

But how may it be common sense for the auto industry to be run by one with no experience of it? This might be envisioned only through the intervention of some magical power—the process taking place in the dark, or in some closed cabinet. This is the essence of the wish for a czar: "Do it, but don't tell me about it, I'm sure it will be fine." It is the wish to be dominated by a strong beneficent power—the wish, in essence, for enslavement. See the various programs headed over the years by "czars,"—the Poverty, Car, Energy, Drug, et cetera—all exercises in magical thinking. What have they accomplished? Nothing.

How can a country grow rich through "redistributing" the wealth, by driving production overseas through taxation, by a refusal to exploit natural resources? This could be imagined only by those willing to suspend their understanding of the laws of cause and effect—the audience at a magic show.

Curiously, as magicians know, the more intelligent the viewer, the more easily he may be fooled. For the less imaginative and less theoretical *know* that a rabbit may not be produced from any hat which did not previously contain a rabbit; that wealth can accrue neither to an individual nor to a society not committed to the production of wealth, and that no organization may be made more efficient by adding to its bulk.

This delusion of an expanded government's increased efficiency is, in Liberal thought, buttressed by a belief in such a government's increased *fairness*—that more laws and more extralegal or administrative procedures will somehow bring about more and "better" justice than that provided by the Constitution. As some groups, we know, were discriminated against in the past, justice may now best be served by discrimination against *other* groups. This is suggested as a commonsense mechanical device. Psychologically, however, it is magical thinking: awarding to the State non-Constitutional powers, correctly deemed notorious when exercised by the individual.

How may justice be served by awarding to any special group a preference? Such awards may be welcome to the recipients, and their contemplation enjoyable to those of the good-willed who are not adversely affected by the redistribution, but they cannot be just.

Contemporary Liberal sentiment endorses the abrogation or elaboration of law to ensure that *no* one suffers, but the first and most important task of law in a democracy is not to right individual wrongs, but to ensure that no one suffers *because of the State*. And the simple, tragic truth is that this may be accomplished not by a Czar or a committee, or by reorganization, or by accession to office of the Benevolent or Wise, but only by limiting the State's power.

21 | RUMPELSTILTSKIN

Freud posits three main aspects of the mind: the Id, which is the unmitigated urge or nonnegotiable demand ("I want it"), the Ego, which attempts to integrate this demand with the Ego's other conflicting needs ("I know I want unlimited sex, but I also want to stay out of prison"); and the Superego, which is taxed with finding a solution to this hopeless and enervating struggle.

Here is my example of the process.

One finds oneself, in the middle of the night, stopped at a deserted intersection by a red light. The Id says, "What the hell are you waiting for, drive *on*."

"But wait," says the Ego, "what if it is a trap? What if the police are hiding, right behind that road sign?"

"No," says the Id, "their car would not quite fit, and we would see the tires, for the love of God."

"But what if there is a hidden camera," says the Ego. "Is it worth the risk? Why not wait the extra half-minute."

"You fool," says the Id, "there is no danger. You weak fool." This is, of course, intolerable. A random moment at a stoplight occasions a battle for self-esteem and psychic integrity. Even the changing of the light will not still the conflict, for one stands insulted and accused, and the question of what *should* have been done remains unanswered and unanswerable.

However, comes now the Superego.

"No," it says, "It is not that you are weak and foolish. You are, in fact, both worthy and good, and I will tell you why: you stopped at the light because you are a Good Citizen. And you realized that if everyone obeyed only those laws the transgression of which would result in immediate punishment, where would Society be? I congratulate and honor you for your choice."

Everybody happy, well, I should say.

As we have seen, all under the sway of the Nazi regime had to greet each other with the Nazi salute. Many found this, as it was an avowal of subjugation, intolerable. The Id said, "I will not give the wretched salute." The Ego replied, "What does it *mean*? You don't actually have to believe in the Nazis; it's just a simple gesture, and performing it will save your life."

But this interchange, unfortunately, caused the individual to enter into a painful negotiation scores of times a day. To wit: "I *do* it, but I don't *believe* in it. I am not a coward. I am merely making a rational and cost-effective accommodation. I am a worthy person, whatever the Id may say."

How can one eliminate the pain of the continual repetition of a distressing and seemingly insoluble negotiation?

Here comes the Superego with a brilliant solution: let the gesture be consigned to the realm of the unconscious—it turns the continual nature of the repetition from a reiterated pain into a selling point. "Look here," says the Superego, "there is just not enough time in the day to worry about it—we will let the dialogue lapse from consciousness, and replace it with unthinking habit."

But this instance differs from that of the stoplight.

For here we have an unfortunate unresolved remainder. For though the conscious negotiation ceased, the salute survived.

What was the effect, Bettelheim asked, of the now unconscious habitual repetition of a gesture of subjugation? The individual became a Nazi. How could he not? Was he not now pledging, unthinkingly, his loyalty scores of times a day?

A friend reports that she saw a doyenne of the Left at a restaurant and asked her advice on some question of Liberal Doctrine. "Contact MoveOn.org," the doyenne replied, "And do whatever they say."

The struggle of the Left to rationalize its positions is an intolerable, Sisyphean burden. I speak as a reformed Liberal.

How may one support higher taxes and government intervention as an aid to the economy, when all evidence historical and current (cf. Greece), records the disastrous folly of such a course?

How can one support racial preferences and set-asides, when they run contrary to the evidence of the results of all race- or genetic-based programs in history—their existence an incipient invitation to murder?

How can one deny (as the Obama administration insists on doing) that the military threat to the West has a name, and that name is Islamic Fascism?

Et cetera.

These positions, ad infinitum, are incompatible with reason, and one can embrace them only with great assistance, which, unfortunately, for the Liberal, is forthcoming.

That assistance is the Superego, capable of adjudicating all things.

A proposition or a person emerges promising the impossible. ("The New Economy"), or crooning about the unquantifiable ("Change"), and the Liberal finds this soothing sound consonant with his self-image as a brilliant and compassionate individual.

This individual is in the exact position of the confidence man's mark. In fact he *is* the confidence man's mark.

Now, the main problem in structuring a con game is in answering the mark's question, "Why *me* . . . ?"

In the Spanish Prisoner, played for over two thousand years, and seen today in its incarnation as the Nigerian Letter, the individual is appealed to as one of noted repute and standing in the community, as someone who can be trusted with the confidence man's improbable claim.

The mark is flattered. He understands why he has been chosen. He has been chosen because of his excellence. How could one (the Confidence man) who was *that perceptive*, then, be other than honorable also? The question does not arise.

The flattered mark glossing over all inconsistencies, and improbabilities, and indeed, impossibilities, in the confidence man's story, forks out his money.

The Liberal is flattered that he, in contradistinction to his benighted countrymates, has been chosen to advance the policies and doctrines of Liberalism. He, in endorsing them, is part of the Elite, one of those empowered to eradicate those historical evils entailed upon humanity because of the unfortunate delay of his advent. ("We are the people we have been waiting for," Obama campaign, 2008.)

He is the champion of Good, chosen because *someone* (the Candidate) has finally recognized his excellence.

His problem resides in this: that the doctrines, policies, and programs presented for his endorsement are senseless and destructive, and can be so-proved by any slight referral of them to the impartial verdicts of history.

What will the Superego do?

It will ensure that the referral will never occur.

How will it do this? By ensuring that the referral would occur only at the cost of relinquishing membership in the herd.

The Superego cannot increase the *benefit* of compliance (as it did with the stoplight), but will increase the *cost* of noncompliance. Questioning = excommunication.

The Left, in addition to its embrace of the false (higher taxes means increased prosperity for all), and its acceptance of the moot as incontrovertible (Global Warming); must account for the incidental effect of the sum of these decisions. This effect is the destruction of our culture.

All strife to the Left is error, and poverty and all human ills eradicable by new programs. But these revolutionary revisions destroy the human ability to interact, which, in its entirety, is known as Culture.

Note that, under the Statist revisions of the Obama administration, racial tensions have devolved to acrimony unknown in this country for decades. Sexual relations are universally subject to constant revision, and limits on language and behavior, once imposed unconsciously, and learned in family, community, and school, are returned to the conscious mind, erasing spontaneity and ease, and replacing them with consternation and fear.

Our beautiful American language is now subject to revision by those screaming loudest, and we have the enormity of s/he, the clunky continuous reiteration of his-or-her, and so on. This revision is presented by the Left as an aid of equality, but its result is an atmosphere not of happy compliance, but of anxiety, circumlocution, and a formalism destructive of the free exchange of ideas.

Our culture is being destroyed by the Left. What difference that the good-willed do so in the name of Equality? It is being destroyed.

The decision to allow a thirteen-story Islamic Center to be built in the vicinity of Ground Zero may be defensible under the rubric of law; but it is a cultural obscenity, allowable only if the State, the Left, or the individual asserts that every decision must be adjudicated according to the new understanding of the anointed.

The Government sues the State of Arizona for the enforcement of laws the passage of which are not only the right of the state under the Constitution, but the content of which is virtually identical with federal law.

The State of California sentences the farmers of its Central Valley to drought, and their farms to destruction, because a small fish called the delta smelt has been declared endangered.

That our culture is falling apart is apparent to any impartial observer. But what observer can be impartial? Conservatives are aghast; we are shocked at the actions of the Left, and we are astounded that they do not acknowledge these actions' results.

It is not that they do not care. But that they cannot afford to notice, for comparing their actions to the results would bring about either their ejection from the group (should they voice their doubts) or, should they merely follow their perceptions to their logical conclusions, the psychic trauma incident upon a revision of their worldview.

The Superego, here, has made a terrible bargain.

It has offered membership in a group whose size and power allows the individual to submerge his doubts. And then to forget them. But the cost is the surrender of his reason.

He may live his entire life never talking to a Conservative, never reading a Conservative publication, or listening to any news at all save that of the Left. That four hundred Liberal journalists have been revealed as involved in a long cabal to distort that which they offer as news, in aid of Liberalism, makes no difference to the Liberal. It cannot; for he cannot risk his membership in the herd. And he must remain unaware of his bargain. Like the young lady in Rumpelstiltskin.

The Gnome in the story came to offer her release from the Evil King. The gnome, however, was no one *other* than the Evil King, and his demands, like those of the King, eventually became intolerable. Prior to that point, she was dedicated to self-delusion. Maybe, she thought, *this* savior will aid me. Maybe, the Liberal thinks, *this* new iteration of Government Programs will prove useful. Perhaps this previous new panacea has failed (as all its like have failed) because it was Underfunded.

The Liberal is caught. To reject the herd protection is to, inevitably, undergo the shame and humiliation of recognizing his prior, destructive folly.*

So the Liberal stands pat. He, who never talks to anyone outside of this group, accuses the Conservative of being brainwashed; he explains the abysmal performance of Obama by saying "look at the mess he inherited," as if the President did not campaign (as do all politicians) on the platform of cleaning up the prior mess. (Those of the same party as the outgoing incumbent campaign on *improving* his accomplishments—which is to say the prior mess.)

The Liberal is subsumed in the herd. How, then, to explain, as he must, the unfortunate state of things? The herd supplies the answer: blame the Opposition.

---

*For a perfect dramatic representation of this crisis see Alec Guinness in *The Bridge on the River Kwai*. He has spent the whole film building a bridge for his enemies, the Japanese. It is only at the film's end, as he is trying to stop its destruction by his own army that he realizes his crime and says, "What have I done?"

Obama's plans are questioned? Call his opponents Racist.

Palestinian Terrorists are dedicated to the destruction of our ally, Israel? Blame the Israelis for saddling us with a challenge to our delusion of Universal Brotherhood.

The Left, in suspending reason and accountability, is ravaging our beautiful culture.

But the necessity of Culture is a part of human interaction. Strand ten bus riders in a blizzard, and they will extemporize their own culture.

The drive to discard our evolved American culture, to replace it with the "reasoning" of idiot teenagers who have blessed, by their presence, the schools of the Ivy League, results, as it must, in a *new* culture. But in what does this culture consist?

The Nazis and the Communists railed against and discarded religion, and instantly, automatically, created their own religion, each with all the formal trappings and operations of—though with different content than—those religions they displaced.*

So the Left creates its own, *new* culture.

But this culture is confusing, amorphous, and constantly shifting. It not only resembles, it *is* the Party Line, avant la lettre. The confused Liberal must grope, each day, to find how to explain (to his *own* satisfaction, for he will never talk to a conservative) the inexplicable vagaries of his tribe.

How can he do so? "Call MoveOn.org, and just do whatever they say."

In what does this new culture consist? In obedience.

---

*The Nazi swastika was a cross. The USSR's hammer and sickle, just somewhat less identifiably, was one also.

22 | MY FATHER, AL SHARPTON, AND THE DESIGNATED CRIMINAL

What is it that Liberal African Americans have not recognized about the Left? That there is no one home. The Left has abandoned the country, come out against capitalism, exploitation of resources, the free market, and work, and announced its refusal to defend our borders. All this as a matter of principle.

Al Sharpton and those calling (under whatever name) for reparations for ancient crimes are, in effect, suing for crumbs from those they, by that suit, designate as their (somehow) superiors. But they have no superiors. There is no one home. The slave owners, along with the robber barons, and "the interests," have left the building.

Reverend Al Sharpton, in Chris Rock's wonderful documentary *Good Hair*, takes on the overwhelming Asian ownership of hair salons in Black communities. He calls this ownership "exploitation." But who is exploiting the Black community, the Asians who, perceiving a need, are catering to that need, or the Reverend Sharpton?

The Asians, like the Jews, immigrants one hundred years ago, saw both a market and a vacuum of power, and responded. They saw in effect that *no one was there*.

My father bluffed his way into Northwestern Law on the GI Bill, having (perhaps) finished two years of community college. He graduated first in his class. I asked him what his secret was, and he explained that *he didn't realize how little was required of him*.

President Obama announces every day (and his presidency could, indeed, be reduced to this announcement and its results) that the West is finished: with capitalism, with Democracy, with self defense, and that anyone who wants it can have it. Will our opponents, those declared and those indeed stunned into wakefulness by our lassitude, be any less likely to respond to opportunity than the Asians in Harlem?

The same rules governing commercial real estate must govern geopolitics—how could it be otherwise, as each are only expressions of the universal nature of human interaction?

If the other fellow has damaged his property, if he has mismanaged it, and depressed or miscalculated its value, if he does not engage in its supervision and upkeep, it becomes a Bargain, and the bargain *will* be snapped up by the observant.

Where do these conditions of mismanagement and unconcern apply more frequently than in the case of property that is inherited ("shirtsleeves to shirtsleeves in three generations" being proverbial)?

Our forebears struggled and fought and died to establish and to preserve and broaden those freedoms they bequeathed us, and which have made us the most prosperous country in history. To denigrate our culture and traditions, to turn our back on our place and duty in the world—to, in effect, live off the interest and call it Humanism, or One-Worldism, or re-distribution of wealth, is an act of folly like that of any thoughtless and weak (not to say ungrateful) inheritor of wealth.

But the Liberal West must hide from itself its dysfunction, noting only those trends and occurrences indicative not only and not even primarily of the success of its theories* but of their *rationality*.

To defend the practice of the irrational consumes any organism's energy and, as with the Reverend Sharpton's cry of "exploitation," blinds the irrational to better uses of his time and power. What is to prevent African Americans from either opening their own hair

---

*Any theory put into practice may have its failure ascribed to underfunding, insufficient time for results, or the unfortunate, still insurmountable burdens placed upon it by a previous administration—this being the totality of the Obama administration's explanation of its dismal performance.

salons, or, like the Asian Americans, casting about for a need to fill and filling it (as Reverend Sharpton has)? Nothing.* And those who do so are rewarded according to the rules of the free market: "Give me something I want or need and I will pay you for it." Mr. Rock's film, in fact, contains a striking instance of a successful Black-owned business, Dudley's Hair Care & Cosmetics, which produces and distributes a vast amount of hair, skin, and makeup products to the African American community.

To defend the irrational or inconsistent becomes, in the dysfunctional organization, the *prime* goal—and any other use of energy secondary—for the dysfunctional organism's life, that is, its ability to function as constituted, depends on the devotion, among its members, to fantasy.

Here is an example. President Obama, in a speech in July 2010, declared that the Government should be ready to support Green Business—that if anyone wanted to create these jobs, the Government would be there to help.

What was the help? He was offering rebates. But what are rebates but tax cuts?

To suggest that giving back (to approved entities) *some* of the money drained from them in taxes, and to characterize this as "help," is like a mugger pausing in administering his beating and characterizing this pause, to his victim, as assistance.

If, as President Obama announced perceptively, cutting taxes creates jobs (as it does; as anyone not blinded by theory knows: when taxes are raised, businesses close), then why not cut *all* taxes?†

This inconsistency is ignored only by those who benefit from it (the administration), and the confused (Liberals).

---

*Compare Marcus Garvey's "Up, you Mighty Race, you Race of Kings. You can accomplish what you will." (recorded 1921)

†That the President only wants to cut taxes to those enterprises he deems politically productive is, of course, understandable. This is called "Politics." It does not, however, synchronize his matter-of-fact admission that tax cuts create jobs with his, then, irrational insistence on helping the economy through raising taxes.

Why not, O Liberals, vote to cause the Government to keep its filthy hands off the possessions of its citizens, and let those citizens and their country thrive?

It's not the largess of Government which is required (the money existed *before* they confiscated it—it simply was not *theirs*) but its reduction. This can only be brought about by reducing taxes, for government and taxes are each the secret name of the other.

To whom is this, in his sober moments, other than evident?

To defend and continue the practice the irrational, and thus necessarily destructive, consumes energy and time which cannot be expended on production, innovation, *actual* revision, or on anything else. For the dysfunctional group—a state or family—congeals around and must spend increasing amounts of its energy defending a lie.

The lie may be that Daddy is not abusing little Susie, or it may be that increased taxes, Government intervention, and One-Worldism somehow bring stability to our country, and bring to its citizens not only health and prosperity, but Salvation (called, in 2008, "Change").

The dysfunctional State and the dysfunctional Family have in common an emergency tool for dealing with, defusing, or indicting outbreaks of reason. The sick family employs the mechanism of the Designated Criminal. It is this person who is always doing something wrong, which is to say contrary to his family's interests and destructive of its peace. His thoughts, behavior, attitude, and loyalty may always be called into question; and he is punished, mocked, marginalized, or ignored, as circumstances warrant, which responses in themselves unite and strengthen the threatened organism. How is this Designated Criminal selected, he whose actions and demeanor are all that stands between his family and Happiness? He is chosen by his health. He is invariably the most clearheaded member of the household.

He may be designated because he is passive, or weak, but more usually, because he is not.

For the more clearheaded, healthy, and strong the child is, the more likely he is not only to question, but to rebel against unreason, thus increasing his utility as a recipient of scorn, his condign punishments standing in support of the original proposition of his perfidy.

It is no great leap to discern, in the Family of Nations, this same mechanism—denial and coalescence around a lie.* No reader need waste reflection in identifying the cause of the West's woes—the Designated Criminal State—it is done for us constantly by the United Nations.

*That the West is exploitative, destructive, racist, and finally, unworthy.

23 | GREED

Greed is a sin. It is mentioned in the Ten Commandments, where it is called covetousness, which is to say the wish for that which another possesses. As such it is allied to envy and resentment.

But there is a nonsinful wish for more, and it is called ambition.

How is the sin of covetousness to be differentiated from a legitimate desire for gain?

The Torah cautions us not to go astray after the evidence of our eyes and our hearts "which we are whoring after"—a good harsh word to describe covetousness. Should we go astray, that which was a sin may fall from the moral world into the judicial realm—sin may become crime and, as such, the legitimate concern of the community. The community must protect itself not from ambition, neither from covetousness, but from crimes committed in their pursuit. And the criminal act, as opposed to the merely distasteful or, indeed, immoral, must be clearly delineated, or else there can be no justice. A democratic system and civilization punishes those who take that which does not belong to them according to law.

There is a Liberal sentiment that it should also punish those who take more than their "fair share." But what is their fair share? (Shakespeare suggests that each should be treated not according to his deserts, but according to God's mercy, or none of us would escape whipping.)

The concept of Fairness, for all its attractiveness to sentiment, is a dangerous one (cf. quota hiring and enrollment, and talk of "reparations"). Deviations from the Law, which is to say the Constitution, to accommodate specifically alleged identity-group injustices will all inevitably be expanded, universalized, and exploited until there remains no law, but only constant petition of Government.

We cannot live in peace without Law. And though law cannot be perfect, it *may* be just if it is written in ignorance of the identity of the claimants and applied equally to all. Then it is a possession not only of the claimants but of the society, which may now base its actions upon a reasonable assumption of the law's treatment.

But "fairness" is not only a nonlegal but an antilegal process, for it deals not with universally applicable principles and strictures, but with specific cases, responding to the perceived or proclaimed needs of individual claimants, and their desire for extralegal preference. And it could be said to substitute *fairness* (a determination which must always be subjective) for *justice* (the application of the legislated will of the electorate), is to enshrine greed—the greed, in this case, not for wealth, but for preference.

The Left's current sentiment for the confiscation of benefits legally earned, but to them offensive, is Greed.

To wish to abrogate a legal contract between employer and employee because a nonparticipant feels someone got too much money is greed. It is not greed for money, but covetousness born of envy—the desire for that which legally belongs to another. That those in favor of this may not want the actual money for their own use is beside the point—they want the enjoyment of the power to strip the money from another. They may not use the confiscated funds to buy a car or a meal, but the billionaire who earns another million dollars cannot spend it *either*—he, like the offended Liberal, is enjoying the warm glow of its possession. A rampant and untrammeled glee, an unchecked ambition for gain is, in the individual, called miserliness; in the society which strips him of it, it is called Socialism.

Who is to decide what is too much? Various religions demand or suggest tithing, and the State demands taxes; both are based upon the principle of proportionality—that is, the surrender of a percentage of earnings.

This seems to be both fair and just. Do some cheat on taxes? Of course—but the Legislature, in its wisdom, has passed laws criminalizing this behavior—not because it leaves the individual with "unearned wealth," but because it deprives the society of its just *legislated* share.

Do some avoid taxes through cunning and chicanery? Of course. But there is a line, as in any business, between fraud and sharp practice. And the individual is free to figure his taxes according to his consideration of his own best legal interest. Should he cross the line, he is free to go to jail.

It is the business of government to tax the individual sufficiently to support the legitimate operations of Government. The identity of these legitimate purposes is a matter of debate, which may begin in society at large, but must culminate in the Legislature. When the greed of the Legislature oversteps the will of the People, and its understanding of the role of government, they may be voted out.

———

What institution is more greedy than Government?

What individual more ravenous than the Perpetual Candidate who is every politician?

We are all subject to envy, covetousness, and greed (else why would we find them in the Ten Commandments?). The purpose of religion and of morality is to limit these corrosive influences on the mind and soul. The purpose of law is to control the destructive actions which spring therefrom.

But not all the actions of ambition spring from Greed. One may grow wealthy through hard work, through persistence, or, indeed, by chance or lucky accident. (Many gullible purchasers of western land in the nineteenth century found themselves duped, in the discovery that their beautifully described property was oozing black sludge, which sludge, on the invention of the automobile, made them and their descendants wealthy beyond belief.)

And one may be greedy as the Horse Leech's Daughter, but, absent luck and crime (dealt with above), he may not gain wealth. Greed is a sin. Ambition is a virtue. Society may express its appreciation of the fine distinction through gossip, but the law cannot take notice of anything other than crime. Greed does not create wealth.

Barring luck and crime, wealth may only be created through satis-fying the needs of others.

A motion picture studio and its bosses may be as greedy as they like, but they can only gain through the public's desire to buy tickets. Are the producers and the studio and network heads greedy? Per-haps; consumed and devoured by covetousness, perhaps; but they only grow rich through bringing pleasure to the audience.* And this holds true of every other good and service. In the Free Market the indi-vidual can prosper only through providing for the desires of others.

But are there not cartels and so on? Of course, but they, if merely noxious, are to be borne, or dealt with through withdrawal of custom; if actually illegal, they are the province of the law, and if immoral, that of society, which may deal with them under the law or change the law.

But what of the massive collapse of the housing market?

President Obama spoke of "predatory lending." But how can lending be predatory which is not usurious? It cannot. No one forced the virtually cost-free loans upon the borrowers. They took the loans *in hope of gain*. The banks *made* the loans in hope of gain. Is either side greedy? The actions of the banks may have been ambitious, but what, otherwise, is the nature of a business? And the borrow-ers' desire to get the best possible terms at the lowest cost, had the market not failed, would have been hailed as genius. It is disingenu-ous, then, that the borrowers, having lost, are championed by those who enjoy identifying them as victims.

(Imagine two golfers. One suggests an unusually high bet on one hole. The other accepts. The first man wins, and the loser explains: "I thought you were just kidding." Well, perhaps he did, and perhaps he did not, but the question is not what he thought, but would he [hav-ing *accepted* the bet, kidding or not] have accepted the money had he won? Had the housing market continued to rise, would the borrowers have accepted the gain? Of course. As would you and I. How, then,

---

*May they grow rich through misleading or defrauding the stockholders? Of course—if the first, let them be voted out, if the second, prosecuted.

can the loans be called "predatory lending"? Only by suggesting the borrowers' incapacity to form a legal contract. On what basis?)

That the borrowers lost is unfortunate. But had they won *they would have taxed the next buyers* with the increase in their property's value, rewarding and applauding themselves not only for their foresight but for the bravery of their investment.

Absent luck there is no gain without risk. One may risk one's savings, one's time, one's energy, and so on, but inherent in the Pursuit of Happiness is risk; and the essential freedom of our Democracy is the freedom to risk, that is to *try*, which has made us the most prosperous nation in the history of the world.*

Some success is borne, by the public, and not envied. There was much outcry when a director of the stock exchange was awarded a vast golden parachute, and fury over the salaries of various executives whose businesses have failed. But who suggests that the contract of a highly paid pitcher be torn up because his team did poorly, or that a movie star whose last film flopped return his salary?

But, one might say, the highly paid money manipulators, stock market operations, et cetera, *performed no service*.† Perhaps they did,

---

*In my family, as in yours, someone regularly says, "Hey, you know what would be a good idea . . . ?" And then proceeds to outline some scheme for making money by providing a product or service the need for which has just occurred to him. He and the family fantasize about and discuss and elaborate this scheme. Inherent in this fantasy is the unstated but ever-present truth that, given sufficient capital and expertise or the access to the same, the scheme *might* actually be put into operation (as, indeed, constantly, throughout our history, such schemes have), bettering the lives of the masses and bringing wealth to their creators. Do you believe such conversations take place in Syria? In France?

†This is the widely noted fallacy that "work" must contain a physical element of actual labor. That one who merely "writes things down," or "plays with figures," is not performing "work," but is merely "a manipulator."

But what of the man who sat on a rock, and came up with the idea of a wheel, or the idea of a bank, or the theory of relativity?

Is there an element of gambling in the stock market? Of course there is, and you and I participate in it either directly, or through choices and purchases we each make on the basis of our predictions of a likely rise or fall in prices.

But let us assume a worst case—that the manipulators, beyond aiding any beneficial transaction (buying and selling of futures in order to, potentially, regularize the cost of commodities), or indeed just gambling (buying and selling futures solely to make money from their fluctuations), are engaged *solely* in "rigging the market," and other sharp practices.

and perhaps not, but a lot of people who gave over their money to them *thought* they did.* And one must reason that the money

---

"Do you not see abuses," the Liberal says. "In fact, do you not see *inherent* abuses in: the money market, the insurance industry, and so on—should they be allowed to continue unchecked?"

And the Liberal is not wrong in his outrage. But what human agency cannot be abused, and abused to the point of outrage?

And might not the Liberal, given an ironclad tip on a stock, consider acting on it, *whatever* his disdain for the stock market's "practices"?

The problem is that if Government can be invoked and employed to arbitrate over every outrage, it may be invoked constantly. For outrage is a feeling and its invocation and adjudication subject to no objective test. The job of the Government is only to make and administer *Laws*.

The Liberal, in his legitimate, or at least supportable, "outrage," has, quite literally, had his feelings hurt.

But if the State is called upon to take more power in such a case—if *no* "outrage" is to continue unchecked, then, inevitably, Government will sooner or later check *everything*; it will (as we see) respond to *all* calls to intervene; not only to control the stock market and health care, but insurance, auto sales, secondhand smoke, and the labeling of the caloric content of food, and so on. Why? Because each intervention increases the power of the respondents.

Legislators and executives live, quite literally, by their ability to find a "pressing cause"— this buys them the airtime they require for reelection, and provokes the anxiety for which they offer themselves, to the voters, as the only cure. See "Global Warming," which made Al Gore a billionaire, and the Global Initiative which have done the same for Bill Clinton.

The Liberal is not wrong to be concerned about malfeasance and sharp practice and misdirection. He is wrong to think that much of it can be controlled by that organization which is the prime exemplar and beneficiary of these methods.

The question, finally, is, what is the correct and effective and just use of Government power? And the answer is neither contained in nor indicated by the feelings of the affronted. It is the United States Constitution.

Is it not tragic that x or y has been harmed in such or such transaction?

Yes. And it is tragic that the blunt but effective tool for the pursuit of justice is as easily exploitable as any other power; and it is tragic that many cannot see it.

*If the Government is to protect all citizens from every possible harm deriving from their choices, from every possible "bad" choice, it is not illogical, in addition to refunding money from legal investments gone bad, to refund the purchase price of most cosmetics. A friend of mine, long deceased, fled Nazi-occupied Poland with her family. She came to New York and was, for a while, supported by her fellow Polish Jew, Helena Rubinstein. One day she said, "Helena, how can you sell these inert white creams to the public, you are selling them *nothing*. Helena responded, "I am selling them the most valuable thing in the world: I am selling hope." (In conversation with Noma Potok, ca. 1979)

If the Government were to debar before—and to compensate after the fact for any actions characterizeable as "foolish"—it would, at first examination, have prohibited both the electric light and the toupee.

these folks played around with came, originally, from investors interested—I will not say "greedily," but "intensely" in an increase of the entrusted funds. It is not "fair" to execrate the failed CEO and to exempt the failed pitcher. It is irrational. As the idea of "fairness" is, itself, irrational.

———

The baseball pitcher brought us some enjoyment, so he does not fall, in our Jacobin dreams; but if we did not possess the excess funds to dabble in the stock market, its director has brought us neither enjoyment, reward, nor hope of the same, so we award ourselves the enjoyment of his humiliation.

The socialistic spirit of the Left indicts ambition and the pursuit of wealth as Greed, and appeals, supposedly on behalf of "the people," to the State for "fairness."

But such fairness can only be the non-Constitutional intervention of the State in the legal, Constitutional process—awarding, as it sees fit, money (reparations), preferment (affirmative action), or entertainment (confiscation).

Ivan Boesky, stock manipulator and convict, said, in a speech at the University of California at Berkeley in 1986, Greed is good.

Greed is not good, greed is bad. Ambition is neutral, and the distinction is subjective, sometimes difficult, and no business of the State.

Who is to say that the success we applaud (that of the pitcher or quarterback, for example) stems from one and not the other? Can we know? Is it our business? It is not, save in a theocracy, whether Puritan, or its current remanifestation as Socialist—Humanist.

We cannot know, neither is it our business to know, what is in another's heart. We can judge the results of his actions and reward them should they meet our needs. When we are no longer free to do so, we will have eliminated not Greed but Free Enterprise, and with it, all other freedoms.

24 | ARRESTED DEVELOPMENT

I was teaching a seminar on dramatic structure at a university. All was going well, until I suggested that the heroine of the story we were constructing be kidnapped by some Arab terrorists. One student asked, "Haven't the Arabs been picked on enough? Why," he asked, "did you specify *Arabs*? As terrorists." "*I* don't know," I said. "They came to mind, perhaps as Arab terrorists bombed New York." Another student suggested the Pakistanis might be the villain of this piece, and a third said, "*That's just not funny.*"

But, my golly, I said, can the piece have *no* villain? Are we to suggest that, since any actor must *himself* have characteristics, we strive to create a featureless villain, to our choice of which then, could be ascribed no attempt at derogatory racial or social comment? Whereupon the class degenerated in a way which, seemed to me, must be rather usual, for the students lapsed into rather stilted and formulaic repetition of pronouncements.

Everything, it seemed, was political, and their job was to inform the ignorant of it. The Ignorant, in this classroom, were myself and the young woman who suggested the Pakistanis. A young Idealogue broadened his thesis, it was not only the responsibility of the dramatist, he taught, to refrain from stereotyping, but to use every aspect of the drama to *enforce* upon the public a humanitarian view of the world. Homosexuals, for instance, he said, should be seen kissing onstage whenever possible, was it not an outrage that the part of Blanche in *A Streetcar Named Desire* was always played by a woman? Why could it not be played by a *man*?

"Well," I said, "it *could* be played by a man. *Streetcar* is essentially a gay fantasy written by a gay writer, and clothed in straight terms." This gave the young fellow pause, for he was not sure if my comment supported or opposed his thesis.

For, in fact, he was not sure what his thesis *was*, but I think it could be reduced to this: all speech should be susceptible to his review on the basis of a series of precepts which, while they could not be cogently *enumerated*, might be inferred from the generalized precept that all people are equal, and anyone from whose actions a dedication to this principle could not be constantly inferred was a subhuman swine.

"Well, all right," I asked, "are homosexuals human?" He answered that of course they were human. "Being human," I asked, "are they entitled to the same rights as any other human?" "Of course," he replied. "Well, then," I said, "if one of those is the right to entertainment, might we not study to entertain them, by learning how to structure a play?"

But the class had ticked over into what I recognized was a usual stage of progression; someone had taken the high ground and shouted "racist," or "homophobe," first and loudest, and all who did not wish to be so branded must submit to his dominance, for did he not speak in the name of all the Good?

"All *right*," I said. "Here's my favorite joke: What did Custer say when he saw the Indians coming?" (PAUSE) " 'Here come the Indians.' " This was met with that pause we all know, within which the right-minded search for a clue as to the comment's indictability. Was it a criticism of the Native Americans? How could it be otherwise? On the other hand, were *not* these people actually *called* Indians? "Here come the Native Americans," of course, does not scan. And so on, ran that dreary brutally foolish pause which was the end of the class and is the end of Liberal Education.

———

What is Liberal Education? It has become an indoctrination in aggressive Identity Politics, a schooling, that is, in the practice of indictment, assault, exclusion, and contempt, all of which contradicts the statement of Universal Humanity upon which all its educational "ideology" rests.*

But here was my question: On leaving the university, what would these Young Stalinists *do*? Who would pay them for the ability to bravely proclaim, "That's not funny?" In what society could they live?

They were and are the children of privilege—in some the privilege is inherited, and the cost of college meaningless, in some the cost is huge, and families suffer; but in all cases the privilege taught, learned, and imbibed, in a "liberal arts education" is the privilege to indict. These children have, in the main, never worked, learned to obey, command, construct, amend, or complete—to actually *contribute* to the society. They have learned to be shrill, and that their indictment, on the economy, on sex, on race, on the environment, though based on no experience other than hearsay, *must* trump any discourse, let alone opposition. It occurred to me that I had seen this behavior elsewhere, where it was called a *developmental difficulty*.

A nine-year-old boy is rowdy—he needs to run, to subvert, to climb, to misuse, to expend his energies and explore.

Our civilization, incapable of dealing with this natural phenomenon through immemorial means (discipline, order, sport, parental punishment, the military) deems the behavior pathological, and administers wholesale diagnoses, sanctions, and drugs.

Boys are boys and need both to discharge and to learn how to *correctly* discharge and moderate those impulses appropriate to this as to any stage of their development. The strong, wise, or trained teacher or parent must learn when to say, "Sit down," and when, "Go out and play"; when "I'm calling the police," and when "Knock it off." But we have lost the power to discriminate.

---

*Here is a sad story. I was due to return to this university, recently, to teach for a few days, but I came down with the flu, and at the last minute had to cancel my trip. Here is what I missed. The students referred to above had provoked or been provoked by a professor to file a complaint against me, for making "racially derogatory comments." This complaint had been picked up by the school newspaper, which announced that a campus-wide "town hall meeting" was being convened to vote on whether or not I was to be barred from appearing on campus. *That's* not funny.

A woman on a transcontinental flight was having problems with her three-year-old twins. She swatted them, the stewardess came over to correct the mother, and the mother and she had some words. On landing, the mother was taken off the plane, indicted and convicted of terrorism, and served three months in prison. For she had disrupted a flight, and had spoken rough to a flight attendant and that, it seems, is now a Federal Crime.

———

The wise society must deal with transitional periods of youth. The young are confused, frightened, energetic, and require not stringency, neither laxity, but *guidance*, which will consist sometimes of the one and sometimes of the other. The guidance required by the rowdy nine-year-olds is also required by college students: They are full of idealism, but have no experience. They may so easily be subverted into sloganeering, for it gratifies the ego and, more importantly, *obviates the fear of the unknown* (adulthood). If everything one needs to know one knows *now*, there is no need to learn discernment, or to *choose*—there is no wisdom greater than "people are people." And if all oppression must be stopped and there is nothing further to learn, then *you* are the fellow to *do* it. This demagoguery looses the student from the very constraints of thoughtfulness, courtesy, respect, circumspection, and patience, which, at age twenty-one, it is his final chance to learn. These habits, even absent a marketable skill, may help him begin to earn a living. But the recitation of aggressive, invidious slogans meant to shame stand little chance of doing so.

It is not that this Liberal Arts Student has too much leisure, he has nothing *but* leisure. I have spent forty years sitting alone at a typewriter, and will report that it takes time, and effort, trial and error, to learn how to structure one's day productively when there is no one there but you.

It is impossible that the eighteen-year-old, in the laissez-faire of the Liberal Arts courses of Identity Politics, can do so. Of course he will look for certainty, and he will find it in the herd. Being equipped with neither experience nor philosophy, he will adopt the cant of those around him; and his elders, far from correcting him, *endorse* him, and, indeed, charge him for the experience, and call it "college tuition." But it is Socialist Camp, and creative not of productive Citizens, but of intolerant, uneducated, and incurious graduates, who now, at age twenty-one or twenty-two, must either look for work bagging groceries, or defer the trauma of matriculation by a further course of "study."

"Are gay people people too?" I asked the student, and he said that of course they were. "Are they aware of that fact?" I asked him. And he responded similarly. "Then why," I asked, "as they are aware of the fact, would they find its repetition on stage entertaining?"

"Ah, but," he said, "the straight people should see it."

"Ah, but," I said, "the straight people don't care. They may reward themselves for the ability to be bored by a play with a Good Message, but they, just like the gay people, come to the theater to be entertained. Your enlightenment is insufficient to capture the audience's attention for two hours. Would you like some hints on how to do so?"

But the class was over, and I left feeling like a fool, and sad. For the class members were not stupid, they were, as they should be at that age, idealistic; and the university's disinterest in educating them to be of use in their society had turned their natural energy and idealism into a developmental difficulty. They were being drugged with self-indulgence.

———

I believe that the Liberal Arts University has had it. Like bottled water, the expense and the illusion of exclusivity are still attracting buyers, but what do they buy and what is it worth? The elite schools sell certification, which perhaps has some theoretical value in some theoretical marketplace, though little in the institutions into which these graduates pour.

What family or graduate is going to benefit from a degree in film or gender studies or, indeed, English literature? What are these people going to do, save spread the gospel of the use of their particular discipline in the hope of obtaining a place in the continuation of the farce?

We scoff at the hereditary Mandarin positions as "Keeper of the Buttonhook," or "Strewer of Rose Petals in the Back Garden," but what else is "Associate Professor of Gender Studies"? It means the particular institution wishes to display status by the conspicuous waste of treasure and time and so inveigle the insufficiently investigative (parents and students) to come, buy its hogwash, and swell its coffers. But as the economy implodes, there will be fewer and fewer students and families blinded by the display, and more and more sitting down at the kitchen table with paper and pencil, asking the question, "What do I *give*, and what do I *get*?" which is the essence of responsibility, and it's a question of which the developmentally challenged youth are unaware.

Scrooge asked, "Are there no Prisons? And the Union workhouses? Are they still in operation?" and I might ask the same of the Trade School, the ROTC, the Military, the Boy and Girl Scouts, the Synagogues and Churches which have, traditionally, functioned to aid the youth toward a matriculation into society, and so to an actual sense of self-worth. But the sloganeering of the Liberal Arts school teaches the young not self-worth, but arrogance, and much of the rage and rancor these sloganeers project against the supposed unenlightened oppressors is uncathected rage against the adult generation which has abandoned them to the rowdy and inappropriate disruptiveness of their own devices.

Children crave discipline. Its absence frightens them, for they know themselves incapable of independent function; and the placards and "revolutionary Humanism" of today's college students are nothing other than the four-year-old's tantrum: he throws the tantrum in front of and for the *benefit* of his parents; he acts out his aggression in a protected setting. The child whose parents are absent, who is in the care of others, will not throw a tantrum, for he recognizes no one cares, and he had better figure out how to get his needs met in an environment not disposed to tolerate his nonsense.

25 | OAKTON MANOR AND
CAMP KAWAGA

In the fifties, Camp Kawaga was the Chicago Jewish summer camp. At Camp Kawaga (D.M., summers 1955–58) they played a recording of Taps each evening. It was preceded by a recording of "Ave Maria," sung by one of the counselors with artistic ambitions. But the Camp was Jewish exclusively.

And on Sundays we had "Chapel," at which, in the spirit of the Jew endeavoring to intuit the content of Unitarianism, the camp director read a poem by Douglas MacArthur.

The General had written, in love, a poem not to, but *about* his young son Arthur, and the poem had, somehow gained a wider distribution.

"Build me a Son, Lord," it ran, "who will be strong enough to know when he is weak, and brave enough to face himself when he is afraid," et cetera, closing, after the conclusion of the recipe, with, "And then I, his father, may dare to whisper 'I have not lived in vain.'"

I remember thinking, aged eight, that this was hot stuff.

I came across the poem after fifty-some years, in William Manchester's biography of MacArthur, *American Caesar*, and found, reading the first few words, that I could quote the whole from memory. So I suppose it had made an impression.

But, on reflection, it's a poem not about the General's relationship to his son, but about his relationship with God. It is a direction to God from his superior, General MacArthur. Perhaps if the General wanted such a son (as I am sure he did) he might have taken a hand in the process himself, asking God for guidance rather than for expedited delivery.

Much later I discovered Kipling's "If," a note not from a man to God, but from a man to his son.

As an American I was spared this poem's ruination by its, to the British, outrageous ubiquity, it holding a place in the British literary consciousness like that held over here by *The Great Gatsby* and *Moby-Dick* but not, unfortunately, by "Stopping by Woods on a Snowy Evening."*

I found Kipling's sentiments marvelous, an exhortation to his son to be strong and brave, careful and considerate.† This is advice I give my own son, my profound desire for its reception colored by my knowledge of my own shortcomings.

Like that speech by Polonius, it is the plea of every father watching his son leave home: "Forgive me, I've done everything wrong, I have done nothing right. I was, as a model, insufficient, and as a preceptor, hypocritical. Here is what I *wish* to have said: Our time is almost done, and I have taxed you with my pomposity and garrulousness and officiousness, and you have been supremely patient with me. But perhaps you might listen for just this last time, in the hope that these words might aid you."

———

I have learned from my old German friend Ilse various helpful old-world phrases. One is: "Boys are different."

And, indeed, they are. Very like each other, and very different from girls.

After three daughters, a son is a revelation. Watching him and his friends one both sees and remembers, boys want only to explore, to fight, to test, to climb, break and rearrange everything they see. They will find a way to ruin a featureless, titanium chamber.

*We were told, as young literary students, that Robert Frost had a lover's quarrel with the world. Better had he had an actual fight.

†"If you can keep your head when all about you are losing theirs and blaming it on you, if you can trust yourself when all men doubt you, but make allowance for their doubting, too . . ."

Our American school system (public and private) is against them. It is no wonder the boys have developed or been diagnosed (which is to say marginalized) as possessing a whole alphabet full of acronyms, which may be reduced to "I give up, *drug* them."

But here is a truer view of boys, from Tolstoy.

He described Karenin's impatience with his young son Sergei. Sergei is looking out of the window, and Karenin is trying to get him to describe, "a verb of *action*." But Sergei, we are told, is patiently trying to remove his attention from the progress of a butterfly, and his ruminations about the nature of air, sun, and the world, in general. Sergei is trying to be polite to his father, and his father is berating him as a dunce, but the boy was wondering at the nature of the Universe.

A blunter writer might conflate our school's anti-male bias with a societal inclination to cease exploration and production, and let the land revert to fallowness. We seem to be taxing ourselves to death in an effort to arrive at a magical formula which will allow us to survive without either production or exploration.

Traditionally women dealt with the home and men dealt with the World. Men and women are both parents, but only one of them is created to be a mother. That there is no difference can be asserted only by those who have not raised children.

Boys are born to contest with the world, and if we are going to breed out of them that ability, the land is going to lie fallow.

————

The other aspect of our Jewish Chicago Summer was Oakton Manor. This was our marvelous, knotty-pine equivalent to the Catskills, just over the Wisconsin Line. Here the kids had activities every day under the supervision of counselors, while the wives got a break from motherhood. The men came up on the weekends, and the adults smoked, drank, danced, and were entertained. Do such resorts exist anymore? It was a Jewish Haven, both catering to the human preference for recreation in the midst of one's kind, and redressing the contemporary exclusion of Jews (Restriction) from many hotels and resorts.

Our lives today seem more stratified, or contained, by wealth than race. This is, thermodynamically, a shame, for one needs more energy to relax sequestered by wealth, than protected in simple settings by one's clan; for wealth, as opposed to race, certainly has degrees, and so these differences, even in seclusion, may create envy and anxiety.

———

Being among my people is a delight.

Jews associate exclusively with Jews. Though we may identify the momentary agglomeration as based on wealth, politics, location, profession, or avocation, a quick check will reveal the group (even if made of enemies of Israel, or of the Jewish Religion itself) is made of Jews. We Jews live among ourselves. I love it. And all the carping about Israel, or mooing about the Palestinians, or about the emptiness of Religion, is a constant in Jewish life, and is, in fact, the descant of the Torah.

The Jewish proclamation of disaffection is like the constant head and body movements of the blind called "blindisms." The blind use these to locate themselves in space.

Our Jewish bitching is, similarly, a proprioceptive maneuver, used to locate in space our wandering, border culture.

Many Jews are confused about or opposed to the existence of the Jewish State, and, in their ignorance or muddleheadedness, wish it away. Much of this disaffection is laziness, for if Israel were gone, these anti-Zionist souls believe they might dwell in an unmitigated state of assimilation, any pressures of which might conceivably be combated by an effortless supineness.*

We were strangers in a strange land, and we are still strangers in a strange land—but the land is less strange than any in which we

---

*Many anti-Zionist Jews feel "outrage" at Israeli "enormities." That the identity and true nature of these supposed "enormities" vanishes upon investigation or contemplation is beside the point. The actual and truly disquieting enormity of Israel is, to them, its existence—because of which a largely anti-Semitic world forces them to *choose*. They, as opposed to non-Jews, are forced to have an *opinion* on a difficult and dangerous topic; and they would rather not. They are angered not at Israel nor at world anti-Semitism, but at "the Jews."

have dwelt. How to make it less strange still? To cease pretending and enjoy the benefits of liberty, security, and success, and defend them as an American, rather than posing as a "citizen of the World."

For here the assimilated (Liberal) Jew simply expands the neurosis of Diaspora thinking: the United States offers Freedom to all, and there is no one here I need to placate; but this position suggests self-examination: "If this is so, why do I feel dislocated?* Perhaps there is a *wider* polity whose 'Good wishes I must seek.' I will call it 'the World,' or 'World Opinion.' Or, 'What might I apologize for . . .' "

Why would any American Jew wish to become a "citizen of the World"? This fantasy is akin to one who believes in the benevolence of Nature. Anyone ever lost in the wild knows that Nature wants you dead.

*The Jew feels dislocated as his lived life is different from that which he imagines he lives. He is indelibly a Jew, associates with his kind, and denies his essential nature, his heritage, and his co-religionaries in their distress. "To summarize, contrary to the claim that is constantly reiterated, Israel has no right to use force to defend itself against rockets from Gaza, even if they are regarded as terrorist crimes." (Noam Chomsky, " 'Exterminate All the Brutes': Gaza, 2009") Of *course* Mr. Chomsky feels that all is not right with the world—his hobby is promoting the cause of people who want to kill him.

26 | FEMINISM

One might say that the politician, the doctor, and the dramatist make their living from human misery; the doctor in attempting to alleviate it, the politician to capitalize on it, and the dramatist, to describe it.

But perhaps that is too epigrammatic.

When I was young, there was a period in American drama in which the writers strove to free themselves of the question of *character*.

Protagonists of their worthy plays had made no choices, but were *afflicted* by a condition not of their making; and this condition, homosexuality, illness, being a woman, etc., was the center of the play. As these protagonists had made no choices, they were in a state of innocence. They had not acted, so they could not have sinned.

A play is basically an exercise in the raising, lowering, and altering of expectations (such known, collectively, as the Plot); but these plays dealt not with expectations (how *could* they, for the state of the protagonist was not going to change?) but with *sympathy*.

What these audiences were witnessing was not a *drama*, but a troublesome human condition displayed as an attraction. This was, formerly, known as a freak show.

The subjects of these dramas were bearing burdens not of their choosing, as do we all. But misfortune, in life, we know, deserves forbearance on the part of the unafflicted. For though the display of courage in the face of adversity is worthy of all respect, the *display* of that respect by the unaffected is presumptuous and patronizing.

One does not gain merit from congratulating an afflicted person for his courage. One only gains entertainment.

Further, endorsement of the courage of the affliction play's hero was not merely impertinent, but, more basically, spurious, as applause was vouchsafed not to a worthy stoic, but to an *actor* portraying him.

These plays were an (unfortunate) by-product of the contemporary love-of-the-victim. For a victim, as above, is pure, and cannot have sinned; and one, by endorsing him, may perhaps gain, by magic, part of his incontrovertible status. (An ancient poker adage has it that the Loser can't get enough to eat, and the winner can't sleep. Its application to the postwar West, I leave to the Reader.)

But a synergistic elaboration of the essence of the victim play was that the Afflicted could in no wise be portrayed as flawed. But, if they could not be flawed (that is, if they had not made, as heroes of the drama, a wrong choice), how could they be the fit subject of a drama? They could not.

———

My first personal experience of Political Thought in the Arts dates from my first commercially produced play. This was *Sexual Perversity in Chicago*, which ran, for some time, off-Broadway at the Cherry Lane Theatre in New York.

A woman critic at the *Village Voice* accused me, in a review of this play, of misogyny. Why? Because misogyny was a subject of the play.

In my play, two couples, two men and two women, contend. The younger man and woman, Dan and Deborah, have fallen in love, and the older pair, respectively, their best friends, scheme to keep them apart. A common, and, I thought, inoffensive theme. But the champion of the Oppressed took against me. How odd, I thought, for one might have supposed the title, characterizing the behavior in the play as *perverse* might have allowed the poor critic, if not some enjoyment, at least a guide to her conjectures as to my motives. (Cézanne's labeling various still-lifes as dealing with *fruit*, for example, sparing his critics the misapprehension that they were portraits of the table.) But, no.

I have received many close-this-play reviews over the years, and that is both part of the cost of my doing business, and one of the prices of a Free Press. The same Constitution which protects my right to write my plays, shields the right of the critic to write drivel. Why do I instance this long-ago hatchet job?

Because, to this day, nearly forty years after that review, I am asked, in lectures, classrooms, and interviews why I hate women.*

———

A rhetorical question is essentially an attack, and this protracted attack must be laid, not to the account of the poor writer at the *Village Voice*, but to that "movement," for which, I presume, she thought she spoke: the "Feminist Studies" so beloved of our great Universities.

I found these attacks upsetting first because I am a sensitive fellow, and, second, because, to the contrary, I love women. I've been privileged to have spent my life surrounded by them; and it seems to me a matter of course that men and women *should* get on well together, which was, after all, the theme of *Sexual Perversity in Chicago*.

Here is another question spawned by the University: Why do I not *write* for women? (This expounded by the students, I believe, burdened by the rigors of studying both feminism *and* drama.)

The answer, I *do* write for women, is unsuccessful in averting wrath, for the wisdom inculcated by the University is not, it seems, of that weak variety which bows before fact. I have written many plays and parts for women; nearly as many as I have written for men, and, probably as many as any other dramatist of my generation, man *or* woman. But the question, again, is not a request for information, but an attack. Well, that's all right.

———

I came across an old trunk, full of bills and posters, playbills, and correspondence of my youth. The correspondence was almost exclusively of two kinds, rejection slips and love letters.

I remember of the rejections, at the time of their receipt, that I, after the first momentary blaze of indignation, felt, of the producers, agents, and publishers who had rejected my work, "too bad for *you*,

*I do not hate women. I do not like *that* woman.

who are going to be the loser thereby"; and I remember feeling at the time, of the letters, and feel still today, a gratitude for and wonder at the generosity of women.

A writer's life is lived, and, I think, must be lived, in solitude. For it is a dialogue with one's own thoughts, and, often, a dialogue *about* one's own thoughts; and the corrosive nature of this struggle is often unpleasant, devouring one's time and weakening one's capacity for simple human interaction. This is a minuscule price to pay for the privilege of earning one's living as an artist; but the price, though small (if it is a price, and not, rather, an *attribute*), unfits the writer, or, at least, unfitted me, for participation in a wider society. I need to be alone. And am very grateful that this state has been not only ameliorated but beautified by the society of my wife and my children, many of whom are women.

————

Part of the Left's savage animus against Sarah Palin is attributable to her status not as a woman, neither as a Conservative, but as a Worker.

The intellectual elite which is the Left can preserve neither its hegemony nor its pretensions in the light of facts, for the fact is that Governments cannot create wealth. Wealth, and prosperity, is creatable only by workers, which is to say, by those who are going to employ their gifts, their time, and their energy and intelligence to *create something others might want*. Every worker knows this: work hard, and get ahead. (May the hard-worker be overlooked, or gulled from his just reward? Of course; but the potential reward for his application is *completely* denied to his brother who *will* not work.)

Sarah Palin was a commercial fisherman. She actually *worked with her hands*, and, so, she like Harry Truman, was, to the Left, an object not only to be dismissed, but to be mocked. For the Left loves "the workers" only in the abstract; to find that they not only exist as individuals, but are willing to *bet their subsistence* upon their principles of hard work and thrift—this, to the Left, is an unanswerable indictment of Socialism, Globalism, and Statism. The enemy of the

Intellectual is not the Capitalist, but the individual, which is to say the Worker.*

———

A few words about Marilyn Monroe.

> A student, lawyer, teacher, artist, mother, grandmother, defender of animals, rancher, homemaker, sportswoman, rescuer of children— all these are futures we can imagine for Norma Jeane. If acting had become an expression of that real self, not an escape from it, one can also imagine the whole woman who was both Norma Jeane and Marilyn becoming a serious actress and wise comedienne, who would still be working in her sixties, with more productive years to come. But Norma Jeane remained the frightened child of the past. And Marilyn remained the unthreatening half-person that sex-goddesses are supposed to be. It is the lost possibilities of Marilyn Monroe that capture our imaginations.—Gloria Steinem, foreword to *Coffee with Marilyn*, by Yona Zeldis McDonough

Marilyn Monroe, then, though her work brought and brings delight to literally hundreds of millions of people, although she created for herself one of the most revered icons in show business, had an impossibly successful career, though she did this through persistence, talent, hard work, and guts, must be dismissed by the wiser, nonworking Left, which finds her neither a serious actress nor comedienne. She did not, sadly, fulfill the vision which Gloria Steinem had for her, because she was not an intellectual—she was an actual worker.

In a more equal world, a top-down world, a world of equality

---

*"So the life you describe—one of responsibility, looking after your family, contributing back to the community—that's what we want to reward," President Obama, to a working-class questioner at a town meeting, September 20, 2010.

A study of Black "Toasts," that is, song-sagas, records a couple of ditchdiggers singing, while, above them, a folklorist makes notes on their quaint ways. The folklorist tires, takes out a pocketknife, and, absently, begins throwing it into the ground. One of the ditchdiggers interpolates, into the toast, "We're down here, and we're 'most dead. He's up there playing mumblety-peg." (Bruce Jackson, *Get Your Ass in the Water and Swim Like Me*)

(as envisioned and enforced by the Left) Ms. Monroe might have been taken in hand (by whom?) early on, and cured of her unreal escapist self (her talent), and still be alive playing Mother Courage in some Resident Theatre somewhere.

Can this be Feminism? A dismissal of the greatest comedienne in the history of the screen because her work did not meet the high standards of Gloria Steinem?

Is it possible that the wise Ms. Steinem mistakes the performances of Marilyn with the person? She does conflate, and seems to connect causally, Marilyn's screen persona with her use of sleeping pills, suggesting that she killed herself (an open point) because she was "denied the full range of possibility" and, so, was forced to disappoint Gloria Steinem.

Would Ms. Steinem be happier if Marilyn had lived to play Medea and Queen Elizabeth? Is she ignorant of the working life span of an actress? Did she never laugh or smile at one of Marilyn's performances? Of course she did, but now she wants to throw it in reverse and, having derived enjoyment from her work, derive further enjoyment from her superior sad understanding of Marilyn's essential "slavery." Marilyn, though vastly wealthy, though widely accomplished, though revered worldwide (and to this day) was somehow a "slave to men." Why? Because she was a woman, and acting, thus, was somehow not "an expression of her real self."*

What balderdash. Shame on you, Ms. Steinem, for promoting hypocrisy. For, anyone who might be foolish enough to nod along with your sanctimony, will, along with you, the next time they watch one of Marilyn's films, laugh and smile; you, then, are promoting a dual-consciousness, an indictment of that which one enjoys, of a legitimate pleasure brought about through the work and the talent of an actual human being, who, in your sad lament, you belittle and

---

*And note, Ms. Steinem, that it is not the job of an actor to "express her real self." (Which of us knows what his real self is?) It was her job to *entertain the audience*. That was her *job*. And she did it as well as anyone who ever acted. What entertainment has ever come from your beloved solipsism? Would *you* go to see such a performance—an evening of someone "expressing her true self"?

patronize. Were or are *you* smarter or more talented than Marilyn Monroe? Make me laugh.

And where was the Left, and where the Feminists, during President Clinton's savaging of Juanita Broaddrick, Gennifer Flowers, Paula Jones, Susan McDougal, and Monica Lewinsky? These women, who suffered, if anyone has ever suffered, "workplace harassment," were dismissed from consideration by the Left, who mentioned their struggles *not at all*; and Monica Lewinsky, a Nice Jewish Girl from Brentwood, working as an intern in the office of the most powerful man on the planet, was treated to the silence of the feminists as she was accused, by her employer, the President of the United States, while he was committing perjury, of being unbalanced and, perhaps, of having had a "bad childhood." How, by the Left, can this be excused? It cannot. But it may be partially explained—Flowers, Jones et al., were dismissed by the Left not merely because they accused the Left's avatar, but because of their *class*. They were, to the Left, "trailer trash," and so, de-facto, undeserving of a hearing yet alone a defense. The Feminists of the Left were voluble in their indictment of Justice Thomas, in Anita Hill's, at best, "he said, she said" controversy; using racist language and innuendo against him unheard in this country in decades. They supported Tawana Brawley's improbable claims of rape up to, and, indeed, *past* the point at which they had been proved fraudulent and her testimony found perjured. But what of the death of Mary Jo Kopechne by drowning? What feminist spoke up for the dead victim? Or against the man who drove her to her death? He remained an icon of the Left for the rest of his life. Are those feminists, then, spokespersons for the Rights of Women? Demonstrably not. They are not even spokeswomen for the rights of *Liberal* women—Ms. Kopechne was working for a Democrat, as was Ms. Lewinsky. They are advocates only of the positions of the Left—at *whatever* cost to women. If Feminism does not consist in the actual defense of actual women, what in the *world* are those people talking about?

———

Matrimony and monogamy have forever been linked with property and inheritance, the nuclear family, in the West, having been decided upon through trial and error as the most effective unit for preservation of both.

In the sixties, the Commune emerged as a riposte to the nuclear family. This was an autonomic re-creation of not only preindustrial, but pre-agrarian life; it was the Return to Nature, but the Commune, like the colleges from which the idea reemerged, only functioned if Daddy was paying the bills, for the rejection of property can work only in subvention or in slavery. It is an illusion that we all can share, that there is naturally occurring wealth, and that the constituency with which we all will share it is expansible. It is only in a summer camp (College or the hippie commune) that the enlightened live on the American Plan—room and board included prepaid—and one is free to frolic all day in the unspoiled woods.

Liberalism is a parlor game, where one, for a small stipend, is allowed to think he is aiding starving children in X or exploited workers in Y, when he is merely, in the capitalist tradition, paying a premium, tacked onto his goods, or subtracted from his income, for the illusion that he is behaving laudably (cf. bottled water).

So the Socialists want to do away with the notion of Property, and, so inclined, they want to do away with marriage. The Right sees an erosion of marriage (evidenced by sex education, cohabitation, homosexuality, single motherhood, abortion), and understands it as a moral affront. But it is additionally, and, perhaps, more basically, an attack on *property*. If the very poor and the very rich can breed without a stable home into which to introduce their children, then what of inheritance? The poor do so, as their children will perhaps be taken care of by the state, or by their grandparents; the rich, as they consider the child an affordable luxury, whose sustenance will not significantly affect the parent's fortune. What of the middle class, upon whose fortunes the future of our country rests?

Monogamy and property came about as human beings developed away from the life of the cave and the savannahs; the question of their usefulness seems to signal a desire to return to that pre-agrarian state: all will own everything, children will be raised by a "village," no human being need make the commitment of marriage, they may simply follow the dictates of their hearts.* These dictates, however, everyone of a certain age knows, are sometimes misleading. And they are, at certain points in life, not only damned near irresistible, but are many times in opposition: the desire to breed promiscuously, and the desire to fall in love, for example. Here the organism is endeavoring to adjudicate not only its societal but its *genetic* course, for, as the desire for unfettered procreation, strengthened as the societally imposed condition of *marriage* is weakened, the chemical urge is ratified, and human beings may self-select for greater sexual athleticism (mass nonfamilial breeding), rather than for "falling in love" (monogamy), which, we see, is already coming to be thought effete.

See the lyrics of songs. These, in my youth were moony, about the One Boy and Girl, then became about the joys of Freedom from Entanglement, and the folly of love, and now, in rap music, actually assert the desirability of spousal abuse and misogyny. Here we have a glimpse into the operation of evolution, and how the social and the genetic are linked; human life will change not because we have eaten more or less leaves off the trees (*pace*, the environmentalists) as if we were giraffes, but because we have become infected with the bacillus of socialism—destroy the family, and trust the State.

But to follow the reasoning one step further, is it possible that the actual delusion of Socialism is a reaction to scarcity or to the perception of scarcity? That the herd, troubled by a burgeoning world population, has simply decided to stop: to stop breeding, to stop producing (the Net Exports of Goods & Services fell from -$78 billion in 1990 to -$669 billion in 2008) to stop consuming (green move-

---

*Senator Clinton wrote that it takes a village to raise a child. But she, as the good mother she appears to be, would not consider having her daughter raised by a village, which she would, correctly, see as a dereliction of duty as the kid's mom. A village neither can nor should raise a child. That, as the Senator knows, is the job of the Family. Further, where *are* these supposed villages the Senator would like to reconstitute as orphanages? We are no longer a rural population, and the small communities the Senator names as the village's assigns have, in the main, been destroyed by Government good intentions.

ments) and exploring (environmentalism)—that the herd reaction to *supposed* scarcity is a return to the savagery of the savannah, which, after the fact, is rationalized as Socialism?

I saw a Prius on the street, with a bumper sticker reading "The only nuclear reactor I want is 93,000,000 miles away." Fine, but if one rejects nuclear, and coal, and drilling for oil, what will run the presses that print the bumper stickers?

The battle between Left and Right can be seen to take place on a chemic level. The Right says one *must* breed, one must produce, and explore, to keep our civilization vital and strong. The Left says we must stop doing *all* these things, and simply widen the herd. That if we widen the herd sufficiently there will be no more struggle and, so, no more anxiety—thus those institutions which *sequester* property to the use of its producers (the nation-state, marriage, etc.) may be and, indeed must be discarded as divisive and productive of rancor. The blather about "Americans' image in the world" is an instance of this unconscious implication of a fraternity of the good-willed, from which we, because of (fill in this space) have been excluded.

———

What would make the Islamic Jihad happy? Our death, according to their repeated assertions. How might one placate them? One cannot (see the State of Israel's efforts over sixty years). What, then, is our Image in the World?

Socialism is attractive because the *effects* of individual enterprise are unforeseeable and the weakened individual is incapable of dealing with anxiety.

One could not predict air travel in 1850, or penicillin in 1920, or the personal computer in 1940. One can, no less, predict today the marvelous and less than marvelous effects of free enterprise, either for the nation or the individual. The effects of the Socialism at the heart of the Left's agenda, on the other hand, are completely predictable: a disappearance of the nation-state, and its conquest by the stronger-willed. This horrific vision offers only one benefit: it is completely predictable. See the Jews pleading with Moses to go "home" to slavery. "Were there not enough graves in Egypt?"

(Exodus) But the magic return to nature seems to awaken no fear, for then we will simply love each other, share everything, and care for the earth of which we are stewards. Well and good, but under what system of laws? And what of those who, *though* recipients of our wisdom, want something more than or different from that which we have in our kind wisdom awarded them?

And who will guide this return to nature? Will there be many attempts to simplify our lives, and do away with pollution, and disease, and poverty, and care and worry, or will there be just the one, that of the State, from which all blessings flow, which never wanes but always waxes in power, and which cannot be wrong?

And how would the leaders of such a State be chosen? By vote? And how would they raise the money for their campaigns? Or should we all simply mass behind a leader so charismatic and well-spoken as to induce in the electorate that state of bliss which, though it may momentarily be indistinguishable from madness or satori, necessitates eventual return to a world made more complicated by our surrender?

———

A man the bulk of whose income is taxed has less incentive toward monogamy.

A weakening of monogamy will weaken and eventually destroy the ability of the family, *any* family, to transmit familial values and wisdom. This function will be taken over by the State (to a large extent it has been—see social studies classes in school and identity politics in college).

School vouchers are a grand idea, if for no other reason than they allow the family choice of institutional tenor and bias. An amusing school in my neighborhood has a billboard upon which one of their staff posts, weekly, ultra-Liberal and diverting messages. This week we find, "What about nationalizing the banks . . . hmm?" We have seen, in the past, also "Leaks—some good, some bad."*

---

*The B.P. Gulf oil leak, that is, was bad. The leak of thousands of classified military documents by Julian Assange on Wikileaks was good. Why?

This, in addition to brightening my drive time, is perhaps a good idea generally. Consider if each school were allowed, or indeed forced to post on a sign its political bias. It would make the job of parents easier. Well-to-do parents have a choice; everyone should have a choice, if for no other reason than to weaken the power of the State to form good-willed programs of social indoctrination.

27 | THE ASHKENAZIS

I am the tag-end of that generation of Jews linked to the Ashkenazi Immigration.

The Ashkenazi, the Eastern European Jews, were, in the main, unassimilated in Europe. They lived in the Pale of Settlement, banished there by the Tsarina, in 1772, and, save in extraordinary circumstances, were barred from residence in cities. They were poor, they lived apart from their neighbors who, periodically, descended upon them, in Pogroms, notably, in my grandparents' time, during which over two thousand Polish Jews were killed, 1903-1906. My grandparents left, on my mother's side in 1918 and, on my father's in 1922. Those who stayed behind, in Warsaw, and on the Bug River, the Russian-Polish border, died, killed by Stalin or Hitler.

My grandparents came to the United States. My paternal grandfather, Jack, made a bit of money investing in Chicago real estate with his brother-in-law in the twenties, lost it all in the Crash, and lived as a traveling clothing salesman, on the road throughout Illinois, Michigan, and Indiana, gone five days a week.

My father's mother was deserted by her husband, my grandfather. She raised her two boys, my father and my uncle Henry, by herself, in the Depression, working at an assortment of jobs, the highest paid of which was as a clerk in the Fair, a downtown Chicago department store.

All four grandparents came here with nothing—with little or no command of English, and all their children went to college, and, if not on to great success, to comfort and stability. The boys enlisted in the Army, the girls got married young and were—as was then the norm—housewives.

I and the people I knew, my friends and their families, had a close relationship with the immigrant generation. On Friday nights we went to celebrate Shabbos at the grandparents' house. We celebrated the Jewish holidays together, we heard their stories of life under the tsar and under Stalin; of pogroms, raids, forced enlistment— dragooning of Jewish males for twenty-five years of military service; of attendance (of my great-uncle) at the first Zionist Conference in Basel in 1897. Other than that, we, in my own as in many Ashkenazi families, had little or no Family History. Every house had the samovar, which, along with the Shabbos Candlesticks, was all that remained from the Immigration—indeed, it was usually all that came over. By my teenage years, the samovar, in our house and that of our friends, had first been turned into a lamp, and then had vanished. The Shabbos candlesticks remained, but, on the passing of the grandparents, were not used. For we were assimilated Jews.

What did this mean?

Arthur Hertzberg in his *The Jews in America*, writes that religion in the Jewish home was always transmitted through the father. It was he who took the four- or five-year-old boy to shul, wrapped in a tallis, and who insisted upon the child learning Hebrew. In Eastern Europe there were not degrees of observance (Orthodox, Conservative, Reform), there were merely Jews.

And, Hertzberg points out, the deep secret of the Ashkenazi Immigration was the abandonment by the father of his immigrant family. Perhaps as many as one-quarter of the women and children of the Ashkenazi immigration were abandoned. Then who took the sons to shul? No one.

My father was not raised in an observant tradition. Nonetheless, he, like most of the men in our circle of acquaintance, insisted upon a degree of observance, which, however, was so dilute that it could be described as merely an assertion of connection. This dilute Judaism was brought to America by the first Jewish immigrant wave, the German Jews. These came in the mid to late nineteenth century, mainly, from the cities, where they have been admitted, in some number in Germany, since the mid-century. Now they, in America, looked down upon the unwashed, unlettered, and "medieval" Russian-Polish, the unassimilated "foreign" Jews.

These German Jews had established their own, assimilationist religion, Reform Judaism, first in Germany, then in England, and then in America, with the founding of the Hebrew Union College in 1875. This was an attempt to blend in, to consider Judaism merely as different in outward expression from Christianity.

In order to lessen the difference, to increase the possibility of assimilation, all outward show of religious difference was not only frowned upon, but abominated. Not only had Reform Jews, by my bar mitzvah, eliminated the *peis* (the sidecurls), but also kashrut (ritual dietary laws), the yarmulke, the tallis, the tefillin, the study of the Torah, and the knowledge of Hebrew. What remained? The reduction of Judaism, and Jewish observance, to a dedication to "social justice."

———

What is the difference between "social justice," and "justice"?

The central tenet of Judaism is devotion to God's commandments. The aim is to allow a closeness to the Divine, and an implementation on earth of the Divine Will, which is that we should dwell in harmony and peace. This last is to be accomplished through a devotion to Justice. As per Deuteronomy, "Justice, Justice shall you pursue." The human capacity for justice, thus, is imperfect; for the Torah does not say justice shall you *do*, but "shall you *pursue*."

Justice means choice. Justice, thus, *essentially* must cause pain: to one of two litigants; to the assaulted who sees the assailant go free or to the family of the convicted, et cetera. If the choice did not require adjudication, that is, if it were resolvable through goodwill and compromise, why would it tax the time and energy of the courts? Justice means inflicting pain upon one party. How may one do so in accordance with Divine principles, overcoming one's human imperfections, one's desires (for acclaim, for revenge, even for peace), in the lack of absolute certainty as to facts and intent?

Only, so we are taught, by recourse to law. By recourse to and devotion to those laws made impartially, without respect to individuals, and applied impartially.

This is the great contribution of the Jews to the world; for Western law is founded upon "Judaeo-Christian principles," and these are founded upon the Jewish principles laid down in the Torah (for, as much as the beauty of the Gospels inspires, its spiritual commandments can only be implemented through mechanical human actions, which, in the West, are based upon judicial codes deriving originally from the Jewish law—the Torah).

The ultimate reduction of these codes is the saying of Hillel (the Torah while standing on one foot): "What is hateful to thee, do not do to thy neighbor."

The formation and execution of laws which take into account human frailty, and acknowledge the limits of reason, which cause the judges and litigants, the accused and the accuser to refer to impartial existing statutes in order to allow the least-partial, and so most fair (though imperfect), of decisions, was the essence of that practice which is currently known as Orthodox Judaism, and was known, before Western Assimilation, as Judaism.

Male Jews historically devoted themselves, if possible, to the study of the Torah and Talmud—of those laws which regulate human behavior. The highest status, in the shtetl, the village of Eastern Europe, accrued to him who was the most learned. Riches, then as now, were prized, but the highest status available to the rich man, was the *support* of the students of Torah, and the institutions of its study.

This millennia-old history of reverence for Justice could not be eradicated in the two generations between my grandparents' immigration and the baby boom. The *mechanism* at the center of this pursuit, however, was not only lost, but forgotten.

The assimilated Jews, raised as immigrants, in families, which, for whatever reason, ceased Jewish observance, retained their cultural love of Justice, but were ignorant of the historical methods of its pursuit.

Judaism became Ethical Culture, or Reform Judaism; its cultural inheritors were the leading population of SDS, American Buddhism, est, the Hunger Project, MoveOn.org, various cults, and the Democratic Party.

Of this last, how could it be otherwise? The Republican Party of my youth was the party of the rich, of the Country Club (in my youth the South Shore Country Club, scant blocks away on Lake Michigan, was Restricted, which is to say, closed to Jews).

The Democrats of my parents' generation revered Roosevelt; my parents came of age in the Depression, and Roosevelt's New Deal seemed to them the benignant socialism which might be the answer to the perennial Jewish quest for Justice.

Contemporary economic thought* makes a strong case that the New Deal prolonged the Depression by a decade, and would have extended its unfortunate sway but that it was stopped by the war.

The National Recovery Act of 1933 set prices and wages, created the inevitable shortages, and drove the small businessman out of business. It was stopped, ironically, by a couple of Jewish poultry merchants, who pleaded with the Republican Supreme Court for common sense (*Schechter Poultry Corp. v. United States*). And the Republican Supreme Court struck down the National Recovery Act.

———

Jews of my day were Democrats, were Liberals. Everyone in the acquaintance of my parents' generation supported the NAACP and the ACLU, knew the Rosenbergs were innocent and Whittaker Chambers guilty; no one would cross a picket line; and for a Jew, to vote Republican would have been as for him to endorse child sacrifice.

The question not asked *then*—for we knew no Conservatives—but asked *now* by the Liberal of the Conservative Jew is: "Don't you care?"

But we, the Jews, even given our historical dedication to Justice, had, in our assimilation, forgotten that justice could only be

*Amity Shlaes, *The Forgotten Man*; see also Milton Friedman and Thomas Sowell.

achieved through law, and that the application of law meant the necessity of, at the very least, disappointment to at least one and more probably both of the parties involved in dispute. That, thus, the utmost expression of care was not the ability to express sympathy, but the ability to *control* sympathy and execute *justice*. Sympathy to the wicked, we were taught, is wickedness to the just. (Meiri, on the Talmud); that the legal codes and procedures were the property of the entire population, which based its actions upon their predictability, and that laws and judges who chopped and changed according to their sympathetic nature, which is to say, according to their "feelings," were, thus, immoral.

This expression of "sympathy," as in the action of most of contemporary Big Government, is the usurpation by the elected (or appointed) of the rights of others. The judge who forgot the admonition in Proverbs, "Do not favor the rich, neither favor the poor, but do Justice," who set aside the laws, or who "interpreted" them in a way he considered "more fair," was, for all his good intentions, robbing the populace of an actual possession (the predictability of the legal codes). He was graciously giving away something which was not his.

"Don't you *care*?" is the admonition implicit in the very visage of the Liberals of my acquaintance on their understanding that I have embraced Conservatism. But the Talmud understood of old that good intentions can lead to evil—*vide* Busing, Urban Renewal, Affirmative Action, Welfare, et cetera, to name the more immediately apparent, and not to mention the, literally, tens of thousands of Federal and State statutes limiting freedom of trade, which is to say, of the right of the individual to make a living, and, so earn that wealth which would, in its necessary expenditure, allow him to provide a living to others.

The literate Jew (or, for that matter, non-Jew) could refer to the very Torah and there find the story of Nadab and Abihu, sons of Aaron, and thus priests. They, overcome by zeal, stole into the sanctuary and burned incense in contravention of the Divine Law, and were consumed by the fire.

They erred, some say, on the side of Devotion, but they erred nonetheless, for they contravened the law, which is both written and derived from an understanding of the Divine, which, though it may be gainsaid by the atheist, is probably understood by him under a different name, that name being "conscience."

Rabbinical thought holds that all sins are the Sin of the Golden Calf: Moses told the Jews to wait, as he was ascending the mountain to talk with God; the Jews did not wait, but, instead, built a golden image, and worshipped it.

But note that, though we understand their sin, and may accept, indeed, that it is the type of *all* sin, it was committed while Moses was yet undescended from the mountain, that is, before the Jews even *received* the Law. That is to say, they held in their heart some conscience,* some knowledge of the Divine which caused them, on discovery of their act, shame at what they, even uninstructed, understood as a transgression.

All healthy people have a conscience; those born without it are known as psychopaths, and treated, for all our philosophic sophistication, as monsters.

———

"Don't you *care*?"

Well. I am a Jew, and I am an American, and I am a new-minted Conservative. I care about Justice and suffering, and wonder, as has every sentient being in history, about the disparity in society of wealth and happiness, and about the seemingly inevitable corruption of our representatives, and about the imperfection and apparent injustice of many of our laws.

The revelation, of my latter years, is that *all* good people care, but that they may be, legitimately, divided as to the means to address and the potential to understand and to correct disparity, sorrow, and injustice.

I have come to see that disparity is inevitable—that there will always be rich and poor—but that disparity need be neither perma-

---

*Which word's most basic meaning is "awareness."

nent nor systemic, and that programs designed to impose equality of result, though perhaps beautiful in prospect, have weakened every society in which they have been practiced, and lead, eventually, to dictatorship and tyranny. The record shows that those same corrupt or corruptible, which it so say, human, individuals we call "the government," will, as their power to tax and spend increases, become or pave the way for the accession of monsters.

Government programs of confiscation and redistribution are called the War on Poverty, or the New Deal, or Hope and Change, but that these programs are given lofty names ensures neither that their intentions are lofty, nor that even, if so, they will or *could* lead to lofty results.* A clearheaded review of these caring governmental subsidies, whether called welfare, or aid to Africa, or farm subsidies, reveals waste, subvention, and corruption, and tends to the enervation and the ultimate destruction both of the recipients and eventually of those taxed to provide the officeholders with the mantle of "sympathy."†

What is "social justice"? It is not merely an oxymoron. It is, inherently, the notion that there is a supergovernmental, superlegal responsibility upon the right-thinking to implement their visions.

But "society" cannot implement visions. It will develop along its own lines, the inherent ethos of the time bringing about, unpredictably, change, according to unfathomable laws, which, when adjudicated according to precedent, become the written laws of the land.‡

The great advances in Justice which have made our country not only great but good are essentially the broadening of its definitions

*If the distribution of benefits according to a person's genes is wrong, if absolute renunciation of such is a hallmark of a just society, then affirmative action must be as injust as chattel slavery. Is it less pernicious? For the moment, yes; is it less unjust? No. It is a distortion of law, which is to say, of conscience, in the name of sympathy—it is the sin of Nadab and Abihu.

†How could it be otherwise? There is only so much money, and the government cannot provide "aid" to everyone. Whose claim, then, will be smiled upon? Only that which enhances the power of its administrators. What human being, in office, would do otherwise? He who is pure-of-heart? How in the world would he have been elected?

‡These laws are the great possession of the American people, and they change as the ethos of the time changes, the fugitive slave law being superseded by the Fourteenth Amendment, for example.

of those worthy of protection. This is the attempt to find justice through equality of opportunity. This is antithetical to that equality of result beloved of the Left; one might have one or the other, but they each are the other's negation, and one must choose.

———

I recognized that though, as a lifelong Liberal, I endorsed and paid lip service to "social justice," which is to say, to equality of result, I actually based the important decisions of my life—those in which I was personally going to be affected by the outcome—upon the principle of *equality of opportunity*; and, further, that so did everyone I knew. Many, I saw, were prepared to pay more taxes, as a form of Charity, which is to say, to hand off to the Government the choice of programs and recipients of their hard-earned money, but *no* one was prepared to be on the short end of the failed Government programs, *however* well-intentioned. (For example—one might endorse a program giving to minorities preference in award of government contracts; but, as a business owner, one would fight to get the best possible job under the best possible terms regardless of such a program, and would, in fact, work by all legal and, perhaps by semi- or illegal means to subvert any program that enforced upon the proprietor a bad business decision.)*

Further, one, in paying the government to relieve him of a feeling of social responsibility, might not be bothered to question what in fact *constituted* a minority, and whether, in fact, such minority contracts were actually benefiting the minority so enshrined, or were being subverted to shell corporations and straw men.†

In the waning days of my belief in "Social Justice" I discovered,

*No one would say of a firefighter, hired under rules reducing the height requirement, and thus unable to carry one's child to safety, "Nonetheless, I am glad I voted for that 'more fair' law."

†As, indeed, they are, or, in the best case, to those *among* the applicants claiming eligibility most capable of framing, supporting, or bribing their claims to the front of the line. All claims cannot be met. The politicians and bureaucrats discriminating between claims will necessarily favor those redounding to their individual or party benefit—so the eternal problem of "Fairness," supposedly solved by Government distribution of funds, becomes, yet again and inevitably, a question of graft.

in short, that I was not living my life according to the principles I professed, that I disbelieved both in the probity and in the mechanical operations of those groups soliciting first my vote and then my money in the name of Justice, and that so did everyone I knew. Those of us untroubled by this disparity, I saw, called ourselves "Liberals." The others were known as Conservatives.

28 | SOME PERSONAL HISTORY

My family always put a large premium on the ability to communicate. This is unsurprising as we had, on both sides, and for thousands of years, been stateless wanderers.

My people, the Jews, in addition to being despised as stateless,* have also been, intermittently, prized for the skills that statelessness created. We have had to acquire knowledge, which is the one possession which cannot be confiscated at the border. We have had to learn languages quickly and we have, for millennia, not only honed those skills through cultural endorsement, but selected for them in our breeding.

Those who could master languages could, in our periodic dislocations, survive; those who could not would be deprived of the opportunity to reproduce.

Our cultural ratification of the mastery of Torah, thus, not only spiritually but as a matter of day-to-day existence, fulfilled God's promise: that the Torah would be a Tree of Life to those who held fast to it. For the Torah is written in Hebrew, the Talmud in Aramaic, and the Talmudic commentaries by Rashi in their own alphabet; the Chasidic masters taught in Yiddish; and the Talmud Hocham, the person learned in Talmud, is devoted to making connections between one part of the scripture and another, between one language and another, between one *idea* and another.

*As have all stateless people. See Thomas Sowell, *Ethnic America*, his examples including the overseas Chinese, the Indian population of Africa, the Ibo, et cetera.

He is celebrated for his ability to discover and cogently express his comparisons—regularizing the apparently disparate, and finding ambiguity in the supposedly unquestionable: *vide,* the success of the Jew.

The Jews' survival mechanism enabled us not only to survive but to thrive. For the expansion of world trade required not only interpreters but middlemen and merchants, whose bonds transcended the national, who shared not only a common language but a moral system, who, as they were strangers everywhere, had no recourse other than allegiance to their particular sovereign, and whose business probity would be beyond question. Why beyond question? Because, as Jews, our lives were subject to the mere *whim* of the native population—why would they, who could "kill us for the sport," hesitate to do so at the suspicion of malfeasance?

———

The paradigm of Joseph, who was second only to Pharaoh, is repeated over and over again not only in the Western World but in Arabia, where, intermittently, the most trusted advisors, ministers, and doctors were the Jews.

See President-Elect Obama, whose *first* appointment was the White House chief of staff, Rahm Emanuel, a Jew; see Madeleine Albright, secretary of state under Bill Clinton, who discovered in late middle age that she was Jewish; see Kissinger in his relation to President Nixon. Disraeli, most trusted prime minister to Queen Victoria; Lord Beaverbrook, that is Max Aitken, closest ally of Churchill, and so on. The observable fact is, shockingly, that the world *trusts* the Jews.

The great American phrase has it: "He beat him like a redheaded stepson." We Jews have been, since antiquity, the redheaded stepson of the world, which is to say, the Designated Victim. Having no country, we were a convenient object of loathing. Now, having a country, we retain our historical position in the world's eyes as "usurpers"—as if it were possible to house anyone otherwise than on land to which *someone* must have had some previous claim. (The State of Israel was, in the main, purchased, at exorbitant rates, from the Turks, it was created as a British mandate ratified by the League of Nations, its existence as a State later ratified by the United Nations. It has existed by universally acknowledged right of self-defense. It has been under attack continually since its inception, and, time and again, it has vanquished its attackers, pushed them back, and then *returned to them the lands from which they attacked*.* And yet, uniquely, in the history of the world, there are supposedly good-willed souls shrieking that its existence is a crime.) Well, the world distrusts foreigners, and however helpful a servant may be, he will pay for his acceptance when the silver teaspoon disappears; for his master-employer-host, will then react against his own supposed "generosity."

————

So my people learn languages, which, historically, include the languages of law, medicine, finance, and the arts.

Our ability to master tongues is seen in the standup comic, who, like me, is essentially a societally supported smart aleck, and in his unemployed brother. This no-good brother is known as the Luftmensch, which means the fellow who lives on air. The Luftmensch survives through his ability to manipulate language, to be sufficiently charming, entertaining, and diverting to slip through life without doing a goddamn thing. This person was, in my father's language, known as a "bum." Growing up, I always believed that this was to be my place in the organization.

I could talk a great game, but as far as anyone (myself included) knew, I never did anything.

I loathed school. I never opened a schoolbook, I failed every test given to me (I was sent back from second to first grade, and was enrolled in remedial reading classes). It never occurred to me to point out the books that occupied all my leisure time, and suggest

---

*I challenge the reader to supply any other example in history of such behavior. Were the perennial returns acts of altruism? No. They were undertaken at the insistence of the United States and the United Nations. But this merely begs the question: Why was Israel, uniquely in Modern History, held by the world to possess its legal State only as an act of sufferance, and, attacked, required to surrender land it had won from its attackers?

that perhaps they left me little time for Dick and Jane ("Oh Dick, see Spot run. Run, Spot, run. Jane, see Spot run," et cetera).

The habit, inculcated at school and at home, of thinking myself a failure persisted through my school career, and, of course, it is to this ingrained assumption that I, in moments of despair, confusion, or indeed, boredom, default.

For, Common Wisdom (and what are the schools if not forcing houses for such?) can never be phenomenological; it must always be operational. The schools and the media must exist, that is, to disseminate and to inculcate and endorse only that "knowledge" already approved by the mass. This is neither a risible nor an unimportant function, as society must, to function, share attitudes and information likely to induce cohesion, but these studies bored me to death.

As a kid I loved comic books. My favorites were, unsurprisingly, the adolescent male fantasies: Superman, Batman, and so on.* I never was a fan of the Archie comics, which were a lighthearted (that is, to me, worthless) look at essentially harmless juvenile hijinks. But one aspect of the Archie comics intrigued me. He was bracketed by two young women: blonde-haired Betty, who loved him, and black-haired Veronica, whom he loved but who scorned his advances. A close examination, however, revealed that, aside from the color of their hair, they were the same girl.

I have tried to apply this insight to many situations in life, and have found that it often answered. We subdue feelings of powerlessness with the illusion of choice; addicted to cigarettes, we are convinced that we are Camel rather than Lucky people; Coke rather than Pepsi people, Democrats rather than Republicans,† and so on.

---

*This genre, the Superhero who must hide his "everyday" identity, is a creation of and the fantasy of the Jews. Superman (Siegel and Shuster), Batman (Bob Kane, né Kahn), and the Marvel Superheroes, created by Stan Lee (born Stanley Lieber), were the fantasies of the outsider who was accepted, indeed revered, *only* when he was saving society, that is, doing that from which someone else benefitted; otherwise, he was ignored—a nonentity. Clark Kent couldn't even get a date.

†What Conservative has not had the experience of concluding a discourse with a Liberal friend in which the Liberal acceded to all the Conservative's points but on being asked, "Well, then why do you vote Democratic?" replied, "I'm a Democrat."?

These staunch loyalties, in addition to gratifying our feelings of perceptiveness, are the placeholders for those doctrinal differences, which once plagued the Christian West.

I knew, though I could not articulate, that while the schools existed to inculcate *habit,* they had and could have no interest in the dissemination of *knowledge.* This is not to say that schools did and do not spread information, of course they do, both good and bad, but this information, reducible in its benign form to the three Rs, can be learned as easily or more easily outside of school, where it is less apt to be tainted by the spurious though amusing doctrines which of late have come to characterize our Education System.

School bored me. And I was so sunk in the shame of my failure there that it took many years' distance to see that school bored most everybody. As an autodidact, know-nothing, or "enthusiast," and as one self-deprived of the benefit of "common knowledge," I was inspired to create that unified theory of existence which, in its wholesale appearance is called philosophy and in its retail, drama.

———

Darwin tells us there must be variation in order to create balance. Balance cannot exist without variation.

Socialism suggests a state of balance, which, once having been established, will never alter.

This is the dream of the return to the Garden of Eden, of a rejection of the current, unfortunate struggle which, in total, is called: civilization.

Darwin writes, in *On the Origin of Species by Means of Natural Selection*: "We shall best understand the probable course of natural selection by taking the case of a country undergoing some physical change, for instance, of climate."

The elections of 2008 were characterized by vicious, indeed vitriolic, feelings and expressions of rage on either side, each side thinking the other on the brink of destroying the world.

The fervor, verging on panic, of each side might be attributable directly to the question of climate change; each side, that is, sensing a diminution of resources, expounding its own strategy for species survival; and each side accusing the other of concern not for the survival of the *species*, but only of its own moiety. The Left claims that it must save the world as the climate is changing, the Right that it must save the world from the Left's irrational and foolish fears, e.g., of climate change.

Both the Left and the Right are, whatever they appear to be addressing, and however they cloak it as a concern for values, or civil rights, or tradition, are each essentially concerned, finally, with a scarcity of resources. The Left sees the earth polluted, wild lands disappearing (indeed, having already disappeared), species extinction, vanishment of fossil fuels, and it counsels that the sky is falling, and that any who cannot see it are, each day, and in all their endeavors and acts, worsening the problem.

The Right shares this concern about resources and productivity, but counsels increased exploration and exploitation, free capital to fund innovation, and a stronger defense against those outsiders who would appropriate those resources which are ours. (Those resources the Left asserts belong not to us, but to "the world, and future generations.")

Now, no adherent of either view is going to live his life in congruity with all, or even most of the precepts he believes himself to endorse. For while he espouses them, his life, day to day, whether on the Left or Right, is lived pretty much the same as that of his ideological opponent—utilizing or conserving more or less the same amount of goods, and "ruining the world" or "living out his life," using the same amount of water, air, and oil. The hatred occasioned by the late election then *must* conceal a deeper sense of impending change.

This ideological division, after the election, has deepened. The Left, seeing its pet fear of climate change debunked*, has moved

---

*"The scientist behind the bogus claim in a Nobel Prize–winning UN report that Himalayan glaciers will have melted by 2035 last night admitted it was included purely to put political pressure on world leaders. . . . Dr. Lal's admission will only add to the mounting furor over the melting glaciers assertion, which the IPCC was last week forced to withdraw because it has no scientific foundation." (David Rose, *The Daily Mail,* January 24, 2010)

"Climate scientists allied with the IPCC have been caught citing fake data to make the case that global warming is accelerating, a shocking example of mass public deception that could

on to health care—maintaining its ineluctable eschatology and, as usual, merely relabeling it.* The fear of the Right, based upon the preelection behavior and pronouncements of then Senator Obama, was of devolution of America into a Socialist State. This fear, unfortunately, has not been dispelled, but ratified by his behavior as President. The hotheads on the Right want those on the Left sequestered as fools and madmen, and those on the Left want their counterparts on the Right killed.

———

Abortion, same-sex marriage, and birth control, whatever else they are, are a displacement of anxiety on the Left about the state of our civilization, as are offshore drilling and the right to own firearms (for example) to the Right; the Left frames its arguments around the essential goodness (barring the Right, Israel, and the Jews) of all humankind; the Right—around the race's observable pursuit, as individuals and states, of its own ends, irrespective of its pronouncements (the Tragic View).

The ascription to leaders of supernormal powers is a recurring

———

spell the beginning of the end for the acceptance of man-made climate change theories. On Monday, NASA's Goddard Institute for Space Studies (GISS), run by Al Gore's chief scientific ally, Dr. James Hansen, announced that last month was the hottest October on record. 'This is startling,' reports the *London Telegraph*. 'Across the world there were reports of unseasonal snow and plummeting temperatures last month, from the American Great Plains to China, and from the Alps to New Zealand. China's official news agency reported that Tibet had suffered its 'worst snowstorm ever.'" Paul Joseph Watson, PrisonPlanet.com.

"Similarly, the *Washington Post* announced in July 2001 that Peruvian glaciers were rapidly retreating because of global warming. Their expert? . . . Benjamin Morales, 'the dean of Peru's glaciologists.' Morales said, 'The temperature was rising very slowly until 1980, and then' – he swept his arm up at a steep angle. However, had Morales looked at the climate records of surface temperature or satellite-measured air temperatures (at elevations where glaciers reside), he would have discovered that since 1979 Peru had been experiencing a cooling trend." John R. Christy, "The Global Warming Fiasco." Christy is a climate scientist at the University of Alabama in Huntsville whose chief interests are satellite remote sensing of global climate and global climate change.

*Fear of Global Warming was, in the seventies, and as propounded by many of the same scientists, a fear of Global Cooling. See also Malthus's early-nineteenth-century assurance that as population outstripped agricultural production, Humanity must soon and inescapably starve. See also the Y2K scare, antinuclear hysteria, and the *yearly* assurance that some new influenza is going to devastate the population.

aberration (called the Election Cycle) which entertains us, and licenses those thoughts, words, feeling, and actions usually kept in check, and it is perhaps no accident that the election cycle (formerly called "elections") is growing and will continue to grow to be continuous, just as, to the preverbal mind, "The Woods are Burning." The Left thinks the Right (America) is ruining the world. The Right thinks the Left is ruining the country. I endorse the latter view.

29 | THE FAMILY

The effective organ for the transmission of cultural information is the family. For, the children, though we know they are never listening, are always watching.

Not only attitudes but mechanisms for social interaction are learned from earliest infancy: this is how a group operates, this is the role of the breadwinner(s), this is the role of the dependents, this is how a *covenantal* group conquers stress and oppression, this is how that group deals with questions of religion, race, national service, charity, injustice.

If the family as a cohesive covenantal unit does not exist, attitudes toward these universal situations must be learned by the individual later in life, when he is both conscious of and burdened by his pressing personal needs—that is to say, when he is not supported by a family.

He must, then, imbibe or acquire these attitudes mechanically, his consciousness affected by the lack of the surety of the home— where one learns, as a child, by observation not by consideration. He is, then, prey to his intellect. What does this mean? He must now trust his intelligence to choose between various courses of thought and allegiance: so he is likely to choose that course which flatters his intellect. But the intellect is an inadequate organ for working out the myriad interactions of a society.

"Good ideas" go bad, and the intellect, rather than be affronted by its failure, will ascribe the reason elsewhere (e.g., the inevitable

French "*Nous sommes trahis*" and the Liberal "The program *itself* was good—it had insufficient funding").

But the interactions of the family were not based upon reason, and so, not liable to casuistry. They were based upon the generationally bequeathed experience of previous families; experience so deep and ingrained that it could neither be absorbed nor parsed by reason. ("This is how one treats one's wife, one's husband; this is the correct way to express disapproval, the correct way to ask for help, for indulgence, forgiveness, solitude," et cetera "*in our community.*" For the family exists to inculcate those laws which will aid the child in the wider world—the world as experienced by its parents and *their* parents. Do we truly want to give this function to the State?)

———

Written rules and laws are only and can only be codifications of the unwritten rules which precede them. These unwritten codes of behavior have been worked out over millennia. The child learns them through constant observation, not through indoctrination. The child who has not been exposed or subject to these rules (treat your elders with respect, take care of your possessions, always defend your family members, do not bring bad companions into the house, never speak ill of or to your family, etc.) may come to think them arbitrary (cf. my generation of the sixties), and endeavor to create rules of his own, based upon his reason, which is and can only be (to a child) a conveniently self-excusatory name for his desires: copulate freely, do not marry, do not respect, but mistrust all authority, demand governmental support, base political choices upon feelings rather than experience, do not bother to learn a trade, et cetera.

Curiously, the brightest (or, perhaps, the highest achievers) of our educational system go to the elite universities where intelligent young people are misled into the essential fallacy of Liberalism: that all society and human interaction is susceptible to human reason, and that tradition, patriotism, marriage, and similar institutions are arbitrary, and stand between the individual's spontaneity and his ability to create a perfect world: that the individual's reason is supreme, that he is, thus, God.*

The child imbibes the lessons of civic virtue, religious devotion, marital behavior, restraint, self-esteem, and self-sufficiency in the home. If the home is destroyed, or its influence negated or derided (as it was both by Welfare, and as it is in today's Liberal Arts "education"), he is hard-pressed to come, through the force of his own reason, to a practicable ethical view of the world. His need for order, then, can easily be warped into the view that there is something wrong with "the world," and that this dysfunctional world requires his participation in a grand new scheme to put things right. This scheme may be called Marxism, Socialism, Fascism, Cultural Revolution, or "change." It is attractive not to the supposed "victims" of the old order, the poor, the "colonialized," the "oppressed," but to the deracinated affluent.

"Family Values" is, unfortunately, a vacuous term, implying an affinity of understanding. This affinity actually exists (on the Right), but renders the term dismissible (or, indeed, risible) to the Left. A more universal term might, simply, be: "family." To learn the rules of a family is the first essential step toward learning the rules of a community.†

---

*"So the life *you* describe . . . that's what *we* want to reward." (President Obama, September 20, 2010; emphasis added) Can one imagine a statement more chilling from the elected leader of a Democracy?

†Here is an example: Family members may hurt each other; it is impossible, in the intimacy of the family, not to transgress feelings, and, indeed, not to break laws. Family members might steal from each other, and the victim might feel anger, rage, disappointment, and similarly imaginable feelings. But that a disgruntled family member might denounce another to the IRS is beyond anathema.

We all understand the difference. Yet where is it written? The written law proceeds from the unwritten law. The unwritten law is worked out over millennia, through actual human interactions. It is learned through immersion in the unit-in-question: the country, the city, the profession, and, first and most importantly, the family.

This is why the Torah, the Five Books of Moses, is the story of a *family,* and how the lessons learned therein extend horizontally and vertically and construct the society. All dictators work first to destroy the family; the Liberal State, in its insistence upon secularization, globalism, "diversity," and so on, apes this operation of a dictatorship.

30| NATURALLY EVOLVED INSTITUTIONS

We are hovering over spheres of thought barely accessible either to psychology or to philosophy. Such questions as these plumb the depth of our consciousness. Ritual is seriousness at its highest and holiest. Can it nevertheless be play?

—Johan Huizinga, *Homo Ludens*, 1950

Children on a playground are perfectly adept at designing a fair game. They collaborate on its design not only *though,* but *so that,* they may compete when the design is finished.

It is the sine qua non of the design that the game's rules be simple, and apply universally, for, without this, there may be triumph, but there will be no sport.

The game is a special case (as per *Homo Ludens*), it is, in effect, a sacred observance, where peace means not *stasis,* but *fairness.*

The rules of all sport evolve toward fairness, and the current hoopla about performance-enhancing drugs is due not to their immorality, but to the disruption of the spectators' ability to root intelligently if drugs are involved.

The job of the referee, like that of the courts, is to ensure that the rules have been obeyed. If he rules, in a close case, sentimentally, he defrauds not only one of the two teams, but, more importantly, the spectators. The spectators are funding the match. As much as they enthuse over their favorite team, their enthusiasm is limited to that team's victory *as per the mutually understood rules.* (Who in Chicago exulted over the triumph of the 1919 Black Sox?)

The product for which the spectators are paying is a *fair contest*, played out according to mutually understood and agreed-to rules. For though it seems they are paying to see success, they are actually paying for the ability to exercise permitted desire, and so are cheated, even should their team win, if the game is fixed. To fix the game for money is called corruption, to fix the game from sentiment is called Liberalism.

———

Let us note that the referee, in a close call, may be wrong—but this is also a part of the game. No referee is other than human, and our cat-calls are part of the pleasure of the thing. He may also be corrupted, which is a profound betrayal of both the laws and the unwritten precepts of sport; or he may (having, to his mind, miscalled a previous close decision), warp his judgment in a *current* case, in an attempt to rectify his previous error (Liberalism; see: Affirmative Action). In such a case, however, to whom is he being fair? He is merely abrogating to himself a supralegal ability to act in the name of an abstract concept: justice, and in contravention of the only possible device for its implementation, law.

The good ref, then, would be aware not only of all the rules of the game, but of his own capacity for sentiment. He would consider his pay, in part, a reward not only for his scrupulousness over the rules, but over his own good intentions.*

———

Both children agree: one gets to cut the cake, the other gets first choice. They have worked out the knotty problem, for they have foreseen that though the statue pictures Justice as blindfolded, her hands are filled, one with a scale and one with a sword, to prevent her from pulling the blindfold down.

And what of the boy- or girlfriend?

---

*Else we, the spectators (the electorate) are paying not to see how the teams progress, but how the ref feels on that particular day (legal activism).

This institution, like baseball, is evolved from the unwritten law. It is a naturally occurring phenomenon and relationship, bearing, to the common understanding, more justice, rectitude, and force than the marriage contract.

Marriage contains a built-in mechanism for dissolution. But how do a boyfriend and girlfriend become divorced? They have no recourse to lawyers, or legalisms. They must, simply, tell each other the truth, or suffer the remorse of betrayal and betrayer. Many, I have observed, get married, because they don't know how, otherwise, to break up.

In the boyfriend–girlfriend, or the institution of the best friend, we see most forcefully the operation of the unwritten law. It has been noted that one might say, "My husband hit me," but one never hears, "My best friend hit me." This is a covenantal relationship, like that of the boyfriend and girlfriend, and it is understood as such, and, so, as *unmodifiable.*

Note, the marriage may be modified by a prenuptial agreement, by usage (an "open marriage"), by divorce or separation, or any number of mutually agreed upon or fought-out amendments. The relationship of the Best Friend is unmodifiable, because it's based upon the unspoken understanding of complete loyalty.

The boy- or girlfriend, similarly, is a sort of best friend with the added component of sexuality. Many might cheat on their spouse, but to cheat on your girlfriend raises the question, not only to the perpetrator, but to any with whom he might share his transgression, "Why?" The covenantal bond here is stronger than the legal.

"This is my wife" conveys less information than "This is my girlfriend"; for the first may, but the second absolutely does inform the community of the speaker's state of mind, intention, and expectations and demands for community performance. Here the two, having entered into a covenantal relationship, inform the community of their expectations of respect of the new member, such expectations being nonnegotiable.

Marriage, though sanctified through millennia of usage, is a codification of this primordial, prelegal urge to monogamy; just as the rules of sport are all an elaboration of the school yard wisdom of the pie: the (momentarily) better team has scored the touchdown, it must then kick off to the (momentarily) lesser team, which now will have the benefit of possession.

James Michener writes (in *Kent State: What Happened and Why*):

> The leadership of the movement [SDS] handed down the famous dictum, "Smash Monogamy"; this meant that husbands and wives or sweethearts who were getting too addicted to each other, had to split up. The idea was that if a man became too attached to a woman, it might impede his judgment if he were ordered to perform some dangerous task, or to involve him too deeply if he saw his girl being sent out on a mission from which she might not return. So the edict went out, "smash monogamy"; that's when the phrase became popular, "I'm prepared to make the ultimate sacrifice." This meant that, as a husband, you were prepared to turn your wife over to the guy next door (p. 149).

What did the SDS fear? The tendency of a person in a covenantal relationship to think rationally, thus, morally. They, like all radical groups, sought to subvert the conscience.

How to turn the nice middle-class boys and girls of my generation into the Killers of the Weathermen? They begin by exhorting each other to betray the one covenantal relationship they knew and respected—to sell out their sweethearts.

After that, everything is moot, for the betrayer has chosen his new community and they all must now abide by the same laws or suffer the shame of a degraded conscience.*

––––

The first rule of tinkering is, of course, "save all the parts."

But in dismantling the social fabric, the parts cannot all be saved, for one of them is *time.* Time, we were told, is a river flowing end-

*See the Nazis' insistence on involving as many as possible in the murder of the European Jews. Those who complied had burned their boats, inextricably wedding themselves to the Nazi cause, as to be conquered meant to risk execution as murderers.

lessly through the universe and one cannot step into the same river twice. Not only can we not undo actions taken in haste and in fear (the Japanese Internment), but those taken from the best of reasons, but that have proved destructive (affirmative action); the essential mechanism of societal preservation is not inspiration, but restraint.

The two children with the pie *will* work it out, their only alternative is calling in an adjudicator, a parent. But the adult can only call in Government, control of whose *own* desires merely moves the problem to a less manageable level. For this new entity has to be provided for in some way, and it, or its assigns, either through good intentions, through corruption, or through the world's favorite process of elaboration, will eventually get *all* the pie.

31 | BREATHARIAN

Countries, like any organism, come into being, and mature, decay, and die. Any successful life form attracts: adherents, exploiters, imitators, sycophants, and parasites, as life can only live on life.

Bernard Cavanaugh was a mountebank in 1841. He claimed the ability to exist on no nourishment other than pure air. At his request he was imprisoned in a cell, and survived there, ostensibly without food, for a period of several months, after which he emerged healthy and having actually gained weight.

The effect, contemporary magicians tell us, is not difficult. Food may be secreted in or around the body, in clothing or actually woven into the cloth from which the clothing is made. It may be formed into the bricks, paint, plaster or bars of the cell, or passed by a confederate.

The only difficulty in the effect's performance is the secretion and disposal of excrement.

The Socialist vision, similarly, is a trick. Man cannot live on air. He must live on food, and the other goods and necessities of life produced through the physical effort and thought of him and his contemporaries.

As civilization progresses and population grows, new and more productive methods must be developed to deal with both foreseeable scarcities and unforeseeable disasters and progressions.

Each of these new methods is, originally, the inspiration of one or a small group of individuals who think differently from their fellows.

Not all of these inspired visions are effective or effectible, so the various visions must compete—no government organization is wise enough to determine in advance which of a number of equally strange visions will succeed.

In order to compete, these visions need private funding.* As many of these inspirations originally seem impossible to accomplish, or, indeed, insane (the airplane, the radio, television, the automobile, the computer), the funding must come from those with sufficient disposable wealth to engage in what is, in effect, gambling. The competition between these competing visions eventually benefits all—if unfettered it will eventually discover new foods and methods of cultivation, of travel, new fuels—as it has throughout the history of free enterprise. For the potential reward of success is enormous— this incentive is the engine of progress, and its absence or stifling leads to stagnation and decay.

The Government can neither invent the automobile, nor, indeed, actually oversee its effective and economic production. It has bailed out General Motors and Chrysler, and this subvention will be seen to be not only an abrogation of the rule of law (the cancellation of obligations), but a vast waste of funds; for just as the camel is a horse put together by a committee, actual "government cars",— should we devolve to that—cars put together under the supervision of a board of majority government appointees, will be neither fish nor fowl, nor sufficiently safe, efficient, attractive, affordable, durable, or fun. How could they be? They won't be made by automakers— that is, by those in love with either cars, gain, or a combination of the two, but by apparatchiks. Who would buy such cars?†

The Government can make work, in the main, only by appropri-

*Is the Government capable of funding actual innovation? It is disposed to fund only that which benefits the current officeholders. I tax the readers to supply instances to the contrary, and remind them that, for years, the Government has funded only that "science" which supports the fiction that the earth is warming, that it has marginalized or debunked information to the contrary, and that it has called this process, "research."

†See Government Healthcase (Obamacare). on the verge of bankrupting the country, and so attractive to the individual buyer that his failure to avail himself of it will be a Federal Crime.

ating those jobs already created by private enterprise, and doling them out less efficiently. A perfect example is the Civilian Conservation Corps of the New Deal, which, as Thomas Sowell has pointed out, was merely giving twenty thousand shovels out to do the work which could be accomplished by fifty bulldozers. Why not then, as he suggested, enlarge the paradigm, and replace the shovels with three million teaspoons? Government intervention in private enterprise is the death of private enterprise (cf. East versus West Germany; Havana versus Miami; Palestine versus Israel). Has the case not already been settled?

Government intervention is, in fact, a form of savage or precivilized thinking, as if a primitive tribe looked at the man who invented the wheel and reasoned that he was depriving an entire contingent of the tribe, the Bearers, of work, and so killed him and burnt his supposed improvement.

Let us note also that the ever-hungry politician, Socialist though he may be, when possessed by the urge for higher office, applies first and always to some combination of the Interests he will, with a wink toward them, eventually denounce. He *must*—for where is the money he runs on going to come from save from those who *made* it?

The stifling of free enterprise by Government, whether wholesale, in Communist Cuba, China, East Germany, Russia, et cetera, or piecemeal, under the New Deal, led at *best* to shortages.* Under totalitarian regimes, it eventually led to famine and slavery, as governments insisted upon the continuation of the destructive and absurd failed systems, and instituted speech and thought control to stifle consideration, and to ban utterance of the most obvious conclusions.

These totalitarian states kept—and keep—their citizens enslaved, imprisoning those who oppose and shooting those who try to escape their Socialist utopias. These totalitarian states must eventually embark on war as the only way remaining to feed their starving

---

*Thomas Sowell cites the severe housing shortage in wartime San Francisco. At the conclusion of the war, the government restrictions on housing were lifted, and the housing shortage disappeared immediately, *in spite of* the influx of the returning servicemen.

masses—through the accession of the land and goods of the more productive. These states, in preparation for war, habitually indict the more productive as "enemies of the People," "colonialists," or "oppressors of the Weak." See the UN's continual denunciation of Israel, the Arab bloc's insistence that Israel is an aggressor state; and the reiteration of peaceful Nazi Germany's simple pleas for "Lebensraum."

But, unfettered, we human beings are capable of fulfilling each other's needs and of prospering thereby. Our prosperity will be in direct proportion to our ability to fulfill the needs of others. The Scare Words of the Left—Greed, Exploitation, Colonialism—are identical with those employed by totalitarian states to indict the more prosperous whose goods they covet and whose successes they must indict to divert attention from their own monstrous behavior.

How can one live on air?

One cannot. And the recurrent Liberal call for Government control, for Welfare, Government bailouts, reparations, and confiscatory taxes, is nothing other than this transparent, silly claim. All life needs to consume. And to consume we must produce. The Government cannot produce, it can merely confiscate, intrude, and allocate according to some plan pleasant to the capacity or cupidity of the current officeholders.

Just as in any totalitarian state, the Government can and will explain its depredations, and the inattentive may endorse these blunt and transparent efforts as "humanitarian," until the appearance of actual shortages is sufficient to discommode even those sufficiently privileged to have thought themselves immune from the Good Works.

But for anyone to consider himself immune requires a studied ignorance of both history and human nature.

One may smuggle in the food, the problem is to explain the accumulation of the effluvia: shortages, unemployment, and inflation.

What is the one institution which will not suffer through confiscation and the abrogation of the rule of law? Government.

Bill Clinton out of office will wax fat upon the various charity schemes bearing his name, and President Obama, on retirement, will proceed to his own particular dukedom.

Marie Antoinette suggested that the starving populace Eat Cake. She was reviled. But at least she understood that they had to eat something.

With thanks to Ricky Jay.

32 | THE STREET SWEEPER AND THE SURGEON, OR MARXISM EXAMINED

What are the interests of the people? Not the interests of those who would betray them. Who is to judge of those interests? Not those who would suborn others to betray them. The government is instituted for the benefit of the governed, there can be little doubt; but the interest of the government (once it becomes absolute and independent of the people) must be at variance with those of the governed. The interests of the one are common and equal rights: of the other, exclusive and invidious privileges.

—William Hazlitt, "What Is the People?," 1817

A privileged adolescent may see the street sweeper and wonder why he is paid less for his job than is the doctor. As the sweeper's job is both essential and disagreeable, perhaps, this young philosopher might muse, he should be paid as much, or perhaps even more.

This is Marx's vision: from each according to his ability, to each according to his need,* taken through one permutation, and substituting *merit* for *needs*. For today we may view the notion of a Government determining "needs," as naïve—who would not exaggerate his needs if simply to do so would gain him more governmental largess? Further, we may, in our enlightenment, see that everyone has *different* needs—one may wish more leisure, another more pay,

---

*The terrible danger of these formulations lies in the excision of the subject—"*the Government shall take* from each according to his ability," and "*the Government shall give* to each . . ." etc.

et cetera. But "merit" is an equally subjective concept, and, like need, its acceptance as a tool for the determination of desert merely empowers the judge.

"But what about," this adolescent wonders, trying out his new toy: "*merit.* Does not the street sweeper, as he also works and sweats, *merit* as much as the physician? Does not the performer of an unpleasant task *merit* as much as or more than one who works in comfort and with status? Must government not recognize the worth of this contribution, and do away with the inequality in the treatment of the lowly applicant?"

But the problem unrecognized by the privileged adolescent, the problem is not the term, but the equation; for the true horror of the equation is the tacit presumption of a *mechanism* to distribute services and goods. And what would that mechanism be, but the totalitarian state?

Acceptance of the notion that there exists an equation under which the State may fairly and honestly control human exchange leads the adolescent down the road of folly—increasing taxes to increase programs to increase happiness to allow equality—which ends in dictatorship.

For in the adolescent vision the street sweeper ceases to be a citizen and becomes an applicant, presenting himself to Government and demanding compensation based upon his "merit," or "goodness," as a member of society who contributes as much as the physician, but is treated, on payday, as less than equal.

The adolescent, in his imagination, stands at the side of the street sweeper, reminding him of his "equality," and urging on him the courage to press his claim.

Justice is corrupted by consideration, not of whether or not the accused committed the crime, but of supposedly mitigating factors of his childhood, race, or environment. If weight is given, in extenuation, to his supposed goodness to animals or to his mother, he is then liable to leniency based not upon the needs of the citizenry (protection), but upon the criminal's ability to dramatize his plight. If he may entertain, and play upon the emotions of the judge and jury, if he and his defenders may flatter the ability to "be compassionate," and call it courage, society is weakened. Laws, then, decided upon in tranquility, without reference to the individual, and based upon behaviors, are cast aside or vitiated by reference to merit, fairness, or compassion, all of which are inchoate, subjective, and nonquantifiable.

It is not the Government's job to determine what is "fair," but to determine what is just—the only tools granted to it derive from a clear set of guidelines, the Law, designed first and last, *to limit the power of government*.

Possessing such a set of laws, the individual may have a reasonable expectation of freedom from Government intervention. As long as he abides by these laws, which under our Constitution apply not to classes of *people* but to classes of *actions,* he may plan and act in peace.

It is not the Government's job to determine merit. Even if it were, upon what criteria? For we are not all-wise; Thalidomide was hailed as a wonder drug, the airplane and automobile scorned as toys.

We may say of the Framers that they did not account for the fact that some may have had an affluent childhood, or that it is more onerous to sweep streets than to manage hedge funds. That this is an oversight on the part of the Framers is clear to privileged adolescents. Unclear to them is the plight of anyone unskilled and desperate for a job, and the monstrous capacity of Government for destruction when indulging in "feelings" (see not only Affirmative Action, but the Japanese Internment, the *Dred Scott* decision, the idea of "hate crimes").

The adolescent, the Marxist, and the Liberal Left dream of "fairness," which can be brought about by the State, forgetting that, in order to pay the street sweeper and the physician the same, one must raise the wages of one or lower the wages of the other.

How can Government raise the wages of the street sweeper? Only by taxing its citizenry, which is to say only by overriding the *societal* decision that the skilled worker is entitled to higher pay than the unskilled.

This decision was never pronounced by Authority, nor blessed by any authority other than the free market. It was arrived at through interaction of human beings perfectly capable of ordering their own affairs; and this group decided, through innumerable interactions known as the Free Market, that some jobs should be better paid. Why? Because of the job holder's education, because of his skill, *or for no defensible reason whatsoever* (for example, the shape of their chins).* Is this folly? Would it be greater folly to allow the Government to decide the criteria by which newscasters were appointed?

In the newscaster we see the operation of the free market. Is it "fair" to pay him tens of millions of dollars because he has a square jaw? Who is to say?

Phrenologists were once considered scientists for disseminating the hogwash that a person's character may be determined by the shape of his head. The fad passed, but in a top-down, Government-controlled economy, where the citizenry gave to the Government the opportunity to rule its actions upon an inchoate and subjective determination (fairness), our tax dollars might still be paying phrenologists.† For a government will not and cannot admit mistakes. Its members thrive through taxation and by ever widening their spheres of influence, selling influence to the highest bidder. We are still paying oil and wheat subsidies, and it is mere luck that the phrenologists of that day did not have sufficiently skilled lobbyists to ensure their own eternal subvention. You might say it is absurd to claim to determine a person's deserts on the basis of the shape of his head. It is equally absurd to make the claim on the basis of the color of his skin.

Government cannot correct itself—which is why we periodically hold elections. But society, convened as the free market, can and does correct itself, and that quickly, for to tarry is to risk impoverishment. We have paid the big-chinned newscasters fortunes over

*The newscaster.

†As they were once widely used to pay eugenicists—those "social scientists" who advised upon which classes of citizens should be sterilized in order to ensure a healthier population.

the decades, and have enjoyed their solemn ability to correctly read a sheet of paper before a camera. But now the Internet has grown, and the day of the newscaster is passing, and another generation will shake its head in wonder at our "trust" of those with well-shaped chins.

Is it a sin, or is it unfair, that the street sweeper is paid less than the surgeon?* The Left, the Socialist, the privileged adolescent may say "yes," but their prescription is "*You* (the taxpayer) pay him more . . ."

This, which has been called the essence of Marxism, person A getting person B to do something for person C. Is *this* fair? That the surgeon be taxed because some good-willed other would thereby feel momentarily better about himself and his society; that the citizenry be taxed so that the good-willed might implement their vision of a perfect world (sweepers and surgeons paid alike)?

The Leftist would enjoy feeling that his vision brought about some good, but, finally, what is it but the enjoyment of a fantasy? Environmentalists insist on the inviolability of Yellowstone Park, but how many Liberals are actually going to *use* Yellowstone Park? Yet they want to ban their fellows who *do* use it from using snowmobiles.

Why? The snowmobile offends the Liberals' fantasy of the pristine nature preserve. So be it. We are all entitled to our fantasies, but are we entitled to impose their costs upon others? The Liberal is free to pay to achieve his fantasy. What stops him from digging in his own pocket and correcting the pay differential in the two jobs, from actually giving actual money to the street sweeper?

This, in fact, is part of the actual unfairness of those confiscatory taxes which are the inevitable companion of big Government—that the individual is prohibited from disposing of his income in the way he sees fit. If the Leftist were actually more interested in a more "fair" redistribution of income—which is to say, a distribution more

---

*Note that however Marxist one may be, he, if he possesses the funds, is going to take his severely ill loved one to the best doctor he can find, putting aside, for the moment, the question of global inequality in compensation.

in line with his own worldview—let him vote to lower taxes, and distribute his now larger share of his wealth, to the street sweeper.

————

Giving the money to the Government, even that Government which proclaims an agenda with which the Liberal agrees, is folly. For a simple perusal of history will reveal that the money the Government strips from the surgeon to pay the street sweeper, far from ending in the sweeper's pocket, will most likely arrive somewhere else altogether. It will be diverted by Government into "costs of administration," or "a general fund"—or it will—like Social Security—merely vanish.*

Called to task, the only way the Government can appear to make good its claim of Fairness to the Sweeper is to print more money, which is to say, impose a new tax. And the best that can be said of this destructive force of inflation is that, at least, it is a tax which is demonstrably "fair," for it impoverishes everyone.

In addition to actually giving more money of his own to the street sweeper, the Inspired Leftist may, today, without let or hindrance, give more money to the cabdriver, the dry cleaner, the restaurateur, and to all others whose services he employs. He is free to give them more money than they request, and so feel good about himself. But I doubt he will do so. For he does not want to pay what is here visible as essentially an "entertainment tax." "Here, let me tip you, as I am a Big Spender."

No, he refrains from paying above the stated price for goods and services. To do so would reveal to him the idiocy of his position.

In his day-to-day life, the Leftist, like everyone else, wants the dry cleaners, the restaurants, the car dealerships, the gas stations to *compete,* for he knows that only then does he stand a chance of getting a fair (which is to say happy) price.

The Leftist, in his own dealings, likewise strives to compete, in order to gain an advantage over his competitors. He burns to com-

---

*California has, for quite some time, had the highest taxes in the nation. Yet our schools are broke, and the citizenry has put on the ballot an initiative calling for a surtax to fund education. Where did all the *previous* money go?

pete. For if he cannot improve the quality or lower the price of his goods and services, potential customers will take their business from him. He *must* compete, *unless he has access to the power of government.* (This is how lobbyists grow rich, through promise or reality of their ability to subvert the free market through government intervention. What else did anyone *think* they were doing?)

————

If the Government determines that the street sweeper be paid as much as the surgeon, must it not, further, insist that the *bad* street sweeper be paid as much as the good? The bad surgeon paid as much as the superior?*

The Left might say that this is folly, and, of course, it is, and it is practiced every day in affirmative action, and set-asides, in preferences, where the Government, we see, has *already* determined that accomplishment and performance may, and in some cases *must*, be put outside consideration. (See also Union rules, for example in the teachers union, in their intractable opposition to merit pay. They

---

*Is this impossible? It is inevitable. If all medicine is under Government control, the good surgeon, unable to exercise the panache, initiative, intuition, and liberty which may have led him into the profession in the first place, will have no incentive to investigate further than the bad—his desire to spend more time with or use more facilities on a patient will be thwarted by the rules which the Government—in order to control costs—*must* install. To work harder, longer, and, so better than the less accomplished or inspired surgeon will not only be contrary to the terms of his employment, but may, should he persist, cost him his job. Should this seem outlandish, consider the horror tales of doctors not only dismissed but blacklisted by the HMOs which employed them. It is not that the inferior surgeon will be paid as much as the accomplished, but that the wages of the accomplished will be reduced to parity with his lesser colleague—and, as the wages are reduced, so will be the quality, inevitably, of his work, for he will be told that in spending more time he is wasting the Government's money.

But what, you might ask, of that surgeon so inspired that he, *irrespective* of the strictures placed upon him by that Government which has, effectively, reduced him to the status of a medical clerk or technician, what if he, in the age-old spirit of the Hippocratic oath, "bootlegs," his own time, and expends his *own* resources to bring a patient to health according to his best lights? Q. Is this not the essence of the Spirit of Medicine? A. It has been down through the ages, but the tradition, for the reasons above, must cease with Government control. Q. But what if the courageous surgeon, true to his creed, insists in this traditional dedication, in excess of that which the Government prescribes? A. Well, then, shouldn't he be paid more?

claim to educate our children, but insist the bad teacher be paid as much as the good. What lesson, then, are they teaching?)*

This folly will be further elaborated by a single-payer national health system, wherein the bad surgeon *will* be paid as much as the good, and the patient left with no recourse other than application to Government. And which of us, applying to Government for redress, from the smallest traffic complaint to the largest issues of life, has ever come away happy?

If we may not enjoy the benefits of competition we suffer. As we will under Government Health Care. As we will in the Government takeover of the auto industry. The businessman must consider the desires of consumers or fail. It is not his job to determine their "rationality"—what is rational about tail fins? It is his job to make cars people want to buy. But the Government is now in the auto business— will it not impose upon all other manufacturers the same restrictions it imposes upon its *own* cars? It *must*, for, like any other business it will want to drive out competition. And, in so doing, it will kill the remnants of the American auto industry, which will be forced to make cars the American people aren't clamoring for. It will be forced to make cars based upon the Good Intention of Government. But what if these cars are "better"? Better for whom? Ralph Nader killed the Corvair, an innovative, rear-engine, high-mileage, small, low-priced car. Had the Government let the Corvair alone, the auto industry might have seen, thirty years sooner than it occurred to them, that the small, fuel-efficient, rear-engine car was the wave of the future, and we would have been shipping a lot less of our money to Japan.

The Government by the Left is intent on taking from the consumer the freedom to choose between competing enterprises, and what is Freedom but the freedom to choose?

The individual who is a street sweeper and would like to be a surgeon may choose to pursue that course of studies which might lead to that end.

*See the Wisconsin union teachers calling in sick (lying) and employing their stolen treasure picketing the state capital for greater "rights." Many wore T-shirts reading PROUD TO BE AN EDUCATOR.

But, you say, he may not have the ability. Then let him work at that for which he does have the ability, or choose another line of employment which might lead him to a life closer to his vision of his deserts and to his needs. Or let him continue at his job in the hope of advancement, doing his job superlatively while looking for and studying for another more congenial position.

But, this is monstrous, you say; some people are *unfitted* to do so. Unfitted by what? Race? I deny it. It is antithetical to the teachings of Religion, to the Constitution, and to experience.

Some individuals are unfitted to be surgeons by lack of individual intelligence? Of course. Human ability is distributed randomly, and must be so, or civilization would not have advanced. But it is not distributed according to race (an assumption which wiped out two-thirds of my people, the Jews, within human memory), nor upon previous condition of servitude (the "Legacy of Slavery")—the Fifteenth Amendment makes it illegal to withhold the right to vote, to discriminate against anyone on the basis of race, color, or previous condition of servitude. If this is illegal in consideration of the first, most basic right of the citizen, surely it is illegal (as it is ridiculous) to discriminate in *favor* of an individual on such a basis. Might one not take cognizance of such an individual? An individual may, but the Government, correctly, announces here that it refuses to indulge in such obscenity.

To call attention to various supposed defects of *classes* of people, and then to call for "fairness" is the folly of the adolescent, and the trick of the demagogue.

If the street sweeper is paid the same as the surgeon, why should he aspire to better his lot? He *may*, but why should he? J. S. Mill, in *On Liberty*, writes that any man who is rewarded equally for doing a good job or a bad job, would be a fool to put energy into its accomplishment. He will naturally withhold it, and put it elsewhere, where it might improve his status or income.

You or I would withdraw that effort, expenditure of which could not improve our lot (cf. the government employee). Milton Friedman suggested that we all recognize as a joke the notion that someone might say to a Government employee, "Slow *down*, you're *killing* yourself . . ."

That it remains, to the sentimental Leftist, a "shame" that the street sweeper is "underpaid" is itself a shame. But it does nothing whatever to ameliorate the street sweeper's supposed lot. The Leftist may do so by digging in his pocket, but he will not. He wants the Government to do it, and yet he will not ask the Government where it intends to get the money, nor hold the Government accountable for the treasure it has wasted and the chaos its involvement has caused in the past. That the Liberal will not do so is not only a shame, but an inexcusable failure of intellect.*†

"From each according to his ability, to each according to his needs" may be rendered:

Let us empower the State to take x (money, time, possessions, status) from Class A of people; and distribute them to Class B of people.

This, with the underlying nature of the exhortation exposed, is a parsing of Marx's doctrine. Operationally, it seeks to give all powers to the State. Now, why would the adolescent want to substitute *merit* for *need*? (It is an equally destructive, and, finally, absurd construction.) Because he is less concerned with the magical terms than with the unstated postulate of the formula—the hidden exhortation

---

*Some will doubtless cavil that the above is merely a restatement of the Victorian canard that "every man should be happy in the place to which it has pleased God to call him." To the contrary, it is the assertion that he be allowed the freedom to improve himself, the judge of his accomplishments or "worth" to be not the State, but those individuals, his fellow citizens, whom he has pleased with his goods and services. This may or may not be "fair," but it is the basis of a just society.

†Note that even if all elected officials were wise, patient, and capable of all discernment—if they were not the power-mad vote-mad corrupt or corruptible individuals all human history has shown them, in the main, to be—if these officials were actually able to determine solutions to the ancient and heretofore ineradicable problems of unfairness, poverty, greed, and envy—if they were sufficiently capable to supplant the rule of law with their own intuitions, and to codify these intuitions into plans, the plans would still be administered by the same functionaries we see today in Government jobs, with whom we have to deal, pleading, begging, asking, stunned, for justice, and for fairness in the application of the laws (which is to say, for that result we desire).

to empower the State. Why is he less concerned? Because he imagines *himself*, his like, or his representatives as the State. His position, though it presents itself as a defense of "humanity" is a fantasy of power.

———

Absent in the contemporary Liberal worldview is the understanding that things go wrong.

Corporations grow, and (like any agglomeration—a business, a family, an industry), make choices which can prove good or bad. That which is productive today may, if persisted in, prove destructive tomorrow (for example, the New Economy, tail fins on cars, tobacco cultivation, busing, the new math). We, neither as individuals, nor as groups, are perfect. The business which makes terrible decisions will correct itself or will and must be allowed to fail. The current government and (marginally) popular sentiment to support failing enterprises are both examples of a creeping Statism—which is the surrender of individual choice to the State—Constitutionally barred by law from abrogating the rights of the individual—chief among them the *right to fail.**

The Left might say of a failed corporation "tear it down, throw the so-and-so's out, they are corrupt and incompetent and waste our money"; but this is the system which already operates under the title "free enterprise." The next step, that which leads toward Statism and dictatorship is "and give the operation of the thing over to the Government."

This might seem defensible on the grounds of "compassion," as folks will be thrown out of work. But it neglects the fact that the Government is just another organization, liable to the same misjudgments, corruptions, and incompetencies of any others. *With this addition:* it has the power to legislate or otherwise enforce its continued existence, a power that is, ultimately, backed up by people with guns. Replacing free enterprise with state control does not do

———

*Is it not evident that any organization believing itself "too big to fail," will more likely, indeed, inevitably, make disastrous decisions? Why should it not—it is Too Big to Fail. But the first rule of *any* healthy concern is prudence.

away with failure and mismanagement, but merely removes from it the possibility of self-correction.

Why are taxes high? To fund programs proved failures decades ago, and to spawn new programs to correct the errors their predecessors proved incapable of addressing. But the fault was not the nature of those previous programs but their systemic inability not only to affect, but to *name* affectable goals.*

Government is only a business. *Past* the roads, defense, and sewers, it sells excitement and self-satisfaction to the masses, and charges them an entertainment tax, exacted in wealth and misery. It cannot make cars, or develop medicines. How can it "abolish poverty" (at home or abroad), or Bring About an End to Greed or Exploitation? It can only sell the illusion, and put itself in a position where it is free from judgment of its efforts. It does this, first of all, by stating inchoate goals, "change, hope, fairness, peace," and then indicting those who question them as traitors or ogres; finally, it explains its lack of success by reference to persistent if magical forces put in play by its predecessors and yet uneradicated because of insufficient funding.

Should the government support an opera singer whose performances no one attends? (Government funding of the Arts.) Allowing nature to take its course would cause his handlers, manager, coaches, and assistants to seek other employment. One might extend to them compassion, as would any of us (the majority) who have ever been out of work; but do those incommoded by the lack of success on the part of their opera singer have a claim on our tax dollars? Then why do the members of the auto industry or those who have made bad or unlucky judgments financially?

Brief consideration would suggest that the state cannot deal equally with *all* claims for support, that it must choose. On what basis, other than "from each according to his ability, to each according to his needs"? That handy slogan which, in its attractive lack of

*Thomas Sowell replies, to the canard of the Left, "Yes, but what would you *replace* it with?" "When a fire is extinguished, what do you replace it with?"

specificity, led to the death and enslavement of hundreds of millions under Communism.

Further thought would reveal that once government is the *only* business, the final opportunities for failure to be corrected will disappear—whatever party is in power. If the state has assumed all power to distribute funds, its apparatchiks become the *one* Party, which will never allow itself to be cleansed and corrected by failure. Funds will, finally, be allocated, *whatever* slogan is used to obscure the process, according to the need and desires of the politicians. How could it be otherwise?*

Successful politicians look forward to their retirement plan, which healthy plan is their transmigration into the favorite daughters and sons of those businesses they may have pretended to regulate during their years in office, the most flagrant Socialist then becoming, magically, a fan of capital.

---

*Statism must devolve into totalitarianism, as, the state's power growing, political antagonists will find more commonality with each other than with those not invited to the party (the voters).

33 | SELF-EVIDENT TRUTH

He ought to have determined that the existing settlement of landed property should be inviolable; and he ought to have announced that determination in such a manner effectually to quiet the anxiety of the new proprietors, and to extinguish any wild hopes which the old proprietors might entertain. Whether, in the transfer of great estates, injustice had or had not been committed, was immaterial. That transfer, just or unjust, had taken place that to reverse it would be to unfix the foundations of society. There must be a time of limitation to all rights. After thirty-five years of actual possession, after twenty-five years of possession solemnly granted by statute, after innumerable leases and releases, mortgages and devises, it was too late to search for flaws in titles.

—Macaulay, *The History of England* (on Ireland), 1848

The basis of American Democracy is stated as a self-evident truth, that all men are created equal. If that truth is not self-evident, which is to say, if it is not held as dearly as any other moral imperative, there is no American Democracy.

One of the great wrongs of our democracy was the *Dred Scott* decision. Here the highest court in the land asserted its right to contravene the Declaration of Independence, and assert, as self-evident, that there existed two classes of human beings, the Black and the White, and that the Black was not entitled to protection of the Law.

How does this differ from Affirmative Action?

The motive of Justice Taney in *Dred Scott* was, like those wishing "Distributive Justice," based on an incontrovertible view of the universe. That the chief justice's view was the upholding of Black chattel slavery, and that of the contemporary Left an "equal distribution of goods" is beside the point; each is based upon the absurdity that there are two classes of people and that they may be distinguished by the color of their skins.

Lincoln wrote that if slavery is not wrong, nothing is wrong.

It is self-evident that a racialist view of the world *must* result in injustice. That that injustice may be calculated to benefit members of a group which may have been previously oppressed may stand as an explanation for immoral behavior, but it does not excuse it.

Shelby Steele was asked, by a good-willed White person, "What can we"—by which the speaker meant the Whites, and/or the American Government—"do for the Blacks?" He responded, "Leave us alone."

———

Who is wise enough to model human behavior? No one.

Our country has created the most effective and beneficent, the most productive and the most just civilization in the history of the world, by forming laws based upon that shared truth: compassion no less than greed will, in the hands of the State, cause misery. It is not the job of the State to be compassionate, but to be *just*. Should the State provide a safety net for the needy, and the afflicted, to care, in the words of Lincoln (the words of the Torah) for the widow and the orphan? Of course, but it must not legislate upon the basis of *classes* of people, judging their entitlement to state benefits by gender or race. Such a view is both immoral and absurd. The *Dred Scott* decision (in 1857) accelerated and ensured the Civil War.

Our new Justice Sotomayor has declared that Hispanic women are more compassionate than White men. This should disqualify her from sitting on the bench. Why? Is it true? Who can say. Some Hispanic women are probably more compassionate than some White men, but who would want a justice of the Supreme Court who held this belief? Must it not indicate that she would, in a close case, credit the claims or arguments of a Hispanic woman over that of a White man? One would think so, if her belief, unfounded in anything other than her experience, is so strong that she felt, as an officer of the court, safe in proclaiming it.

Further, and more importantly, does one want a Supreme Court justice who feels it important to dispense compassion? Is not her job, rather, to dispense Justice, which is to say, to rule, blind to the attractiveness of the litigants or of their claims, upon the applicability of laws made previously and held to be fair, by legislators ignorant of the identity of litigants?

In the days of the acceptability of corporal punishment of children (well within my memory), the old parental phrase, whilst searching for the strap, was, "This is going to hurt me more than it hurts you." The parent may have believed it, but that did not make it true, and it did not matter that the parent administered the strap in the—in his mind—cause of love; a legal and a moral test would have been for the child to respond, "Fine, then let me whip *you*."

For how would the compassionate new justice respond to a White Male who asserted (with equal right or lack thereof), "I am a good judge, as White males are more compassionate, as is well-known, than Hispanic females"?

Here the case is shown, in its enormity, as congruent with that of the slave masters who considered themselves beneficent, and the slaves better off than freed men and women. To which Lincoln responded, yes, but I do not see any slave owners offering to trade places with them.

———

The human mind may be worshipped, but it cannot be trusted. This is why we have laws. Gene Debs said, "Even if I could, I would not lead you into the Promised Land, because if I could lead you in, someone else could lead you out." I thought this a rather flat and obvious epigram, as a youth. But I don't think so now.

Moses was debarred from taking the Jews into the Promised Land. This could be considered a blessing, as he was to be spared the charade of their behavior in his absence. He got his reward on this side of the river—he was assigned a task, and worked 'til he saw his work completed.

Everything, indeed, must have an end, which is another way to look at the story—that the Five Books end with the Jewish People set free, not only of the authority of Pharaoh, but of that of Moses. If Moses had lived, their history beyond the Jordan would have been one with their history in the Wilderness: revolts against authority and sinful blunders followed by pleas for intercession. With Moses gone, the Jews had nothing between themselves and the word of God, and were free to obey or disobey at will, reap the rewards, or suffer the consequences. If Moses had led them *in*, someone else could have led them *out*.

Demagoguery is the attempt to convince the People that they can be led into the Promised Land—it is the trick of the snake oil salesmen, the "energy therapists," the purveyors of "health water," and, on the other side of the spectrum, the politician and that dictator into which he will evolve absent a vigilant electorate willing to admit its errors.

It is good for the State if the electorate has seen enough of life to notice the similarities between "Lose Weight Without Dieting," and "Hope." The magicians say the more intelligent the viewer is, the easier he can be fooled. To put it differently, the more *educated* a person is, the easier it is to engage him in an abstraction.

It has taken me rather an effort of will to wrench myself free from various abstractions regarding human interaction. A sample of these would include: that poverty can be eradicated, that greed is the cause of poverty, that poverty is the cause of crime, that Government, given enough money, can cure all ills, and that, thus, it should be so engaged.

These insupportable opinions (prejudices, really), function, in the West, much like a routine of magic tricks. The magician pulls a rabbit out of a supposedly empty hat, and while one wonders, "How did he do that?" he is already diverting the audience to a *new* trick—for he cannot give the audience time to dwell upon the effect. Neither can he repeat it—for the trick is a confounding of cause and effect.

We watch the trick, and, in our surprise at its conclusion, remember it as the *demonstration of a proposition.* (I will cause a live cockatoo to appear from the front of my frilly shirt; watch.)

That is what the mind *remembers,* but that is not what actually occurred; for, had the magician said, "Watch my shirt to see if you can find the cockatoo," the audience would *do* so. No, the magician makes a magic pass or two, and the shirt, upon which we had previously devoted *no* attention, gives forth the cockatoo, AS IF FROM NOWHERE. But the cockatoo did not come from nowhere, it *was* the frill on the shirt.

The trick of the politician and his fellow mountebanks, "Earn big money while never leaving your house!" is an inversion of the above: the dupe is *told the proposition* (I will now change the frill into a cockatoo; I will raise productivity and, thus, wealth, by taxing everyone to death, and driving capital out of the market), and then he is distracted from the fact that the trick has no conclusion. The politician says, "Watch closely, watch closely," and then "Wait, wait, *wait* . . ." and, while our attention is diverted, he makes off with the money.

What did he just *do*, the opposition asks? He ruined the economy, took our savings, destroyed our ability to do business, and indebted our grandchildren. "Wait wait *wait*," say the believers, "You *fool*: didn't he say, 'It might take *time*?'" And should the believers grow restive, a *new* effect (crisis) is right around the corner.

———

It takes an effort of will to observe the actual effects of human interactions. And greater effort to accept and then act upon one's observations. Of late, it seems someone has Led Us into the Promised Land, promising all things to all people of Goodwill. And if his, one must admit, rather vague, program (Change and Hope) has not yet eventuated in the Growth of the Magic Tree from the Magic Beans, it is obviously because the tree needs more water. As any but a fool could see.

And we are left not only holding, but *watching* the bag. But the laws of cause and effect cannot be superseded. The Left says of the

Right, "You *fools*, it is *demonstrable* that dinosaurs lived one hundred million *years* ago, I can *prove* it to you, how can you say the earth was created in 4000 BCE?" But this supposed intransigence on the part of the Religious Right is far less detrimental to the health of the body politic than the Left's love affair with Marxism, Socialism, Racialism, and the Command Economy, which one hundred years of evidence shows leads only to shortages, despotism, and murder.

Here they are like the victim of the confidence game, who pleads with the con men to come back One More Time, and turn the handle on the new-bought machine which turns cardboard into hundred dollar bills.

Perhaps "you can't cheat an honest man" because the struggle to live honestly has of necessity created the habit of honest observation.

The honest man might observe, for example, that no one gets something for nothing; that politicians go in poor and come out rich; that the Government screws up everything it touches; and that the Will to Believe is best confined to the Religious Venue, as, to practice it elsewhere is just too damned expensive.

34| HOPE AND CHANGE

Of patriotism he did not know the meaning;—few, perhaps, do, beyond a feeling that they would like to lick the Russians, or to get the better of the Americans in a matter of fisheries or frontiers. But he invented a pseudo-patriotic conjuring phraseology which no one understood but which many admired. He was ambitions that it should be said of him that he was far-and-away the cleverest of his party. He knew himself to be clever. But he could only be far-and-away the cleverest by saying and doing that which no one could understand. If he could become master of some great hocus-pocus system which could be made to be graceful to the ears and eyes of many, which might for awhile seem to have within it some semi-divine attribute, which should have all but divine power of mastering the loaves and fishes, then would they who followed him believe in him more firmly than other followers who had believed in their leaders.

—Anthony Trollope, *The Duke's Children*, 1879

We are a democracy, and as such do not generally elect our best people to office. How could we? They weren't running.

Those wishing to be elected must appeal, in the shortest time, to the greatest number. They are generally those comfortable with, enamored with, or incapable of understanding the potential harm of questionable generalities, which is to say, of mumbo jumbo. As with the football team, we like to elect the attractive to positions of management. Quarterbacks are handsome, as the most handsome kid, starting from the days on the sandlot, is elected quarterback; and, since the days of the first televised debates, the more attractive candidate usually wins. Attractive people are, more than the less favored, used to getting their way without effort, and so may possess that relaxation in front of a camera which may pass for assurance. We forget that most candidates are, in public appearances and those presentations we accept as debate, not only reading prepared speeches written by others, from a teleprompter, but, in response to questions, listening to cues from an offstage staff of experts, relayed to inner-ear receivers.

A politician I knew was fond of relating an anecdote his father had told him about Franklin Roosevelt. When Roosevelt died, the man's father came upon a workingman crying. "Why are you crying," he asked, "did you know him?"

"No," the man replied, "*he* knew *me*."

Good story. But what can it mean? That Roosevelt "understood the fellow's pains and troubles"?

If so, then he likely would have been more circumspect before tearing apart an economy the workings of which he neither understood nor wished to.

"*He* knew *me*" means that the fellow *felt* Roosevelt knew him. How was he brought to that feeling? By the President's actions? More likely by his presentation. For Roosevelt spoke soothingly. He was a good radio performer, he had good writers, and so the listener was *soothed*. "We have nothing to fear but fear itself," is, indeed, a nice phrase—in the event, it would have been truer had he added, "And an out-of-control and ignorant Government intervention in our daily business."

———

We long ago ceased expecting that a President speak his own words. We no longer expect him actually to know the answers to questions put to him. We have, in effect, come to elect newscasters—and by a similar process: not for their probity or for their intelligence, but for their "believability."

"Hope" is a very different exhortation than, for example, save, work, cooperate, sacrifice, think. It means: "Hope for the best, in a process over which you have no control." For, if one *had* control, if one could endorse a candidate with actual, rational programs, such a candidate demonstrably possessed of character and ability sufficient to offer reasonable chance of carrying these programs out, we might require patience or understanding, but why would we need hope?

We have seen the triumph of advertising's bluntest and most ancient tool, the unquantifiable assertion: "New" in what way? "Improved" how? "Better" than what? "Change" what in particular? "Hope" for what?

These words, seemingly of broad but actually of no particular meaning, are comforting in a way similar to the self-crafted wedding ceremony.

Whether or not a spouse is "respecting the other's space," is a matter of debate; whether or not he is being unfaithful is a matter of discernible fact. The author of his own marriage vows is like the supporter of the subjective assertion. He is voting for codependence. He neither makes nor requires an actual commitment. He'd simply like to "hope."

———

My generation has a giddy delight in dissolution. Mark Rudd, a leader of the radical group which occupied Columbia in the student riots, said, on taking over the administration building, "We got a good thing going here. Now we've got to find out what it *is*." This student radical, on taking the high ground, called for "change,"* undifferentiated from improvement, or any specific improvements. Most changes later specified were either obviously or later proved to be other than improvements: separate dorms for Blacks, student representation on the Board, ROTC off campus, rejection of Government funds for research, and, to date, divestment of any university funds in Israel, and the barring (or booing) from campus of any Zionist, inter alia. To inspire the unsophisticated young to demand

---

*Correspondence from a friend: "I remember, as a student at Columbia, Mark Rudd and his ilk would storm the Dean's office and burn our transcripts. Of course he never bothered to ask whether we wanted them burned or not." (R.T., 2010) But it was change.

"change" is an easy and a cheap trick—it was the tactic of the Communist Internationale in the thirties, another "movement."

The young and spoiled, having not been taught to differentiate between impulses. Frightened of choice, they band together, dress, speak, and act alike, take refuge in the herd, and call it "individualism." But the first principle of a responsible human being—a man or woman who must support him or herself, or their dependents— a principle so obvious that its actual statement seems fatuous, is not to alter that which prospers. For the self-employed, for the business-person, to consider doing so is an absurd act of self-destruction—it is "New Coke."

Why is the call attractive? It appeals to the Jacobin, the radical, the young, and those who have never matured—the perpetually jejune of my generation. We were self-taught in the sixties to award ourselves merit for membership in a superior group—irrespective of our or the group's accomplishments. We continue to do so, irrespective of accomplishments, individual or communal, having told each other we were special. We learned that all one need do is refrain from trusting anybody over thirty; that all we need is love; that war is unhealthy for small children; that all people are alike, and to judge their behavior was "judgmental"; that property is theft. As we did not investigate these assertions or their implications, we could not act upon them, and felt no need to do so. For we were the culmination of history, superior to all those misguided who had come before, which is to say to all humanity. Though we had never met a payroll, fought for an education, obsessed about the rent, raised a child, carried a weapon for our country, or searched for work. Though we had never been in sufficient distress to call upon God, we indicted those who had. And continue to do so.

Those we loved, "the oppressed," were those whose consciousness we denigrated sufficiently to presume they would believe in our pretensions. (This is why the Left prefers the Arabs to the Israelis. It, mistakenly, considers the Arabs backward, and, thus, stupid. And this is also why the Left obsesses over our country being "liked.")

But how manipulable are we? We have been exhorted and have encouraged each other to empty the national treasury, to chain our children to inflation, debt, and a decreasing standard of living, taxed business sufficiently to ship overseas those jobs which would support our progeny and our country. And we have abdicated our position as a world leader, as if our desire were not for security, but for exploitation—another example of that decried Colonialism which the Left sees everywhere, which cry is the one trick of the Remittance Men who make up the United Nations.*

What greater act of colonialism than to bind a segment of our own population to shame and poverty through government subsidy and by insistence that they be judged by lower standards than the populace-at-large? We have created a permanent underclass through the ignorant and sententious operations of the mis-educated and ignorant. And we compound the legislative enormity by insistence in education on "diversity," and "multiculturalism." These are a codependence similar to the insistence in the prewar South on the Biblical support for Slavery.†

———

The sleepy child of my youth said a Pledge of Allegiance at the beginning of school, and then was done with it. This was a ritual acknowledgment that we lived in a good land, and in a good society, and that our elders wished us to continue it. How different from the constant insistence on the "celebration of differences" which one finds in today's schools.

Who are the performers of this show, and for the benefit of whom?

*"Things change. The world's best rapper is white, the best golfer is black, and France is accusing Israel of Colonialism."—Jacob Dayan, Consul General of Israel to the United States

†"Multiculturalism" and "diversity"—now insisted upon as a basic tenet of education, is, of course, directed at Whites. What Black or Hispanic enclave or group insists upon the presence of Whites? Why should they? Why, then, is the White population devoted to this show-and-tell? It is the essential counterweight to affirmative action—the postmodern version of busing. The enormity of these programs is less that they, fatuously, endorse the exposure of whites to People of Color, but that they *operationally* support the inverse, the idea that these People of Color benefit from White condescension. As such, "diversity" is the stalking horse of affirmative action—it is a happy proclamation of Black inferiority.

They are parents, teachers, administrators, and school boards, indulging in a cheap orgy of self-congratulation. And, worse, they insist the children smile along. For all children know that each person is different, that each home is different, that each religion and each race has its own customs—and the properly brought up child will treat these differences with not only respect for but a deference to their adherents' privacy. That these happy, colonial ceremonies of "Diversity" stem from Goodwill on the part of someone I do not doubt. But they are intrusive. I do not imagine Black communities and schools growing giddy over "White History Month." Are these practices intended to correct ancient injustices? This is not the job of the schools. Their job is to teach the kids to read and write; and, having taught them to read, to expose them to those documents and principles which *unite* us as a nation. To expand their brief into the correction of social injustice is improper and intrusive—like the teaching of sex education: it is simply none of their business.

Diversity (and "multiculturalism") is a pat on the head from the White members of my generation sufficiently inexperienced and self-absorbed to feel they are entitled to "bless their inferiors."

35 | THE SMALL REFRIGERATOR

My daughter had an heiress in her elementary school class.

The two were discussing their various bedtimes. And the heiress said that every evening, at ten o'clock, she went to the small refrigerator in her room, and took out her usual snack: fresh berries and organic yogurt dripped with honey.

My daughter asked, "Who puts it there?"

The heiress paused for a while, and said, " . . . I don't *know.*"

The great fault of my generation is not ingratitude but incomprehension. *Someone* must make the money. *Someone* must provide the goods and services we all enjoy. *Someone* must look ahead, and struggle or be inspired to create those things which will improve our lives. It is not only the production of goods which requires money, it is invention. It needs the investment capital necessary to devise and gamble upon those wildest schemes which become the automobile, the airplane, modern pharmacology and medicine, the computer. The money has to come from somewhere. And it comes from the productivity of the American worker, his urge to create, his desire to consume, and his willingness to invest.

The Left sees only waste and greed. But the plastic bottled water from Fiji is no less destructive of the environment than the bottled soda from Akron, Ohio; and the American Military and its leaders are no less subject to both altruism and error than the leaders of Greenpeace, MoveOn.org, and so on.

The Left is ignorant of this: we are all in it together. The person before you in the traffic jam has as much right to his journey as you do to yours. You alone did not pay for the road, the road was built through tax dollars for the benefit of all, and carping about urban sprawl and desecration of the seashore and woodlands is finally just elitism—they are owned by all.* The fellow with the snowmobile is as entitled to use it in the National Park for his vacation as is the millionaire to fly the private plane down to his beachfront house in Hawaii. The taxes are progressive, but the commonality—the environment and the blessings of democracy, are there to be enjoyed by *all*. A high income should not allow a greater say in the disposal and control of natural resources. Why is the Sierra Club's desire to restrict access to and use of common land more worthy of respect than the oil drillers, who, after all, will be distributing the oil to consumers? You say some of the oil drillers will get rich? Why not? If their actions benefit the consumer. And the investor. Why not?

Who puts the snack in the refrigerator? *Someone* does.

The flow of traffic on the highway can be seen as a blot on the landscape, but only by the unthinking. A moment's thought would reveal that the offensive vehicles and their offensive exhaust bring to the offended the goods they require, bring to the theatres the viewers whose ticket purchase pays for the moviemakers' mansions, bring to their various workplaces those whose productivity makes the country strong and safe. One might say, "but there are so *many* of them, clogging the highway." Yes, and you and I are two of them, and no more entitled to the space than anyone else—unless a higher income rate (or, indeed, a "more advanced view") entitles one to a higher percentage of government services. (Which is, finally, the position of the Sierra Club.)

The great fault of my generation is ingratitude. The ignorance stemming therefrom leads to folly destructive of that very world which, while it may not be the unachievable, inchoate utopia the

---

*As Thomas Sowell said, one might complain that this or that activity "ruins his neighborhood"; but that one does not own his neighborhood—he merely owns his *house*. The attempt to have governmental bodies enforce zoning (and environmental) rules for the benefit of incumbents is a misuse of the power of the State.

Left desires, is a wonderful place to live in, and has given us a great country.

What is this Utopia? It is the vulgate version of Heaven, where the lion lies down with the lamb, and no one is in want, where the believer has seventy virgins, and the supporter of All the Good Causes rests in peace, adored by the recipients of his Goodness.

But will human nature there be abolished? Will not the Politician look around, at this heaven, and see a bunch of sheep ripe for the picking, the womanizer glide among the now docile women, the thief, et cetera. Would not these be their Heaven?

And what of the Heavens on Earth, the Workers' Paradises which foul villains have created? See reports of their operation, of Harry Hopkins's 1930s visit to Russia: "I have seen the future and it works." Of Jane Fonda's trip to Hanoi: "No prisoners of war were mistreated." Of Susan Sontag's visit to Castro.* These are and were lies. The committed were looking at hell, its horror screened, a false-front stage production presented to their happy credulity.†

And yet, the current administration plans for a Socialist Utopia, where wasteful competition is gone, and America is "liked" overseas. But someone puts the yogurt in the little refrigerator.

---

*"The sense of community perceived in Cuba was not only nurtured by the political designs and ideology of the system, but had its subterranean reservoirs and supports in the stereotype of the joyful, life affirming attitude, attributed to the musically gifted song-and-dance loving natives, their natural and politically engendered vitality." Susan Sontag wrote, "The Cubans know a lot about spontaneity, gaiety, sensuality, and freaking out. They are not linear, desiccated creatures of print culture.'" (Paul Hollander, *Political Pilgrims*, quoting Susan Sontag's *Some Thoughts*)

†In his book *Political Pilgrims*, Paul Hollander quotes Simone de Beauvoir on her visit in the 1950s, to China: ". . . not a model prison; it was simply the only one in the city area . . . what a difference between this and the American system. (Here) they have a field for sports at their disposal, a big courtyard with a theatre where a movie is shown or a play presented every week. The day I was there they were rehearsing a play of their own. There is also a reading room stocked with books and periodicals where they can sit and relax." Quoted from de Beauvoir, *The Long March*.

Please note "the day I was there . . ." the coincidence between de Beauvoir's visit, and the "happenstance" of the staging of the play. Was this woman a complete fool, or just criminally deluded? And, finally, to those who suffered under Mao, and to those on the Left inspired to deny their sufferings, by her recitation, what is the difference?

My ungrateful generation, rich and poor, has been living off a trust fund: the productivity of our parents, and of the two hundred and more years work of those who preceded them. We want the Government to replace those parents from whose support we were never weaned. We, like the infant, think that crying harder makes the breast appear, that the wage earner is a fool not to perceive he is involved in waste, the boss that he is involved in exploitation, and our fellows indictable for their vicious unconcern for Mother Earth. And we wonder why Arab fanatics felt safe in bombing us.

36 | BUMPER STICKERS

A bumper sticker of my youth read "I Would Rather Crawl on My Hands and Knees to Moscow Than Be a Victim of a Nuclear Bomb."

This was the precursor of the gentler, more contemporary "War Is Not Healthy for Children and Other Small Creatures," and "War Is Not the Answer." These of course, present a false choice: between death and surrender. But war may be forced upon one, in which case the choice is not between war and peace, but between defense and death. "War Is Not the Answer" supposes that the bumper sticker is going to be read by those questioning, in the abstract, the relative benefits of war and peace. The identity of those people escapes me.

Other possible readers of this philosophy might be those intending us harm—the bumper sticker here, acting, presumably, as a deterrent. But as the motto is attached to the hated possession of a despised, to their mind, depraved and subhuman denizen of a loathed civilization to the obliteration of which the reader has dedicated his life, its deterrent value is debatable.

To understand the motto's deeper meaning, one might consider its antecedent. For, aside from identifying the driver to his philosophic like (such fraternity based upon another driver's possession of the same bumper sticker), it is a call and an exhortation to an actual action, the action being surrender.

The sad but wiser possessor of the wisdom that War Is Not Good, in that it brings harm to the innocent, neglects to take into account that it is precisely for this reason that terrorists engage in it. "We spent several days being chauffeured, in that foreign land, by the

206

nicest man, and we engaged in some very good debates, and I think that, at the end of our stay, we established some common ground." Which of us has been sufficiently blessed as to have been spared the recitation of the Reasonable Cabdriver, and of the ensuing triumph of true humanitarian diplomacy?

But war occurs in the absence, the failure, or the impossibility of diplomacy. What common ground was there between Hitler's desire to turn the world into a Nazi slave state, and the West's desire to remain free? Or between the Arab vow to obliterate the Jewish State and the Israelis' intention to remain alive and in possession of their country?

What is one to do if one's opponent has determined that war *is* the answer—and if such opponent, further, obstinately holds to its position in spite of the well-meaning's attachment to his car bumper of a suggestion to the contrary?

Well. If we look to the "Hands and Knees" progenitor of today's more postmodern expression, we see the answer is preemptive surrender.

For it did not occur to the author of "Hands and Knees" that the choice is false, that one need *neither* be the victim of a nuclear bomb, *nor* crawl on one's hands and knees to Moscow. One may arm oneself sufficiently to dissuade one's opponent from War, and display sufficient resolve in the face of his threats, that he believes that our weapons, should their need arise, will absolutely be deployed.*

Fifty years of that Cold War so decried by the Left kept the peace, and *kept* the nuclear bombs from being deployed. Had a sufficient number *actually* or figuratively crawled on their knees to Moscow (for example, Tom Hayden, Jane Fonda, Susan Sontag, and the radical Left *tout entière*), had they ended our nuclear armament as they ended the Vietnam War, it is possible that Communism, rather than

---

*The Obama administration (on April 6, 2010) announced a new directive regarding our Nuclear Arms—that they will never be employed against a Non Nuclear Power. Such a power, now, is free to use biological warfare, germ warfare, poison gas, and so on, free from worry about response from our superior technology. Whom, in the name of God, does this directive benefit save our enemies?

having fallen, would now be the law of the land in an America turned into yet another of their slave-states.

What can it mean to a potential aggressor—the proclamation that one *will not fight*? Note that such is not a pacifist doctrine, not the ahimsa of the committed Buddhist, nor the inviolable stance of the Quaker, but, rather, a proclamation of good-heartedness in the hope that it will win over the Aggressor State (the USSR, the Taliban, Iran, Al Qaeda).

"There is nothing you can do to me, my children, or my country that will cause me to defend myself," is an accurate paraphrase of "I Would Rather Crawl on My Hands and Knees to Moscow." But, the fundamental religious vows above excepted, there are *some* things the owner of the bumper sticker would do to defend, if not that in which he believes, that to which he is sworn. Would he fight to protect his wife from an intruder, his children from a rapist, his house of worship from an incendiary?

Perhaps yes. Then what, to his mind, is the difference between an individual act of defense and a concerted opposition to criminal, immoral actions on the part of another State? First, the Liberal's feeling of exemption from service; next, his adoration of State Power, which may, most accurately, here be described as "slavish."

If Fidel Castro and Che Guevara rob a few banks, and shoot a few landowners, they may or may not be considered criminals, but if they put up a flag, and proclaim a new Government, and remember to characterize this Government as "For the Workers," they become, in the assessment of the Left, immediately worthy of respect. This hides the deep-seated wish of the Left for the existence of a wise and all-powerful State, a State which will Take Care of the individual, saving him from worries not only about health care, but about every other choice in his life.

The Left worships power, because it feels that power can be used to Do Good, and Absolute Power, could it only be achieved, because it could eradicate evil. The record of all human history does not suffice to eradicate this delusion; neither will the threat of death nor of our country's dissolution. Who would offer the choice between walking on the knees and death by nuclear bomb? Our sworn opponents. The display of the bumper sticker is an acceptance of their proposition—it is preemptive surrender, signaling an absolute refusal—let alone to *fight*—to consider any defense (intellectual *or* military) of the American Way. The same supine love of power, today, in its hatred of Israel, in its love of that Victim Philosophy adopted and exploited by Arab Terrorists, announces surrender of the American Way to those gratified to hear of the choice.

If Peace is Good and War is Bad, and that is the end of the argument, if America and the West are incapable of progressing from the nursery rhyme to a consideration of realpolitik, then War can, indeed, be avoided, simply by giving our opponents everything they require, including, of course, the State of Israel, and the lives of all the Jews worldwide, and of nonbelievers, and the children of the same, and of the lands they possess.

———

In the study of jiujitsu one strives to apply a hold on his opponent and increase the pressure just sufficiently so that the controlled, if he finds no escape, signals his acknowledgment and the hold is relaxed. This is called tapping out. My young son and I were practicing jiujitsu. "In a *real* fight," he asked, "you can still tap out, can't you?"

"No," I told him, "the definition of a real fight is one in which one *cannot* tap out."

"Well then," he asked, "what do you do?"

And I explained to him that in such a case you'd better win.

On his ten-year-old face incomprehension fought with the beginnings of maturity.

37 | LATE REVELATIONS

I did not serve in the military. I was deferred. However, had I not had this deferment, I would not have gone in any case, so the exemption which served me then cannot serve me now.

I knew no one who went to Vietnam. I knew no one who suggested that it was my duty to go to Vietnam. In the many years since my eligibility for the military, I regretted my exemption. I felt the lack of the military experience as a loss, and envied those who had served. It has lately occurred to me that my feelings in this regard were immoral—that a truer or more moral name for my nostalgia was not loss, or envy, but *shame*; and that to characterize it as loss was merely to claim for myself another unearned exemption.

The Rabbis teach that the road to Glory (redemption) must begin with shame, and I ratify their insight in this case; for nostalgia and wistfulness can only intensify through time. They are, finally, just self-involvement in fantasy: an infantile wish for the benefits of a choice one did not make. But shame, a breaking open of the heart before God, leads, so the Rabbis say, to that true self-knowledge necessary for change.

For how can one change who cannot identify and accurately name the problem?

The Obama campaign slogans suggested the opposite: that change (by which one must understand them to have meant *amelioration*) may happen absent not only real effort but the mere psychological honesty necessary for specificity.

I don't think I have changed very much in my life, or in my self, over sixty years.

I was given a gift for dramatizing things, and have had the great fortune to practice it in the most congenial and exciting surroundings and with the salt of the earth. I've used this gift to support myself and my family, and have worked to learn the various skills involved happily—as their increase added to my satisfaction and to my larder.

———

I've worked hard at very few things, chief among them learning how to write a plot. This study involved wrenching myself free of an infatuation with my own talent, and, so, it was an encounter with shame.

I look back on my Liberal political beliefs with a sort of wonder—as another exercise in self-involvement—rewarding myself for some superiority I could not logically describe.

My twenty-year marriage has been an unrelieved joy. (Tolstoy wrote that there is no such thing as "working at" a marriage—that it is all or nothing.) My children and I adore each other; and the vicissitudes I have undergone as part of my profession have either been unavoidable (the press) or elective (whoring around Hollywood).

The question "What would you do differently?" I am privileged to see, as a result of my aperçu about the Military, is not only a foolish but a costly indulgence. The useful question is, "What will you do *now*?"

———

Saul Alinsky was the great "community organizer" of midcentury America.

His was the philosophy (and, I believe, the organization) in which President Obama matriculated on his appearance in Hyde Park. Alinsky and his "organizers" were, supposedly, involved in bringing "social justice" to the community—in redressing wrongs through what might be called, depending upon one's political bent, Street Theatre and Civil Disobedience, or thuggery.

His tactics involved picketing the homes of directors of institutions whose practices he and his organization found uncongenial, clogging the floors of a department store with nonbuyers who would, at the end of the day, place orders COD for purchases they had no intention of accepting, and so on.

I take these examples from his own book *Rules for Radicals* (1971). Also to be found in his book is his threat, to the City of Chicago, of "a shit-in"—a clogging of all lavatories onboard planes and in the concourses of O'Hare Airport: "It would be a source of great mortification and embarrassment to the city administration. It might even create the kind of emergency in which planes would have to be held up while passengers got back aboard to use the plane's toilet facilities."

What did he hope to gain? Power.

Here is this Twelfth Rule of Power Tactics: "*The price of a successful attack is a constructive alternative.*" (Italics his.) "You cannot risk being trapped by the enemy in his sudden agreement with your demand, and saying 'you're right—we don't know what to do about this issue. Now tell us.'"

A "community organizer," then, is one who seeks power. To do what? Whatever he wants. In the service of whom? Of those he designates as "within his community." He may (Alinsky and his cohorts did) seek to force banks to issue mortgages to those unable to pay—his community being the recipients of these "low income mortgages." But in forcing the banks to risk and waste the money of their depositors, he was, finally, not "bringing about social justice," but rationing poverty.

Who did he think he was? He thought he was a fellow who had learned a good trick. And he used it to further what he called "his ideals" but which might at least as accurately be characterized as his "agenda"—for who can know, finally, what were his ideals? Perhaps he just liked causing disruption. Indeed, there is no doubt about it. "It should be remembered that you can threaten the enemy and get away with it. You can insult and annoy him, but the one thing that is unforgiveable and that is certain to get him to react is to laugh at him. This causes an irrational anger." (Ibid.)

So, "the enemy's" anger is "irrational," but Alinsky's furor over "social injustice" is somehow brave and laudable.

———

Hard cases make Bad Law; and hard situations make bad precedent.

That the Freedom Marchers succeeded in the passage of the Civil Rights Act is moot. That they succeeded in changing the nature of our country is undeniable.

Dr. King, the SCLC, and the host of organizations and individuals who risked their lives changed America vastly for the better.

One legacy of their bravery is a penchant, among the well-meaning, to "do good," "march for," and so on, in supposed aid of causes whose worth may be questionable, and whose goals impossible—an example of the first, opponents of Global Warming, and of the second, World Peace.

These well-meaning citizens and celebrities do not risk the maiming and death risked by Freedom marchers, they risk nothing—merely aggrandizing their own self-image, and rewarding themselves for engaging in actions which as they may be *superficially like* those of the Freedom Marchers, can be felt as deserving of merit.

Environmentalists have stopped water to the Central Valley of California, as the flow endangered, they said, some fish. And they got a judge to agree with them. Is this just? To whom? To some fish? To the farmer? Finally, it may or may not be just, but it is grateful to the self-image of the judge.

How wonderful to think of ourselves as heroes, and how often is such a fantasy the result of a feeling of powerlessness. The Left offers the ever-attractive suggestion that one, knowing himself to be (like you and me) a biddable, often confused, flawed human being, may rise above his knowledge by merely announcing his capacity for Herohood.

Candidate Obama said "Selma belongs to me, too." Well, the benefits do (as they accrue to us all), and, certainly, the pride-of-race does—as might also the pride of country, patriotism, for being a citizen of a country whose citizens displayed such heroism—*but the credit does not.*

Neither does credit accrue to those espousing *whatever* causes, who risk nothing in their prosecution; and for the inspired to indulge in extralegal or borderline actions of either civil disobedience or judicial activism is to seek credit for breaking laws whose transgression (in contrast to those at Selma) cost them nothing. Such is a cost-free exercise in self-aggrandizement similar to my "nostalgia" for not having served—it is arrogation of that which belongs to another. This is the essence of the philosophy of the Left.

We may be inspired to break the laws, discard the customs, and to destroy the culture which allowed us the freedom and leisure to so engage ourselves; and I, growing up in the sixties, thought it a grand idea: to bring about Social Justice.

That such actions, whatever their supposed intention, caused havoc and that we who espoused them were responsible for the same, was to me a difficult perception. It still is.

The embrace of Conservatism, my own, and that of anyone coming to it in maturity, necessitates a deep and rigorous survey and evaluation of thoughts and actions, and their honest assessment.

The ability to honestly assess actions and consequences (morality) is not limited to Conservatives, nor are we as individuals more likely than Liberals to make such decisions—save in the political realm.

Given a perception that the greater possibility of happiness for the greatest number lies in Conservative rather than Liberal principles, why is the transition to the first from the second difficult?

One may reason (as I, and many readers have) with honest, intelligent, moral Liberal friends, who may, in one instance after another, grant the validity of one's Conservative theses, and acknowledge the discrepancy between their *own* actions, and their voting habits, but yet not only vote Democratic, but proclaim that nothing on earth could induce them to do otherwise. Why?

It means leaving the group.

It is not difficult to endure, but it is painful to recognize the incredulity and scorn which one encounters from one's native Group (the Liberals) on announcing a change of philosophy. It is shocking. And it is sobering, for it reveals this truth: that the Left functions, primarily, through its power as a primitive society or religion, dedicated *above all* to solidarity, and not only to acceptance but to constant *promulgation* of its principles, however inchoate, as "self-evident" and therefore beyond question. But, as Hayek points out, that something is beyond question most often means that its investigation has been forbidden. Why? Because it was untrue.

How does the Left draw and maintain its unthinking allegiance from people of intelligence, compassion, and goodwill? By offering an illusion. Here is Whittaker Chambers, speaking of the Communism from which he wrenched himself in the 1940s: "Its vision points the way to the future: its faith labors to turn the future into present reality. It says to every man who joins it: the vision is a practical problem of history; the way to achieve it is a practical problem in politics, which is the present tense of history. Have you the moral strength to take upon yourself the crimes of history so that man at last may close his chronicle of age-old senseless suffering, and replace it with a purpose and a plan? . . . The answer is the root of that sense of moral superiority which makes Communists, though caught in crime, berate their opponents with withering self-righteousness."*

We human beings need order. We crave it, and we thrive under it.

How do we adjudicate between our need for order and our need for freedom (for the Left offers only the first)?

By realizing that this determination must be made, and that it can never be made perfectly; and through sufficient maturity to accept the burden of choice rather than submit to the comfort of the Group.

*(Whittaker Chambers, *Witness*, 1952)

38 | WHO DOES ONE THINK HE IS?

"An' I was thinking, Hinnissy" (Mr. Dooley said in conclusion), "as I set in that there coort, surrounded be me fellow-journalists, spies, perjurers, an' other statesmen, that I'd give four dollars if th' president iv th' coort'd call out "Monsoo Dooley, take th' stand.'

" 'Here,' says I; an I'd thread me way with dignity through th' Fr'rinch gin'rals an' ministers on th' flure, an' give me hand to th' prisident to kiss. If he went anny further, I'd break his head. No man'll kiss me, Hinnissy, an' live. What's that ye say? He wudden't want to? Well, niver mind.

" 'Here,' " says I, 'mong colonel, what d'ye want with me?'

" 'What d'ye know about this case, mong bar-tinder.'

" 'Nawthin',' says I. 'But I know as much as annywan else.'"

—Finley Peter Dunne, *Mr. Dooley in the Hearts of His Countrymen*

I am a guy who got his nose broke playing high school football.

I remember very well what it is to look for work. It is my experience that being self-supporting is like shooting free throws: if you hit, you get to shoot again, if not, not.

I believe, like Coach Lombardi, that every man wants to test himself, and is never happier than when he "lays on the field of battle, exhausted, and victorious."

The Chicago literary tradition is born not out of its Universities, but out of the sports desk and the city desk of its newspapers.

Hemingway revolutionized English prose. His inspiration was the telegraph, whose use, at Western Union, taught this: every word costs something.

This, of course, is the essence of poetry, which is the essence of great prose. Chicagoan literature came from the newspaper, whose purpose, in those days, was to Tell What Happened. Hemingway's epiphany was reported, earlier, by Keats as " 'Beauty is truth, truth beauty'—that is all ye know on earth, and all ye need to know." I would add, to Keats's summation only this: "Don't let the other fellow piss on your back and tell you it's raining."

I believe one might theoretically forgive one who cheats at business, but never one who cheats at cards; for business adversaries operate at arm's length, the cardplayer under the assumption that his position will be conducted under the strict rules of the game, *period*.

That was my first political epiphany.

And now, I have written a political book.

What are the qualifications for a Political Writer?

They are, I believe, the same as those of an aspiring critic: an inability to write for the Sports Page.

———

I was born in Hyde Park and grew up on the South Side of Chicago. I hold no brief against someone who is not interested in sports, but I could never trust someone who *claimed* such an interest, in order to advance his own agenda, and then could neither name a member, past or present, of his self-apostrophised "Home Team," nor correctly pronounce the name of their ballpark.*

I can forgive someone who lies, but if he can't think on his feet, he has no business representing my interests. If he can't lie to me, how can I expect him to lie, on my behalf, to the other guy?

———

*President Obama, in a radio interview at a ballpark, was asked if he, as a Chicagoan, preferred the Sox or the Cubs. He claimed he was a Sox fan, twice mispronounced the name of Comiskey Park, twice referred to the umpire as "the judge," and, asked for his favorite White Sox, past or present, could not come up with one name. Sigh.

I have written a political book not because I am an expert but because I am a citizen. I have *published* a political book because other citizens wrote a Constitution denying to our Government the power to control Speech.

I am the beneficiary of those who lived and died to defend our Constitution. I need no permission to publish my work—only the endorsement of another citizen or group who believe they may, financially or otherwise, profit from its publication.

For many, what may be accepted as common sense is only that which comes out of the mouths of experts. But Harry Truman said the smartest man is the farmer, for, while he works all day, he's thinking.

I would add that the smartest man is the immigrant, for he has to assess each situation afresh, and *mechanically*. Which is to say he starts with no misconceptions, and so is very difficult to misdirect—his ability to eat depends upon his ability to figure out the way things work.

Things work in ways both wonderful and stunning, when set next to the way we *think* they work.*

The gap between the two grows naturally, through use and elaboration. It is capable of misuse by those who can profit from it: the politician who would like more patronage money to dispense, the entrepreneur who is selling snake oil, and the investment banker who may be his brother.

What is the difference between equality and fairness? A standard may be applied to the former, which the latter will not bear. The cry for "fairness" is the child's cry. It is, indeed, the first sentence dealing with the abstract which the child speaks, "It's not *fair*."

"Fair," then, may mean "What I want," or, in the altruist, "The way I believe the world should be," but it is, finally, subjective; and an insistence on this subjective standard opens the way both for evil in the name of good (busing), and for the unprincipled exploiters of

---

*Note that, to a parent, most fatuous of pronouncements, that of the childless upon child rearing, which begins, "my *niece* . . ."

any system, (Lenin, Mao, or their contemporaries of various ranks and denominations).

Equality can only, practically, mean, *equality before the law*—this is to say that everybody gets his turn to be heard out by a judicial system which, in the way of the world, is overworked, and indifferent, and may be misguided, or indeed, corrupt.

The question is, "Whom would I want on the jury trying me?" The answer, "Persons like myself," brings us down to the Courthouse when it is our turn to serve, with personal and civic pride counterbalancing the inconvenience.

You and I would want, on a jury tying our case, *not* the expert, *not* the hypothetical or overeducated, but the plumber, the grocer, the carpet salesman, the firefighter, the Marine—a regular person just like you or me.

For *our* case, were it, God forbid, before a court, would be, in our estimation simple, and we would want our jurors wary of abstractions—capable of and experienced in differentiating between simple things: the debt was paid, the debt was *not* paid; he struck me *first*; he promised X and did Y. These are the things the average, undeluded, and undeludable worker deals with every day, the things with which *we* deal when we recall (should we forget) that *we* are workers.

The awe and majesty of the Law are our basic inheritance of freedom. Without these nothing can exist in Freedom: here is the bright line, stay to the correct side and the community will protect you, venture across, and you will be at the mercy of its other name, the State. Likewise, those we call "leaders," were originally understood to function as *representatives*, with one to *preside* over their deliberations.

The imperial Presidency is a bore. No one is perfect, and no man can know or understand all things.

————

On the movie set, there is one person and one person *only* who need possess no quantifiable skills, that is the director. The actor must be able to act, the designer to design, the carpenter to build; the director need be conversant with the technicalities of none of these; his job is to move the project forward, allowing each of the workers involved to do *his* own job. That of the director is to listen to their suggestions, to propose a course of action, and to bring the entirety, happily and simply, to a shared devotion to that course.

The rules of behavior on a movie set are largely the Unwritten Law: who shows deference to whom, when one should speak, when one should be silent, how to deal with unpleasantness, with an excess of zeal, with shoddy work; how to evaluate that which falls short of the perfect. The set is infused with a sense of commonality and dedication not only to the project at hand, but to *training by example* the new workers, by extending and protecting the precious lessons of the past.

This perception was the beginning of my love affair, or, let me say, my recognition of my love affair with America. We do things differently here. We were and are a country of workers and, as such, get along so well that we became the preeminent power in the world. This came about not through a "lust for power," not through colonialism or "exploitation," but as a result of our ethos and cohesion. It begins with the notion that all are created equal.

The definition of "all" has widened over time; and the history of our country, when finally written, will appreciate that this widening was the essence of our Republic; that we, in the process of devotion to the essentially religious goal, the "self-evident truth," managed to shape, through our Industry and through our art, a new and better world.

39 | THE SECRET KNOWLEDGE

The Left is atheist, and, simply because it is atheist, its religious fanaticism is worse than any of the other fanaticisms of history. For the romantic of the past has sometimes, if all too rarely, been restrained by the memory that God is Truth. But the atheist fanatic has no reason for such restraint. There is no reason in principle why the revolutionary atheist should regard truth, and it does not seem that he does so in practice.

—Christopher Hollis, *Foreigners Aren't Fools*, 1936

America is a Christian country. Its Constitution is the distillation of the wisdom and experience of Christian men, in a tradition whose codification is the Bible.

I will not say this Christian country has been good to the Jews, for this suggests an altruism or acceptance, neither of which exist. But America has been good *for* the Jews, as it has been, eventually, good for every immigrant group whether fleeing oppression, seeking prosperity, or, indeed, brought here in chains. The result of a 230-year-long experiment is the triumph of Judaeo-Christian values. We have created peace and plenty for more citizens over a greater period of time than that enjoyed by any other group in history.

This triumph is not due to altruism, nor to empathy, nor to compassion, but to adherence to those practicable, rational rules for successful human interaction set out in the Bible.

These rules and precepts amount, in their totality, as much to a legal philosophy as to a theology.

Practically, they assert the existence of God not as a magical force, making all men good (all men are not good), but as the *a priori* condition of human interaction: accountability. This irreducible understanding, which is the basis of Judaeo-Christian civilization, is that all human beings possess both a conscience and that free will necessary to allow them to either reject its dictates or to formulate them into habit. It is the codification of this conscience as Law, which allows us to adjudicate between both its conflicting claims, and its absence or presence in differing individuals.

The laws, derived from the Bible, and finding their most demonstrably perfect form in the Constitution, assert not man's perfection, but his imperfectibility, and, thus, the inevitability of conflict.

Our Judaeo-Christian teachings acknowledge conflict (between individuals, between them and the State, between them and God) and proceed to suggest (through narrative in the Old and through parable in the New Testament) mechanisms for its most peaceful resolution.

This tradition does not refer, overtly or by implication, to any possible perfect state of Man or of his associations, but, rather, acknowledges his weakness both before his imperfections and before that Power, however named, which gave him both a conscience, and the desire for law.

This power may be understood as metaphysical, and called God, or as a mere cosmic accident, gifting the human species with a unique formation of intellect impelling them to create Law as the most obviously utilitarian path toward effective civilization.

The Bible is an acknowledgment of human individuality. Human society has thrived, historically, as we see in our diverse society, because of the liberty to exploit a random distribution of talents, flaws, and proclivities.

Those States which have, in the name of productivity, racial purity, or, indeed, equality, attempted to limit human individuality have reverted from the civilization of the Judaeo-Christian state to savagery; for they have rejected the teachings of the Bible. One need not even say they died because they rejected God; they died because they rejected reason.

——

There is no secret knowledge. The Federal Government is merely the zoning board writ large.

One may find, in either place, able and even dedicated public servants, but there are no beneficent "experts." For such an expert must be, essentially, but a skilled manipulator of people (the electorate or the legislature). He must be, therefore, a politician (that is, a perpetual candidate), bureaucrat, or demagogue; or he may be a lobbyist or a theoretician, skilled in manipulating or conspiring with the other named groups.

Our jury trial admits the testimony of experts. But the jury, faced with each side's expert but opposed opinion, usually discards both, judging the experts suborned or misled by either their stipend or their theories. They then retire to their deliberations, realizing that, though each side's evidence is presented as beyond the power of the common individual's understanding, they, the jury, are going to have to figure it out for themselves.

So it is with the rest of our self-government. The problems facing us, faced by all mankind engaged in Democracy, may seem complex, or indeed insolvable, and we, in despair, may revert to a state of wish-fulfillment—a state of "belief" in the power of the various experts presenting themselves as a cure for our indecision. But this is a sort of Stockholm syndrome. Here, the captives, unable to bear the anxiety occasioned by their powerlessness, suppress it by identifying with their captors.

This is the essence of Leftist thought. It is a devolution from reason to "belief," in an effort to stave off a feeling of powerlessness. And if government is Good, it is a logical elaboration that more government power is Better. But the opposite is apparent both to anyone who has ever had to deal with Government, and, I think, to any dispassionate observer.

It is in sympathy with the first and in the hope of enlarging the second group that I have written this book.

ACKNOWLEDGMENTS

My son asked me to explain the difference between a Conservative and a Liberal. I went on at some length. He thought for a while and said, "Then, basically, it's the difference between the Heavenly Dream and the God-Awful Reality"—a succinct and accurate compression of those views which I have, at somewhat greater and, I hope, excusable length, endeavored to express here.

———

I had never knowingly talked with nor read the works of a Conservative before moving to Los Angeles, some eight years ago.

I am indebted to very patient friends and teachers I met here, who inspired me to seek some understanding of the political process.

I would particularly like to thank Endre Balogh and Rabbi Mordecai Finley. They introduced me to the works of Milton Friedman, Friedrich Hayek, Thomas Sowell, Shelby Steele, and, so, began my efforts at self-education; and to Jon Voight, who, among other acts of kindness, gave me Whittaker Chambers's *Witness*.

As my reading broadened, I became aware of various nexuses of Conservative thought: I discovered that my radio had an AM band, and that the news and commentary on KCLA from Dennis Prager, Hugh Hewitt, Michael Medved, and Glenn Beck made more sense to me than the bemused and sad paternalism which had previously filled my drivetime.

I am very grateful to my wife and children, for putting up with my virtual monomania as I wrestled with what had become, for me, a new way of considering human interaction; to Sloan Harris for his forbearance, encouragement, and championship of the project; and to my assistant Pam Susemiehl for her patience, good humor, and much appreciated suggestions during the writing of this book.

BIBLIOGRAPHY

Alinsky, Saul D. *Reveille for Radicals.* New York: Vintage, 1969.

———. *Rules For Radicals: A Practical Primer for Realistic Radicals.* New York: Vintage, 1971.

Assagioli, Roberto. *The Act of Will.* London: Wildwood House, 1974.

Bagehot, Walter. *Physics and Politics: or Thoughts on the Application of the Principles of 'Natural Selection' and 'Inheritance' to Political Society.* London: Henry S. King & Co., 1873.

Bagehot, Walter and Mrs. Russell Barrington. *The Works and Life of Walter Bagehot.* 1914. 10 vols. London: Longmans, Green, and Co., 1915.

Bard, Mitchell. *Myths and Facts: A Guide to the Arab-Israeli Conflict.* Chevy Chase, MD.: American-Israeli Cooperative Enterprise, 2002.

Beauvoir, Simone de. *The Long March: An Account of Modern China.* 1957. Phoenix: Phoenix Press, 2002.

Butler, Samuel. *Erewhon: or, Over the Range.* 1872. Ed. and introd. Peter Mudford. London: Penguin, 1985.

Chambers, Whittaker. *Witness.* 1952. Preface. Robert Novak. Washington, DC.: Regnery, [1987].

Chomsky, Noam. *A Hated Political Enemy.* Interview. Allen Bell. Victoria: Flask, 2005.

———. *Chomsky on Anarchism.* Comp. and ed. and Introd. Barry Pateman. Pref. Charles Weigl. Edinburgh: AK Press, 2005.

———. "Israel, Lebanon, and the 'Peace Process'." *Z Magazine,* April 23, 1996.

———. *Middle East Illusions: Including Peace in the Middle East? Reflections on Justice and Nationhood.* Lanham, MD.: Rowman & Littlefield, 2003.

———. "Obama on Israel-Palestine." *Z Magazine,* January 24, 2009. http:// chomsky.info/articles/20090124.htm.

———. "On the US-Israeli Invasion of Lebanon." *Al-Adab,* August 19, 2006.

———. *Secrets, Lies and Democracy.* 1994. Interview. David Barsamian. Comp. and ed. Arthur Naiman. *The Real Story Series.* Chicago, IL.: Common Courage Press/LPC Group, 1998.

———. *Selected Readings on Transformational Theory.* 1971. Ed. and preface. J.P.B. Allen and Paul Van Buren. Mineola, NY.: Dover, 2009.

Competitive Enterprise Institute. *Global Warming and Other Eco-Myths: How the Environment Movement Uses False Science to Scare Us to Death.* Ed. Ronald Bailey. Roseville, CA.: Prima Lifestyles, 2002.

Darwin, Charles. *On Natural Selection: From So Simple a Beginning Endless Forms Most Beautiful and Most Wonderful Have Been, and Are Being, Evolved.* 1859. London: Penguin, 2005.

Dunne, Finley Peter. *Mr. Dooley in the Hearts of His Countrymen.* 1899. n.p.: Bibliobazaar, 2006.

Emerson, Ralph Waldo. *Essays & Lectures.* New York, Library of America, 1983.

Fallaci, Oriana. *The Force of Reason (La Forza della Ragione).* 2004. New York: Rizzoli International, 2006.

Fanon, Frantz. *The Wretched of the Earth.* 1961. Pref. Jean-Paul Sartre. trans. Constance Farrington. New York: Grove, n.d.

Ferguson, Niall. *Empire: The Rise and Demise of the British World Order and the Lessons for Global Power.* 2002. New York: Basic, 2004.

Forster, E. M. *Howards End.* 1910. Introd. David Lodge. London: Penguin, 2000.

Friedman, Milton. *Capitalism and Freedom.* Chicago, IL.: University of Chicago Press, 1962.

Friedman, Milton and Rose Friedman. *Free to Choose: A Personal Statement.* 1980. Foreword. Milton and Rose Friedman. Orlando: Harvest-Harcourt, 1990.

Garrett, Garet. *The People's Pottage.* Ed. and introd. Jon Cook. Caldwell, ID.: The Caxton Printers, 1965.

Gibbon, Edward. *The History of the Decline and Fall of the Roman Empire.* 1781–1788. Ed. David Womersley. 4 vols. London: Penguin, 1995.

Gide, André et al. *The God that Failed.* 1950. Introd. Richard Crossman, M.P. New York: Bantam, 1959.

Glazov, Jamie. *United in Hate: The Left's Romance with Tyranny and Terror.* Foreword. R. James Woolsey. Los Angeles, CA.: WorldNetDaily, 2009.

Goldberg, Jonah. *Liberal Fascism: The Secret History of the American Left, from Mussolini to the Politics of Meaning.* New York: Doubleday, 2007.

Goldhagen, Daniel Jonah. *A Moral Reckoning: The Role of the Catholic Church in the Holocaust and Its Unfulfilled Duty of Repair.* New York: Vintage, 2003.

Haichen, Sun. Comp. and trans. *The Wiles of War: 36 Military Strategies from Ancient China.* 1991. Beijing: Foreign Languages Press, 1996.

Hayek, Friedrich A. *The Constitution of Liberty.* 1960. Chicago, IL.: University of Chicago Press, 1978.

———. *The Fatal Conceit: The Errors of Socialism.* 1988. Ed. W. W. Bartley III. 19 vols. Chicago, IL.: University of Chicago Press, 1991.

———. *The Road to Serfdom.* 1944. Introd. Milton Friedman. Chicago, IL.: University of Chicago Press, 1971.

Hazlitt, William. *On the Pleasure of Hating: Love Turns, with a Little Indulgence, to Indifference or Disgust: Hatred Alone Is Immortal.* 2004. London: Penguin, 2005.

———. *Selected Writings.* Oxford: Oxford University Press, 1991.

Hilfer, Tony. *The New Hegemony in Literary Studies: Contradictions in Theory.* Evanston, IL.: Northwestern University Press, 2003.

Hoffer, Eric. *Reflections on the Human Condition.* 1972. New York: Harper & Row, 1973.

———. *The Temper of Our Time.* New York: Harper & Row, 1967.

———. *The True Believer: Thoughts on the Nature of Mass Movement.* 1951. New York: Perennial Classics, 2002.

———. *Working and Thinking on the Waterfront: A Journal: June 1958–May 1959.* New York: Perennial Library, 1970.

Hollander, Paul. *Anti-Americanism: Critiques at Home and Abroad 1965–1990.* New York: Oxford University Press, 1992.

———. *Discontents: Postmodern & Postcommunist.* New Brunswick, NJ.: Transaction Publishers, 2002.

———. *Political Pilgrims: Travels of Western Intellectuals to the Soviet Union, China, and Cuba 1928–1978.* New York: Harper Colophon, 1983.

Hollis, Christopher. *Foreigners Aren't Fools.* New York: Frederick A. Stokes Company, 1937.

———. *Noble Castle.* London: Longmans, Green and Co., 1941.

———. *The Death of a Gentleman: The Letters of Robert Fossett.* 1943. London: Burns Oates, 1945.

Horowitz, David. *Hating Whitey and Other Progressive Causes.* Dallas, TX.: Spence Publishing Company, 1999.

Hubbard, Elbert. *A Message to Garcia.* New York: Classic Books America, 2009.

Huizinga, Johan. *Homo Ludens: A Study of the Play Element in Culture.* 1950. Boston, MA.: Beacon Press, 1955.

Ingrassia, Paul. *Crash Course: The American Automobile Industry's Road from Glory to Disaster.* New York: Random House, 2010.

Jackson, Bruce, Comp. *Get Your Ass in the Water and Swim Like Me: African American Narrative Poetry from Oral Tradition.* 1974. New York: Routledge, 2004.

Johnson, Paul. *A History of the American People.* New York: Weidenfeld & Nicolson, 1997.

———. *Intellectuals.* New York: Weidenfeld & Nicolson, 1988.

———. *The Offshore Islanders: A History of the English People.* 1972. London: Phoenix, 1992.

Lewis, Bernard. *What Went Wrong?: The Clash Between Islam and Modernity in the Middle East.* Oxford: Oxford University Press, 2002.

Lomborg, Bjørn. *The Skeptical Environmentalist: Measuring the Real State of the World.* Cambridge: Cambridge University Press, 2001.

Lyons, Eugene. *The Red Decade: The Classic Work on Communism in America During the Thirties.* 1941. New Rochelle, NY.: Arlington House, 1970.

Macaulay, Lord. *The History of England.* 1848–1861. Ed. and Introd. Hugh Trevor-Roper. London: Penguin, 1968.

Mackay, Charles. *Extraordinary Popular Delusions and the Madness of Crowds.* 1841. Foreword. Bernard M. Baruch. USA: Noonday, 1972.

Manchester, William. *American Caesar: Douglas MacArthur 1880–1964.* 1978. New York: Dell, 1983.

Maugham, W. Somerset. *The Narrow Corner.* 1932. London: Penguin Classics, 1993.

McDonough, Yona Zeldis. *Coffee with Marilyn.* Foreword. Gloria Steinem. London: Duncan Baird, 2007.

Mencken, H. L. *The American Language: An Inquiry into the Development of English in the United States.* 1919. New York: Alfred A. Knopf, 2000.

Michener, James A. *Kent State: What Happened and Why.* New York: Random House, 1971.

Mill, John Stuart. *On Liberty.* 1859. Ed. and introd. Gertrude Himmelfarb. London: Penguin, 1985.

Mitford, Nancy. *Madame de Pompadour.* 1953. Introd. Amanda Foreman. New York: New York Review Books Classics, 2001.

Montague, Charles Edward. *Disenchantment.* New York: Brentano 1922. n.p.: General Books, 2009.

Moyo, Dambisa. *Dead Aid: Why Aid Is Not Working and How There Is a Better Way for Africa.* Foreword. Niall Ferguson. New York: Farrar, Straus and Giroux, 2009.

Opie, Iona, and Peter Opie. *The Lore and Language of Schoolchildren.* 1960. Introduction, Marina Warner. New York: New York Review Books, 2001.

Paine, Thomas. *Common Sense.* 1776. Ed. and introd. Isaac Kramnick. London: Penguin, 1986.

Pareto, Vilfredo. *The Mind and Society: A Treatise on General Sociology.* 1935. Trans. Andrew Bongiorno and Arthur Livingston. ed. Arthur Livingston. 4 vols. New York: Dover, 1963.

Pence, Mike. "The Presidency and the Constitution." *Imprimis.* Oct. 2010. www.hillsdale.edu/images/userImages/mvanderwei/ . . . /Imprimis_Oct10.pdf.

Phillips, Melanie. *The World Turned Upside Down: The Global Battle over God, Truth, and Power.* New York: Encounter Books, 2010.

Plimer, Ian. *Heaven and Earth: Global Warming the Missing Science.* Lanham, MD.: Rowman & Littlefield, 2009.

Pondhoretz, Norman. *Why Are Jews Liberals?* New York: Doubleday, 2009.

Priestly, J. B. *Apes and Angels.* London: The Library Press, 1928.

Radford, R. A. "The Economic Organisation of a P.O.W. Camp." *Economica.* vol. 12, 1945.

Rand, Ayn. *The New Left: The Anti-Industrial Revolution.* New York: Signet, 1971.

Roots, Ivan, ed. *Cromwell: A Profile.* Gen. ed. Aida DiPlace Donald. New York: Hill and Wang, 1973.

Rousseau, Jean-Jacques. *The Social Contract: On Principles of Political Right.* Amsterdam, 1762.

Shlaes, Amity. *The Forgotten Man: A New History of the Great Depression.* New York: HarperCollins, 2007.

Shute, Nevil. *Slide Rule: The Autobiography of an Engineer*. 1954. London: Pan Books, 1968.

Simons, Anna. *The Company They Keep: Life Inside the U.S. Army Special Forces*. New York: Simon & Schuster Children's, 1997.

Smith, Adam. *An Inquiry into the Nature and Causes of the Wealth of Nations*. 2 vols. London, 1776.

Sontag, Susan. "Some Thoughts on the Right Way (for us) to Love the Cuban Revolution." *Ramparts*, Apr. 1969: 6–19.

Sowell, Thomas. *Black Education: Myths and Tragedies*. New York: David McKay, 1972.

———. *Economic Facts and Fallacies*. New York: Basic, 2008.

———. *Ethnic America: A History*. New York: Basic, 1981.

———. *Intellectuals and Society*. New York: Basic, 2009.

———. *On Classical Economics*. New Haven, CT.: Yale University Press, 2006.

———. *Pink and Brown People and Other Controversial Essays*. Stanford, CA.: Hoover Institution Press, 1981.

Stauss, Leo. *Natural Right and History*. 1953. Foreword. Jerome Kerwin. Preface. Leo Strauss. Chicago, IL.: University of Chicago Press, 1965.

Steele, Shelby. *A Bound Man: Why We Are Excited About Obama and Why He Can't Win*. New York: Free Press, 2008.

———. *White Guilt: How Blacks and White Together Destroyed the Promise of the Civil Rights Era*. London: HarperCollins, 2006.

Szasz, Thomas. *Anti-Freud: Karl Kraus's Criticism of Psychoanalysis and Psychiatry*. 1977. Syracuse, NY.: Syracuse University Press, 1984.

Taylor, Mitchell. "Last Stand of our Wild Polar Bears." *The Toronto Star*, 27 Apr. 2006.

Tolstoy, Leo. *War and Peace*. 1869. Trans. Rosemary Edmonds. London: Penguin Classics, 1982.

Trevor-Roper, H. R. *The European Witch-Craze of the Sixteenth and Seventeenth Centuries and Other Essays*. 1956. New York: Harper Torchbooks, 1969.

———. *The Last Days of Hitler*. 1962. New York: Collier, 1965.

———. *The Philby Affair: Espionage, Treason and Secret Services*. London: William Kimber, 1968.

Trollope, Anthony. *Dr. Wortle's School*. 1881. Ed. and introd. John Halperin. New York: Oxford University Press, 1990.

———. *Phineas Finn: The Irish Member*. 1869. Ed. and introd. and notes. Jacques Berthoud. Illust. T.L.B. Huskinson. New York: Oxford University Press, 1999.

———. *The Duke's Children*. 1879. Ed. and introd. and notes. Hermione Lee. Illust. Charles Mozley. New York: Oxford University Press, 2008.

Trotter, W. *Instincts of the Herd in Peace and War*. 1915. New York: Macmillan, n.d.

Veblen, Thorstein. *The Engineers and the Price System*. 1921. New York: Viking Press, 1944.

———. *The Higher Learning in America.* 1918. Stanford, CA.: Academic Reprints, 1920.

———. *The Instincts of Workmanship and the State of the Industrial Arts.* 1914. Introd. Murray G. Murphey. New Brunswick, NJ.: Transaction Publishers, 1990.

———. *The Theory of the Leisure Class.* 1899. London: Penguin Classics, 1998.

Waugh, Auberon. *Will This Do? The First Fifty Years of Auberon Waugh: An Auto-biography.* New York: Carroll & Graf, 1998.

White, William Allen. *Masks in a Pageant.* New York: Macmillan, 1928.

———. *Some Cycles of Cathay.* Chapel Hill, NC.: University of North Carolina Press; London: Humphrey Milford-Oxford University, 1925.

———. *What It's All About: Being a Reporter's Story of The Early Campaign of 1936.* New York: Macmillan, 1936.

INDEX

Liberals (*cont.*)
  power worshipped by, 208–9
  work shunned by, 29
  world-view of, 59
Lincoln, Abraham, 191
Lincoln, Robert Todd, 54*n*
Listerine, 36
Lombardi, Vince, 216
Long March, The (de Beauvoir), 204*n*
Lost Horizon (Hilton), 32, 33
luftmensch, 158

MacArthur, Arthur, 129–30
MacArthur, Douglas, 129–30
Macaulay, Thomas Babington, 88,
  89, 190
McCormick, Cyrus, 79
McDonough, Yona Zeldis, 138
McDougal, Susan, 140
Mad Cow scare, 73*n*
Madoff, Bernie, 68
Mailer, Norman, 7, 96
Malthus, Thomas, 40, 162*n*
Mamet, David, 8
  childhood of, 217
  schooling of, 158–60
  in turn from Liberal to Conserva-
    tive, 7, 211, 214
Mamet, Henry, 146
Mamet, Jack, 146
Mamet, Noah, 52
Manchester, William, 129
Mao Zedong, 76, 204*n*, 219
Marie Antoinette, 176
marriage, 141–42, 165, 169–70
Marshall Plan, 44*n*
Marx, Karl, 2, 29, 43, 177, 186
Marxism, 43, 46, 166, 179, 181, 195
media, 26*n*, 84–85, 109, 159, 162,
  180–81, 197
merit pay, 183
Michener, James, 170
Milch, Erhard, 70

military, 1, 4, 44, 128, 202
Mill, J. S., 73, 185
misogyny, 135, 142
money, 4
monogamy, 141–42, 144, 170
Monroe, Marilyn, 138–41
Monty Hall problem, 65–66, 67, 68
Moses, 50, 94, 143–44, 152, 166*n*,
  192–93
MoveOn.org, 105, 110, 150, 202
Moyo, Dambisa, 34–35, 36
*Mr. Dooley in the Hearts of His Coun-
  trymen* (Dunne), 216
Muhammad, Elijah, 57
multiculturalism, 15, 39, 200, 201
*Myths and Facts: A Guide to the Arab-
  Israeli Conflict* (Bard), 81*n*

NAACP, 56–57, 150
Nadab, 151–52, 153*n*
Nader, Ralph, 184
Napoleon I, Emperor of the French,
  19, 20
National Recovery Act (1933), 150
Native Americans, 124
natural resources, 1, 34, 40, 64, 73,
  102, 161
Nazis, 32, 57, 60, 70, 89, 93, 105, 110,
  121*n*, 170*n*, 175, 207
Neue Freie Presse, 86
New Deal, 37, 150, 153, 174
New Economy, 187
Nixon, Richard, 157
Noble Savages, 91–95
North Korea, 93
November (Mamet), 5–7
nuclear power, 41, 42, 143, 162*n*

Oakton Manor, 131
Obama, Barack, 37, 54, 85, 106, 107,
  111–12, 113, 138*n*, 162, 166*n*,
  176, 210, 211, 213, 217*n*
  apologies by, 44